A Dictionary of
Vampires

LADY MARGARET *seeks the Spirit of the Storm in the Cave of Fingal,
and there beholds with horror the Vision of the Dead Body of* EARL
RUTHVEN, *taken Possession of by a Grizzly and Fleshless Vampire.*

'A Grizzly and Fleshless Vampire' – frontispiece from *The Bride of the
Isles* (1820) wrongly attributed to Lord Byron

A Dictionary of
Vampires

Peter Haining

ROBERT HALE · LONDON

© *Peter Haining 2000*
First Published in Great Britain 2000

ISBN 0 7090 6550 7

Robert Hale Limited
Clerkenwell House
Clerkenwell Green
London EC1R 0HT

The right of Peter Haining to be identified as
author of this work has been asserted by him
in accordance with the Copyright, Designs and
Patents Act 1988

2 4 6 8 10 9 7 5 3 1

Typeset by
Derek Doyle & Associates, Liverpool.
Printed in China by
Dah Hua International Printing Press Co. Ltd

For

PHILIPPA

with love, again

Acknowledgements

The writing of this Dictionary would not have been possible without the help and co-operation of a great many people and I should like to thank Peter Berresford Ellis, Ron Haydock, William Marshall, Christopher Lee, Ingrid Pitt, Barbara Steele, Dorothy Nixon, Tom Peck, Jeannie Youngson, Gordon R. Guy, Donald A. Reed, Sean Manchester, Donna Crow, Dr Kathryn D. Marocchino, Basil Copper, Stephen Kaplan and the late Peter Cushing. I must also acknowledge my thanks to the staff of The British Museum, The London Library, The Harry Price Library at the University of London, The Theatre Royal, London, Shaftesbury Theatre, London, New York Public Library, The Library of Congress in Washington DC, The Vampire Research Society, London and the Vampire Information Exchange of Brooklyn, NJ. Several newspapers and magazines allowed me access to their files and supplied cuttings as well as photographs for the book including *The Times, Daily Telegraph, Observer, Daily Mail, Daily Express, Daily Mirror, Times Literary Supplement, New Society, International Herald Tribune, Radio Times, Supernatural Magazine, Essex Chronicle* and *Aberdeen Evening Express.* The following publishers have given permission for quotations from their books and the reproduction of a number of illustrations: Little Brown, Constable & Co., Michael Joseph, Foulsham & Co., The Scarecrow Press Inc., and Marvel Comics. The films stills are reprinted by courtesy of The British Film Institute, Hammer Films, Universal Pictures, Border Films, American International Pictures, Columbia Pictures, BBC Enterprises and ABC TV, New York. Other illustrations were supplied by the Yorkshire Tourist Board, Aberdeen City Council and The Count Dracula Society of Los Angeles. The remaining photographs and illustrations are all from my own archives.

Preface

In December 1998 I travelled to Romania to film a television documentary, *Dracula*, about vampires in general, and Bram Stoker and
his classic novel in particular. I was appearing as presenter of the
programme for a multinational series, *Myths of Mankind*, and the
three-week shooting schedule took me from the little seaport of
Whitby in Yorkshire via London to Bucharest and the snow-covered
mountains of legendary Transylvania. It was a fascinating experience as the production crew and I passed through the places made
so familiar by Stoker – the great plain of Wallachia, the towns of
Sighişoara, Bistriga, Brasov, Snagov, Tirgovişte, Bran Castle and the
Borgo Pass – as we went in search of the facts about Vlad Tepes a
Wallachian prince known as 'The Impaler', who was an important
source of inspiration for *Dracula*, and ultimately arrived at the
setting of the mythical castle of the most famous vampire of them
all. . . .

Yet from the very first day of filming at Whitby where, in
Stoker's novel, the undead Count makes his first landfall in
England, to the closing sequences shot high up in the brooding,
pine-covered Carpathian Mountains at *Castel Dracula* – a brash
tourist hotel complete with an elevating model of the Count in a
coffin in the basement – a curious thought kept slipping into my
mind. Here *I* was walking in the places that the author had
described so evocatively, but, with the exception of the English
locations, *he had never actually visited*. Though all great novels
undoubtedly owe much to the imagination of their creator, *Dracula*
is probably one of the very few based, quite evidently on fact, but
in which virtually all the most crucial elements were drawn solely
from research.

The thought made me dwell for a time on the facts and fiction – not to mention the misconceptions and inventions – about vampires and vampirism. Of course, there have been a great many books on the topic and its use in literature, films, stage productions, the arts and in a great many other areas of everyday life from product branding to comic strips. What seemed to be missing was a handy guide to the vampire: perhaps the most gruesome of all figures of terror and yet a universal icon to whom people of all ages have been inexorably drawn, generation after generation. *The Dictionary of Vampires* is intended to help satisfy this craving. For all their strangeness, probably the one thing humanity shares in common with these undead creatures is the fact that they apparently live for hundreds of years – just as our interest has done.

Of course, there have always been those who scoff at the very idea of a reanimated corpse rising from the grave to suck the blood of people in order to sustain its undead existence. Yet such sceptics need only look at the huge body of documented evidence that is available (much of it cited herein), or travel to almost any country in the world to discover that no amount of scepticism has been able to shake *this* belief in its tomb – as writers of fiction have been doing so successfully for the past two hundred years and more.

The great English poet, Lord Byron – who was well aware of this public fascination – wrote in his oriental piece, *Giaour* (1813) that 'the freshness of the face, and the wetness of the lip with blood, are the ever-failing signs of a vampire.' I would suggest that the evidence of these pages proves that there is an unflagging interest in the subject which the passage of time, the advances in science and medicine, and even the arguments of philosophy, have done little to diminish. Nor, I believe, will this change in the new millennium.

PETER HAINING
Boxford, Suffolk
January, 2000

𝕬

Abruzzi Vampires

Abruzzi, the beautiful mountainous area of south central Italy which culminates in the *Gran Sasso d'Italia*, the highest point of the Apennines, has a centuries old vampire tradition. The undead here are referred to as *la strega chi succia il sangue* ('the witch who sucks blood') and their particular target are children, according to G. de Nino in his book, *Usi e Costumi Abruzzesi* published in the middle of the nineteenth century. When the young are seen to pine and waste away, de Nino says, the parents go at once to the priest who will recite the Holy Gospel over the child and arrange for a cross of wax, which has been blessed on Ascension Day, to be hung over the doorway. A little linen bag full of salt is often hung around the sufferer's neck as extra protection against nocturnal attacks. If the wasting continues, a piece of the sick child's hair will be cut and burned in a nearby field as the smoke is believed to drive off the vampire. In some parts of Abruzzi, candles and tapers are burned in graveyards on the first day of November each year to 'show the evil dead the way back to their tombs'. Local tradition also says that vampires can be stopped from entering a house by leaving the dead body of a cat or dog outside, for the undead cannot pass until they have counted every hair on the corpse and this will take them until dawn when they must flee from the rising sun. It has been observed that a great many Italian-Americans are descended from emigrants who came from Abruzzi and Sicily and brought with them to the US the old beliefs that can still be found in some of their communities and where the wearing of holy talismans and medallions is a clear echo of the past.

'Show the evil dead the way back to their tombs' – the time-honoured instruction observed by the people of Abruzzi

Addams Family

Morticia, the mother of the Addams family, who dresses umistakably in a shroud, is one of the best-known female vampires in the media. Her ghoulish family consisting of husband Gomez, Uncle Fester, Lurch, and the dastardly children, Pugsly and Wednesday, were originally created in the 1930s by Charles Addams (1912–1988) in a series of cartoons for the *New Yorker* magazine. Later they all featured in a 1960s TV series (with Carolyn Jones as Morticia), a 30-minute cartoon programme, a 1979 special *Hallowe'en with the Addams Family*, and in 1992 by a $30 million blockbuster Paramount movie starring Anjelica Houston, as a wonderfully vampy Morticia. Creator Charles Addams was fascinated by the macabre all his life and Morticia represented his 'female ideal'; his first two wives both favoured her look, it is said, and he married the third in a Long Island cemetery! His New York flat contained, among other things, a skeleton in a glass case, an embalming block and a Victorian flyswatter which cast a bat-like shadow on one wall. A number of collections of his cartoons have been published including *Monster Rally* (1955), *Nightcrawlers* (1957), the posthumous *The World of Charles Addams* (1991), as well as a novelization based on the TV series, *The Addams Family*, by Jack Sharkey (1965).

Adze (Africa)

The *Adze* is the African species of vampire that haunts graveyards and, sometimes, jungle areas. For much of the time, this member of the undead looks like a small version of the firefly moving swiftly in the night. But tradition says this is merely an illusion, and when it decides to attack, the *Adze* turns into a human being with glaring eyes and enormous, red-flecked lips and teeth. It mostly enjoys the blood of children and can only be destroyed when it is caught in human form and burned alive.

Illustration for Vasilie Alecsandri's famous Romanian poem
'The Vampyre' (1855)

Alecsandri, Vasilie (1821–1890)

Vorn in Bacau, Romania, Alecsandri wrote over 300 poems and more than 50 plays – including the impressive *Despot Voda* (1879) – and played an important role in the development of modern Romanian literature as well as in the political events of his time. He first studied medicine and law, but gave these up for literature and spent years travelling his native land collecting popular traditions and ballads. His poem, 'The Vampyre' (1855), has become familiar to generations of Romanians, although it was not translated into English until 1887 by William Beatty-Kingston for the April issue of the *English Illustrated Magazine*. Several stanzas have subsequently been reprinted in vampire anthologies, though curiously, not the last verse, which is probably the most evocative of all:

> *Then from those dismal depths arise*
> *Blaspheming yells and strident cries*
> *Re-echoing through the murky air.*
> *And, like a serpent from its lair,*
> *Brandishing high a blood-stained glaive*
> *The Vampyre rises from his grave!*

It has been claimed that Bram Stoker (*q.v.*) may well have read this poem prior to writing his classic novel *Dracula*, as his elder sister, Matilda, an accomplished illustrator and literary critic, contributed an article on 'Sheridan and Miss Linley' to the same issue of the *English Illustrated Magazine*.

Allacci, Leone (1586–1669)

Leone Allacci – occasionally referred to as Leo Allatius – was a learned scholar and theologian who published one of the earliest descriptions of Greek vampires in 1645. Born on the island of Chios, he entered the Greek College at Rome and in 1616 received the degree of Doctor of Medicine. He was then given a post at the Vatican library where his subsequent researches and dedicated scholarship earned him the appointment of custodian. Several major works evolved from Allacci's access to the library's vast wealth of material, including *De Graecorum Hodie Quorundam Opinationibus*, published in Cologne in 1645, in which he included information on many traditions from his native Greece, especially that of vampires, or *Vrykolakas* (*q.v.*). He had no doubt about their existence, writing: 'It is the height of folly to attempt to deny that such bodies are not infrequently found in their graves uncorrupt and that by use of them the Devil, if God permits him, devises most horrible complots and schemes to the hurt and harm of mankind.' He added, 'No plague more terrible or more harmful to man can well be thought of or conceived.'

Alp (Germany)

The *Alp* is a female vampire found mostly in Germany. According to legend, she is the spirit of a recently deceased person and will settle on the chest of her sleeping victim, stifling them before drawing blood. Sometimes a butterfly – called an *Alp* – flies out of the creature's mouth before she bites. Tradition says that these creatures are particularly fond of attacking children or lonely travellers, especially those who speak to them in the mistaken impression that they are living women. The prescribed method of driving an *Alp* away is by forcing a lemon into its mouth.

Alucard

Dracula's name reversed has become a popular device for authors and film makers of vampire stories. The title Count Alucard made its first appearance in the 1943 film, *Son of Dracula*, written by the German writer/director, Curt Siodmak (1902–   ), who created the screenplays for a whole series of monster movies in the 1940s and 1950s. The Count was played by Lon Chaney Jnr. Count Alucard was also one of the story-tellers in *Dr Terror's Gallery of Horrors* (1966) played by Mitch Evans and ultimately revealed to be the

'Vampire King' himself. In *Dracula AD 1972* made by Hammer Films (*q.v.*), Johnny Alucard, a teenager, played by Christopher Neame, was responsible for reviving his namesake: the Count once again played by Christopher Lee (*q.v.*). The American movie expert and writer, Forrest J. Ackermann (1916–   ) had also used the name Alucard as a pseudonym in some of his work.

Count Alucard was played by Lon Chaney jnr in *Son of Dracula* (1943)

Ancona Vampire

The beautiful Italian coastal town of Ancona, with its stunning views across the Adriatic, was the location of what was described as a vampire incident in 1952. Widely reported at the time, it has continued to puzzle experts and historians alike ever since. The events, concerning the discovery of a long dead body, were reported in the *Giornale D'Italia*: 'Blood spurted from a corpse which had been buried since 1920 in the cemetery of Aberici di Montemarciano near Ancona. The corpse had just been exhumed in a perfect state of preservation. The clothes were also in very good condition. It was the corpse of a woman who had died at the age of 70 in February 1920. Blood flowed abundantly from the left knee, and it was only after this outflow that decomposition commenced. No explanation has yet been found for this phenomenon.'

Andilaveris

For a number of years the little Green island of Kythnos was plagued by a vampire known as Andilaveris, according to Henry Hautteweur in his book *Le Folklore de l'Isle Kythnos* (1898). The undead man – a 'vicious devil' – rose from the grave at night and would attack any family who had not bolted their doors against him. When unable to find victims, the creature would climb onto the roof of the church in Messaria and in his frustration angrily pass water onto the streets below. Andilaveris' reign of terror on the island was put to an end when his body was taken by day from its coffin by a party of local men led by their priest and rowed out to a small deserted islet where, in accordance with an ancient Greek belief that vampires cannot cross water, he was left to waste away. In this same part of the world, vampires are sometimes referred to as *Anakathoumenos* – the 'snatcher' or 'he who sits up in the grave'.

Asasabonsam (Ghana)

The Ashanti region of Ghana in West Africa, famous for its warlike people, is the haunt of the *Asasabonsam*, a vampire which can appear in the shape of a man, a woman, or even a child. It is described by R. Sutherland Rattray in *Ashanti Proverbs; Translated from the Original* (1916): 'It is a monster of human shape which, living far in the depths of the forest, is only occasionally met by hunters. It sits on treetops, and its legs dangle down to the ground and have hooks for feet which pick up any one who comes within reach. It has iron teeth. There are female, male and little *Asasabonsam*.' Rattray also refers to the *Obayifo*, a kind of human vampire derived from *bayi* ('sorcery'), which sucks the blood of children until they die. Men and women possessed of this power are said to be able to leave their bodies at night and travel great distances to find victims. They can apparently be spotted because they emit a phosphorescent light in the darkness.

Astral Vampires

A theory that vampires are actually the astral bodies of incarcerated or recently dead individuals revitalizing themselves parasitically on living victims, was advanced in the middle of the nineteenth century by a French psychical researcher, Professor Z.T. Pierart. The Professor, who began conducting his research into campirism in 1858, argued in the *Revue Spiritualiste* a few years later that the astral body would be 'forcibly ejected upon the premature burial of a still-living agent'. Then, he said, 'The astral body would vampirize the living in order to nourish the trapped body.' Pierart explained the reason for the legend of vampires by stating that the bodies of these undead do not decay because of 'the vitality which flows from the astral body through the astral cord'. It was also part of Pierart's philosophy that it was dangerous to leave a mirror in the room of a dead person, as the doubling of the corpse by the reflection could also result in the creation of a vampire.

Aswid (Scandinavia)

Aswid is the name sometimes given to vampires in the Scandinavian countries – although the simple *Vampyr* has been much more popular in Sweden for generations. The early narratives from this part of the world, like the ancient *Grettus Saga*, say that there are many living dead in their barrows who wander abroad at night 'like ravenous ghouls'. According to tradition, if an *Aswid* had been a nobleman when alive, then he would first devour the horse and dog buried with him before going in search of the blood of the living. The best form of protection against the *Aswid* is to plunge a sharp-pointed knife into its body.

Australia

In his book, *Vampires and Vampirism* (1924), Dudley Wright (*q.v.*) states that 'the vampire demon is no stranger to Australia.' He cites as his evidence John Bonwick's book, *Daily Life of the Tasmanians* (1918) in which the author writes:

> During the whole of the first night after the death of one of their tribe, they will sit round the body, using rapidly a low, continuous recitative to prevent the evil spirit from taking it away. This evil spirit was the ghost of an enemy. Fires at night kept off these mischievous beings, which were like the vampires of Europe.

B

Bajang (Malaysia)

A vampire-like creature found in Malaysia which is said to usually resemble a large polecat. Local folklore claims that the *Bajang* is the spirit of a stillborn child and requires blood to maintain its undead existence. Sir Frank Swettenham in his book, *Malay Sketches* (1895), states that *Bajangs* 'can, at the dead of night, be lured from the grave by potent incantations' and then used by those who know these secrets to prey on their enemies. For years, the punishment for anyone found in possession of one of these vampires was to be thrown into a river with their hands and feet tied and left to drown – an echo of the practice employed in England of 'ducking' suspected witches.

Baobhan Sith (Scotland)

The *Baobhan Sith* of Scotland are among the most beautiful of vampires – lovely girls with long, golden hair who dress in flowing green robes. The words mean the same as the Irish *banshee*, but these women are described as being 'a kind of succubus, very dangerous and evil'. They mostly appear in groups of four and make a habit of bewitching solitary male travellers late at night. According to the folklorist Donald A. Mackenzie in *Scottish Folk Lore and Folk Life* (1935), the women encourage their unsuspecting victims to dance with them so furiously that the men begin to bleed. At sunrise, the *Baobhan Sith* instantly disappear, leaving behind the bodies of their victims . . . sucked dry of all their blood.

Bara, Theda (1890–1955)

Theda Bara was the Hollywood film star who introduced vampiric elements into the movies and launched the concept of the 'vamp'. She became an overnight sensation in her first starring role as a voluptuous, wanton and cruel *femme fatale* (*q.v.*) in *A Fool There Was* (1915) which was based on the poem, 'The Vampire' by Rudyard Kipling (*q.v.*). She was also one of the first film stars to have a career almost completely manufactured by publicity. Born Theodosia Goodman, the daughter of a Cincinnati tailor, she was claimed by her publicists to have been born in the Sahara Desert, the love child of a French artist and his Egyptian mistress, and was promoted as a woman of mystic powers. Her name is an anagram of 'Arab Death' and she was said to like the taste of human blood! She wore indigo make-up to emphasize her pallor as well as posing with relish alongside human skeletons and skulls. Bara often gave interviews stroking a snake, gloried in her title, 'The Vamp', while a line from *A Fool There Was*, 'Kiss me, my fool!' became an instant catch-phrase. Her later roles in the same vein inspired a whole generation of American girls to dress in vampire-like clothes. Theda Bara's last screen appearance was in *Madame Mystery* (1926) – a parody of her extraordinary earlier eyars – after which she was never heard of again, until her tragic death from cancer.

Baring-Gould, Sabine (1834–1924)

An English clergyman-scholar, Sabine Baring-Gould spent over fifty years of his life collecting and publishing stories about folk-lore and the supernatural which made him a forerunner of other, now perhaps better known writers in the genre, such as

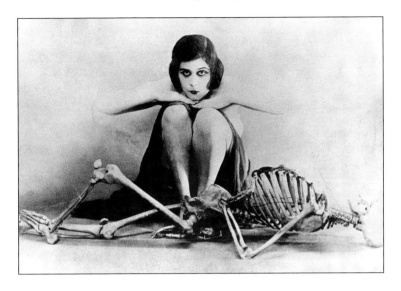

Theda Bara the American actress who created the term 'Vamp' in 1915

Montague Summers (*q.v.*) and Elliott O'Donnell (*q.v.*). Living on the family estate, which he inherited at Lew Trenchard in Devon, Baring-Gould first came to public attention when he wrote the famous hymn, 'Onward Christian Soldiers'. By contrast, his works including *The Book of Were-Wolves* (1865) and *Curious Myths of the Middle Ages* (1866) revealed him to be a man of far-ranging interests with a profound knowledge of the weird and the macabre. *The Book of Were-Wolves*, in particular, which contains a number of true reports of vampires, has proved to be an important reference source on the subject, much consulted by later writers. Bram Stoker (*q.v.*) used it and *Curious Myths* while writing *Dracula*.

Bat, Vampire-

Despite the vampire-bat's fearsome reputation with mankind since the term was first applied in zoology by Linnaeus in the eighteenth century, only three types of bat – the *Desmodus Rufus*, the *Didemus Yungi*, and the *Diphylla Caudata* all found in Central and Southern America – are actual bloodsuckers – and they are all more likely to attack cattle than human beings. Apart from being most active at night and having the ability to detect ultrasonic sounds, these bats are all very agile creatures that can fly quickly, turn somersaults and even walk on the ground at speed. In fact, the bat invariably alights on its victim gently and then steps softly on its large, hooked toes over the skin in order to find a suitable spot. Then it licks the flesh, inserts its incisor teeth into the flesh, and laps up the blood as it comes to the surface. The bat's bite has an anaesthetic quality, while the saliva has an anti-coagulating property which facilitates the flow of the blood. This bite can transmit rabies to a victim which,

Desmodus Rufus – the bloodsucking vampire-bat

in turn, bites just like the victims of human vampires. Scientific study has confirmed that these species of bat all exist entirely on blood.

Bathory, Countess Erzsebet (1560–1614)

Known either as the 'Vampire Countess' or 'The Blood Countess of Transylvania', Erzsebet – or Elizabeth – Bathory was the widow of a Hungarian nobleman and lived in the now ruined Castle of Cachtice (formerly Csejthe) not far from Bratislava in the Lesser Carpathians. Here, it is claimed, she satisfied her bloodlust by the torture and murder of as many as 600 young women. It was after being widowed by the death of her soldier husband, Count Gerencz Nadasdy (the family crest consisted of three wolves' teeth on a blazon) to whom she had been betrothed since she was 11, that Elizabeth, desperate to preserve her fading beauty for a succession of lovers, decided that bathing in human blood was the way to preserve her looks. The blood was mercilessly extracted from naked girls suspended from the ceiling in iron cages of nails or alternatively, by imprisoning females in an 'iron maiden' which, when closed around the helpless victims, plunged metal spikes into them. When the number of the Countess' victims became such that even the local authorities were forced to take action, Elizabeth was tried and sentenced to be walled-up alive in her castle until she died. There has been much debate among historians as to whether Countess Bathory did, in fact, drink blood in true vampire fashion or merely used it as a cosmetic. Her story has been told in several books – beginning with Sabine Baring-Gould's (*q.v.*) *The Book of Werewolves* (1865) (*q.v.*) and the detailed biographies of Valentin Penrose, *The Bloody Countess* (1962), *The Dracula Myth* by Gabriel Ronay (1972), *Dracula Was A Woman* by Raymond T. McNally (1983) and '*Countess Dracula*': *The Life and Times of Elisabeth Bathory, The Blood Countess* by Tom Thorne (1997) – as well as two films, *Countess Dracula* made by Hammer Films (*q.v.*) in 1970 starring Ingrid Pitt (*q.v.*) and *Contes Immoraux* with Paloma Picasso (1974).

'The Vampire Countess', Erzsebet Bathory

Beeleigh Abbey

Picturesque twelfth-century Beeleigh Abbey in Essex is reputed to be haunted by an evil spirit who may also be a vampire, according to its long-time owner, the late Christina Foyle, head of the famous London book store that bears her name. For fifty years – until the spring of 1974 – no one had slept in one particular bedroom which, tradition claimed, was haunted by the ghost of Sir John Gate, beheaded on Tower Hill in 1553 because of his involvement with Lady Jane Grey (1537–1554), briefly the Queen of England. Deciding one night to brave the ghost, Christina Foyle settled down in the four-poster bed and slept soundly until about 3 a.m. when she was awakened by a feeling that everything in the room was shaking. 'I was also surprised to find two teeth marks on my shoulder and another on one of my fingers,' she told *This Essex* magazine later. 'When my doctor saw the wounds he suggested I ought to go to hospital and there I was told I had been infected by a germ unknown for over twenty years. Had I been living in the old days, people would have said I had been bitten by a vampire. Anyway, I shall never sleep in that room again – *ever*.' Nor has anyone else.

Beheim, Michael (1416–c.1472)

Born in Sulzbach, Michael Beheim was a German Meistersinger, poet and writer who lead a rather chequered career and is best remembered for two rhymed chronicles, *Von den Wienern* (1465) and *Leven Friedrichs I von der Pfalz* (1469). However, research amongst the notes made by Bram Stoker (*q.v.*) while writing *Dracula*, which are today owned by the Philip and A.S.W. Rosenbach Foundation in Philadelphia, USA, has revealed that he consulted a work by Michael Beheim, *The Story of a Bloodthirsty Madman called Dracula of Wallachia*. According to Raymond T. McNally and Radu Florescu in their study, *In Search of Dracula* (1994) Beheim read this paper to the Holy Roman Emperor, Frederick III, during the winter of 1463. They add, 'The original manuscript, located at the Heidelberg University library, proved that the historical Dracula [Vlad Tepes (*q.v.*)] dipped his bread in the blood of his victims, which technically justified Stoker's use of the word, "vampire".'

Bertrand, Francois (1824–c.1865)

A tall, handsome young Army Sergeant, François Bertrand became infamous as 'The Vampire of Paris' in 1849 and to this day remains the most direct instance of 'live' vampirism in France. Born at Voise in the Haute Marne, Bertrand displayed a destructive tendency while still a child, and as an adolescent began to cut up the corpses of dogs or horses to experiment upon. By the time he joined the French Army, he was also digging up and dissecting human corpses – and this rapidly became a mania, as he later confessed in prison: 'If I have sometimes cut male corpses into pieces, it was only out of rage at not finding one of the female sex. Some nights I have had to dig up as many as a dozen men before finding a single woman in the common grave at Montparnasse.' When, in early 1849, the number of outrages at the Père Lachaise cemetery, where many famous artists and musicians are buried, had generated stories about a mysterious night creature violating the corpses, the authorities decided to erect a man-trap to catch the fiend, who the press dubbed 'The Vampire of Paris'. Into this stepped Bertand, and although he managed to escape severely wounded, the fragments of military clothing he left behind led to his arrest. During the sensational trial which followed on 10 July, the 'living' vampire freely admitted how he embraced each corpse and then slit open the stomach. Commenting on the evidence presented to the court, historian Ornella Volta has written in *The Vampire* (1963): 'His look must have had a hypnotic power because, like Dracula's, it made animals lower their eyes and tails and slink away in silence as he lay in the graves next to the corpses in order to avoid detection.' However, the sergeant was sentenced to just one year in prison – the maximum for grave violation: the only charge under which he could be prosecuted. During his incarceration, he wrote a confession published by Ambrose

Tardieu as *Bertrand, Deterreur de Cadavres*, after which he dropped from sight, never to be heard of again. As Dr Alexis Epaulard has written in his *Vampirisme, Necrophile et Necrosadisme* (1901): 'All in all, Bertrand was a vampire just as other people are drinkers.'

Blautsauger (Bosnia)

This is the native vampire of Bosnia – a creature which is said to be covered in hair but has no skeleton. It has very large eyes and has the ability to turn into either a wolf or a rat. The *Blautsauger* apparently always carried with it a little of the earth from its grave which it slips into the mouth of sleeping victims. It is swallowing this earth, rather than the blood, which the vampire draws from the unconscious person, that will turn them into one of the undead. Bosnian folklore claims that hawthorn flowers (*q.v.*) scattered around the cemetery where a *Blautsauger* lives will prevent its night-time wanderings.

Bloch, Robert (1917–1994)

Famous as the author of *Psycho* (1959) which Alfred Hitchcock turned into one of the all-time movie classics, Robert Bloch also wrote a number of vampire short stories highly regarded for their originality and black humour. Born in Chicago, he came to fame writing for the legendary pulp magazine, *Weird Tales* – especially his story for the July 1943 issue, 'Yours Truly, Jack the Ripper' in which the London mass-murderer is revealed to be an immortal who sustains his existence with the blood of his victims. Other tales of the same kind include, 'The Bat Is My Brother' (1944), 'Hungarian Rhapsody' (1958), 'The Living Dead' (1967) and 'The Yugoslaves' (1986). Bloch also wrote a novel of vampirism, *It's All in Your Mind* (1971), and completed 'The Light House', an unfinished story by Edgar Alan Poe (*q.v.*), in which he ingeniously introduced a vampire as the cause of the problems.

Blow Vampire

The eighteenth-century story of the vampire of Blow, a village near Kadax in Bohemia, is unique in that the undead, a shepherd, continued his attacks *after* being staked through the body by villagers. The story is told by Gustav De Schartz in his *Magia Postuma* published in 1706 which describes how, after a series of deaths, the peasants of Blow drove a stake through the corpse, but 'the man, when in that condition, told them that they were very good to give him a stick with which he could defend himself against the dogs which worried him.' Notwithstanding the stake, the vampire returned the following night and attacked more people than he had ever done on a single occasion before. When impaled once again, De Schartz states, 'a great quantity of bright vermilion blood flowed from him,' but while in this weakened condition, the shepherd's head was cut from his body and the corpse burned. This, De Schartz declared, was the only way to be sure of killing one of the undead.

Borgo Pass

The Borgo Pass is one of the most picturesque spots in Romania, evocatively described by Bram Stoker (*q.v.*) in *Dracula* though, of course, he never actually visited the area. Situated just to the east of Bistrità – referred to in the novel as Bistritz where Jonathan Harker stayed at the Golden Krone Hotel – the Pass, with its steep sides and mounting rows of pine trees, is now becoming a popular tourist attraction. There are the ruins of two castles in the vicinity, Castle Rodna and Bethlen Castle (complete with a grim dragon insignia), as well as the new Hotel Castel Dracula, 1116m up in the Tihuta Pass which links Transylvania with Bucovina. Built in medieval style, it took seven years to complete and has its own 'Dracula Vault'. Castel Dracula boasts of being the only hotel in the world bearing that name; the only one with a small cemetery placed in front of it; and having a water supply from 'Dracula's Springs'. The air here is also claimed to have the highest level of iodine in Romania!

The picturesque and mysterious Borgo Pass in Romania

Bottling a Vampire

The Bulgarians have a unique method of bringing a vampire's reign of terror to an end – by *bottling* it. The facts have been provided by folklorist N.I. Dumitrascu in the publication *Ion Creanga* (1914):

> There are certain persons who make a profession of this and their mode of procedure is as follows. The sorcerer, armed with a picture of a saint, lies in ambush until the vampire passes, when he pursues him with his Ikon. The undead takes

refuge in a tree or on the roof of a house, but his persecutor follows him with the talisman, driving him away from all shelter, in the direction of a bottle specially prepared, in which is placed some of the vampire's favourite food, blood. Having no other resource, he enters the prison and is immediately fastened down with a cork, on the interior of which is a fragment of the Ikon. The bottle is then thrown into the fire and the vampire disappears for ever.

Boucicault, Dion (1822–1890)

The Irish dramatist and actor, Dion Boucicault, perhaps most famous for his Irish melodrama, *The Colleen Bawn* (1860), also wrote and starred in one of the earliest three-act plays about the undead, *The Vampire*, which opened at the Princess Theatre in London in June 1852. Curiously, the Dublin-born author set his story of multiple murders in Wales during the reign of Charles II, with the finale two hundred years later when the vampire's reign of terror is finally brought to an end by 'a charmed bullet', against the backdrop of Mount Snowden. Boucicault played the central character, 'The Phantom', and a contemporary description says he appeared all in black, his head partially bald on top, his long black hair swept back behind his ears, and his face 'phosphoric livid'. The London critics generally dismissed *The Vampire* as 'tedious trash', and its star 'a moster of absurdity', but the public loved it. In 1887, Boucicault revived his production as *The Phantom*, again playing the lead, and the following year took it to New York where it ran for several months at Wallack's Theatre 'to good applause.'

Bradbury, Ray Douglas (1920–   )

Ray Bradbury is one of the world's best writers of imaginative fiction and the creator of a group of vampires known as 'The Family' who live an existence of almost everyday normality in Middle America. The background is, in fact, very similar to that in which Bradbury grew up in Waukegan, Illinois before moving to Los Angeles with his family during the Depression. Writing was always his passion and some of his early stories appeared in the pulp magazines like *Weird Tales*. The first of his stories of 'The Family' entitled 'The Homecoming' was intended for this magazine, but surprisingly was rejected; instead it was published in one of America's leading glossy publications, *Mademoiselle*, in October 1946, where it created something of a landmark according to historian, William F. Nolan, 'because Bradbury succeeded in making a clan of vampires delightful and presented them to a host of feminine readers mainly unfamiliar with vampires as fiction fare'. The following year 'The Homecoming' won the O. Henry Memorial Award. During his career, Bradbury has written ground-breaking science fiction (notably *The Martian Chronicles*, 1950, which established his reputation), unique fantasy (*Something Wicked This Way Comes*, 1962) and highly original crime and mystery fiction

Ray Bradbury addressing The Count Dracula Society in Los Angeles

(especially *A Graveyard For Lunatics*, 1990), not to mention screenplays for a number of films: all of which have made him internationally admired and respected. His series about 'The Family' has been continued at irregular intervals and now includes *The Traveller* (1946), *Uncle Einer* (1947), *The April Witch* (1952) and *West of October* originally written in the 1960s but not published until 1988. Ray Bradbury has said he has other ideas for stories featuring his unique vampire family and the whole series is long overdue publication in a single volume.

Bran Castle

Pinnacled Bran Castle, not far from the towns of Cluj and Brasov in Romania, has been described as the place which more than any other conveys the atmosphere and look of the age of Dracula. This picturesque fourteenth-century fortress with its multi-level battlements which dominates the pass to Wallachia is full of inner courtyards, huge halls and long, dark corridors, all filled with period furniture, armour and hunting trophies. In the middle of the central courtyard there is a well and beside it the entrance to a secret passageway which leads 150 feet down the mountain to the citadel of Brasov. As the most imposing castle in Transylvania, it was commandeered by Vlad Tepes (*q.v.*) and has become forever associated with his legend and that of Dracula. (Vlad's actual castle was at Arges, where only the ruins still survive, explaining why Bran is often erroneously described as Castle Dracula.) Bran Castle is now run by the Romanian Tourist Authority and open daily to visitors – one of whom has written in the guest book, 'We are all Draculas!'

Bride of the Isles

Among the Gothic 'Bluebooks' – cheap paperback volumes of 38 pages sold for sixpence (less than 2p) during the early years of the nineteenth century – one of the rarest is *The Bride of the Isles* published by J. Charles in Dublin in 1820 and purporting to be

The courtyard of Bran Castle, Transylvania

'Founded on the Popular Legend of the Vampire by Lord Byron.' The story is set among the southern islands of Scotland where vampires were said to flourish, and features a certain Oscar Montcalm, 'of infamous notoriety in the Scotch [sic] annals of crime and murder (who was decapitated by the hands of the common executioner) and was a most successful Vampire, for many were the poor unfortunate maidens sacrificed to support his supernatural career, roving from place to place'. The climax of the action takes place in the famous Fingal's Cave on the island of Staffa with a confrontation between Oscar the vampire and the beautiful Lady Margaret. The little book is now of the utmost rarity and even the British Library does not possess a copy.

Brite, Poppy Z. (1967–)

Described by the *Independent on Sunday* in 1994 as a 'priestess of the vampire cult', Poppy Brite was born in the same city, New Orleans, as Anne Rice (*q.v.*), to whom her work has been compared. Like Rice, she is regarded as being at the forefront of the writers of 'New Gothic Fiction.' She has commented: 'I don't like vampires very much. What I wanted to write about was the Goth subculture (*q.v.*) of which I was an observer and participant at the time, and vampires are such an essential icon in that – and that's how they turn up in my books.' Brite was briefly a student at the University of California, and then had a number of unusual jobs including gourmet candy-maker, mouse caretaker, artist's model and exotic dancer, while writing her ground-breaking debut novel, *Lost Souls* (1993) about a group of drug-crazed vampires, Molochai, Twig and their leader, Zillah, driving across America in a black van, who snort their victim's blood in whisky bottles as they search for more blood and good times. The book was hailed as 'bringing vampires into the era of rock 'n' roll.' Brite's subsequent works have linked her name to that of Edgar Allan Poe (*q.v.*) – who she has acknowledged as an influence – because of their concentration on death and decay. They include *Drawing Blood* (1994), *Swamp Foetus* (1995), an outstanding collection of contemporary vampire erotic short stories, *Love in Vein* (1998), and *Self-Made Man* (1999). Poppy Brite also has the dubious distinction of being the author of what has been described as 'The Most Horrifying Copy Of Any Vampire Novel' – a copy of a limited edition of *Drawing Blood* which survived a fire in a Los Angeles warehouse in which a suicidal arsonist was burned to death. The book, found close to the body, was offered for sale by a local second-hand book-dealer in September 1994 as 'impregnated with the odour of burning human flesh'.

Brontë, Charlotte & Emily

The two Brontë sisters, Charlotte (1816–1855) and Emily (1814–1848), were clearly fascinated with the idea of vampires as their books bear witness. In Charlotte's *Jane Eyre* (1847) when the heroine learns of Rochester's insane wife, Bertha, she speaks of the woman's face thus: 'The lips were swelled and dark, the brow furrowed; the black eyebrows widely raised over the bloodshot eyes. Shall I tell you of what it reminded me? Of the foul German spectre – the Vampire.' Heathcliffe in Emily Brontë's *Wuthering Heights* (1847) also seems to have similar attributes in his predilection for nocturnal wanderings, bloodless looks, his refusal to eat and his ability to drain the vitality of others. Although the authoress does not explicitly say he *is* a vampire, she tempts her readers who know about such things to draw their own conclusions when she writes in the concluding chapter, 'I tried to close his eyes: to extinguish, if possible that frightful, life-like gaze of exultation before any one else beheld it. They would not shut: they seemed to sneer at my attempts: and his parted lips and *sharp white teeth* sneered, too.'

Brown, Mercy L. (d.1892)

The story of Mercy L. Brown, a farmer's daughter of Exeter on Rhode Island, USA, whose body was exhumed by a group of local people believing her to be a vampire, has been mentioned in numerous works including *The Shunned House* (1924), a tale of vampirism by H.P. Lovecraft (1890–1937) (*q.v.*) and J. Earl Clauson's *The Plantations* (1937). According to press accounts in 1892, the wife and three children of farmer George Brown had died in the nine years since 1883, and that January Mercy also fell ill and died. Suspicions that one or other of the dead Browns might be the cause of the mysterious deaths encouraged some of their neighbours to secretly disinter the bodies. All except Mercy's were found to be in advanced stages of decomposition, though hers was still fresh-looking, and when her heart was cut open it spurted blood. The horrified eyewitnesses needed no more convincing that the girl was one of the undead, and burned her heart and liver on a nearby rock. Later, the corpse was reburied, but an atmosphere of unease persisted in Exeter. Indeed, over the years a number of visitors to the grave in Chestnut Hill Cemetery, just to the west of the grimly named Purgatory Road, have reported strange phenomena in the vicinity, all of which have ensured the continuation of the legend of Mercy L. Brown, vampire.

Brukulaco (Greek Islands)

The *Brukulaco* – sometimes known as *Bulcolaccas* or *Buthrolacas* – is another species of Greek vampire, found mainly on the smaller islands. An extremely ugly creature, it has very taut, tanned and swollen skin which makes it sound like a dum when struck and has earned it the nickname, *timpanita*. The vampire has a deep resonant voice with which it tries to lure victims and is said to be the carrier of the plague. Leon Allacci (*q.v.*), the seventeenth-century Greek authority on vampires, says that this species has been 'named from the vile filth' and continues: '*Bruku* means bad, black mud, not any kind of mud, but feculent muck that is slimy and oozing with excrementitious sewerage so that it exhales a most noisome stench, and *laco* a ditch in which foulness of this kind collects and reeks.' According to tradition, the *Brukulaco* is usually the body of a man who has led an evil and wicked life and most probably been excommunicated. The method of killing this vampire is to cut off its head and burn it.

Bruxsa (Portugal)

The Portuguese vampire or *Bruxsa* is female in appearance and possesses the power of flight when she leaves the tomb in order to seek out victims. This member of the undead is said to have become a vampire as a result of witchcraft and is especially dangerous to travellers on their own. American historian, Richard Andree writing in *Passport to the Supernatural* (1972), describes the creature in these words, 'At night she leaves her resting-place and flies far from home in the form of some gigantic night-bird. The *Bruxsas* keep tryst with their diabolical lovers and seduce, terrify and torment lonely wanderers. On returning from their nocturnal journey of pleasure they suck the blood of their own children.' Local tradition says gloomily there is no known method of disposal.

Buchanan, George (1506–1582)

The Scottish humanist and reformer, George Buchanan, who spent a number of years in exile in France for his outspoken views although he ultimately became James I's tutor and keeper of the Privy Seal, was also responsible for unmasking a rogue Scottish priest who used the fear of vampires to keep his congregations in thrall. The priest apparently travelled the length of the country warning his listeners that 'in a field in Scotland full of Brimstone there are tormented souls who continually cry for blood.' But the truth about these vampires, Buchanan explained in his work, *Franciscanus* (1539), was that the priest had suborned a peasant 'whom he presented at learned gatherings as one of these tormented souls returning to earth at night'. However, this man got drunk one night and gave the fraud away, said Buchanan, and the vampires of the Brimstone Field were heard of no more.

Buffy The Vampire Slayer

The American television series *Buffy The Vampire Slayer* became one of the most popular shows of the late 1990s on both sides of the Atlantic, having risen, vampire-like, from the ashes of a poor movie of the same title released in 1992. Created and scripted by Joss Whedon, the movie told the story of a high school cheer-leader, Buffy, played by Kirsty Swanson, who is informed by an old vampire hunter named Merrick (Donald Sutherland) that she is the 'Anointed One', the only genuine vampire killer in the Californian suburb whose old Spanish name was *Boca del Infierno* ('Hell's Mouth'), and she it is who must put down a group of Romanian

Sarah Michelle Gellar – star of the cult TV series
Buffy The Vampire Slayer

vampires led by the 'vampire king' Lothos (Rutger Hauer). The poor box-office returns indicated this might be Buffy's one and only appearance, but in 1996 Whedon revived the idea for TV and soon had a huge success on his hands with Sarah Michelle Gellar cast in the lead, and the British actor, Anthony Stewart Head, as her mentor, Rupert Giles. Explained Whedon, 'Basically Buffy deals with the classic monsters and she's a great role model because she uses her wits and strength to win.' Already a successful actress in horror movies such as *I Know What You Did Last Summer* (1997) and *Scream 2* (1998), Gellar became a heroine with teenage viewers after playing the girl who 'fits in her homework around nightly martial arts and some serious vampire-slaying at the nearest graveyard', to quote *The Sunday Times* in June 1999. Born in New York, Geller was trained at the La Guardia High School for the Performing Arts and does her own stunts in the show – having clinched the part at the audition by explaining that she was a Tae Kwon Do brown belt. She says of the role, 'I love Buffy the character and everything about her, she's strong and smart. What is astonishing is the range of her appeal – I get calls from adults who just love the show. What about vampires? They suck!' The phenomenal success of the show generated its own catchphrase for anything very bad, 'an Ubersuck', a series of books and souvenirs, as well as its own website.

Buo (Borneo)

The *Buo* is the vampire species of Borneo, a creature of the night with piercing eyes, huge teeth and a rapacious thirst for blood. These members of the undead are believed to be very old, most of them being the reanimated bodies of warriors killed in battle. Indeed, some are said to be still wearing the fighting clothes in which they died and even brandishing their antique weapons. According to local tradition, their favourite victims are young women and to ensure that a *Buo* is dead it is essential to cut off the head, arms and legs.

Burton, Sir Richard Francis (1821–1890)

Famous as the African explorer who found Lake Tanganyika in 1858, Burton was a master of languages and disguises whose many journeys in the far-flung corners of the world are described in his books such as *First Footsteps in Africa* (1856) and *Wanderings in West Africa* (1863). He was also responsible for a definitive translation of the *Arabian Nights* (1885–1888). It was while Burton was exploring India that he came across a number of stories about vampires among the Hindus, which were obviously very ancient, and he set about translating the Sanskrit texts. The result was *Vikram and The Vampire, or Tales of Hindu Deviltry* (1870), a volume somewhat overshadowed by his tales of high adventure, but significant in the Dracula legend because Bram Stoker (*q.v.*) met the author and read the book while at work on his classic novel. In introducing *Vikram*, Burton wrote: 'The *Baital-Pachisi* – a vampire of evil spirit which animates dead bodies – is an old and thoroughly Hindu repertory. It is the rude beginning of that fictitious history which ripened to the *Arabian Nights*.' Of the contents, he added: 'The story turns chiefly on a great king named Vikram, the King Arthur of the East, who in pursuance of his promise to a *Jogi* or Magician, brings to him the *Baital* (Vampire) who is hanging on a tree. The difficulties King Vikram and his son have in bringing the Vampire into the presence of the *Jogi* are truly laughable; and on this thread is strung a series of Hindu fairy stories which contain much interesting information on Indian customs and manners.' The book was enhanced by a series of picturesque illustrations by Ernest Griset. Bram Stoker (*q.v.*) met Sir Richard on several occasions in 1878, 1879 and 1886 when the explorer dined with Sir Henry Irving (*q.v.*) and it has been suggested that the vampire book and the tradition in general were among their topics of conversation. Certainly, Stoker was hugely impressed by Burton: 'a dark and forceful man, masterful and ruthless – he is steel and would go through you like a sword.' Something else also struck Stoker: 'When Burton spoke, his upper lip rose and his canine tooth showed its full length like the gleam of a dagger.'

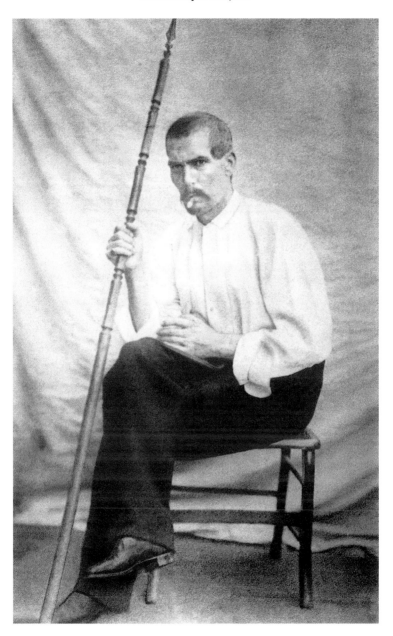

Sir Richard Burton – explorer and vampire storyteller

Byron, Lord George Gordon (1788–1824)

Lord Byron, the English poet as famous for his romantic air of mystery as his great works like *Childe Harold's Pilgrimage* (1812) and the *Bride of Corinth* (1815), was for some years credited with the authorship of *The Vampire* (1819) which had actually been written by his travelling companion and personal physician, John William Polidori (*q.v.*). Byron did, though, have an interest in the subject, for there are elements of vampirism to be found in his 'Fragment of a Novel' (aka 'The Burial') written just prior to Polidori's classic, and the verses of *Giaour* (1813) where he observes:

> *But first on earth, as Vampyre sent,*
> *The corpse shall from its tomb be rent;*
> *Then ghastly haunt thy native place,*
> *And suck the blood of all thy race.*

Remarking on this poem as a whole, James B. Twitchell in *The Living Dead: A Study of the Vampire in Romantic Literature* (1981) claims that, 'It was Lord Byron who, most of all, helped launch the vampire in a fresh direction, one that would culminate with the figure of Dracula.' For his own part, Byron tried to distance himself from the whole tradition, particularly when he wrote to Galignani, the French publisher of an edition of Polidori's book which bore his name, on 27 April 1812: 'I have a personal dislike to vampires and the little acquaintance I have with them would by no means induce me to divulge their secrets. . . . If the book is clever it would be base to deprive the real writer, whoever he may be, of his honour, and if stupid, I desire responsibility for nobody's dullness but my own.'

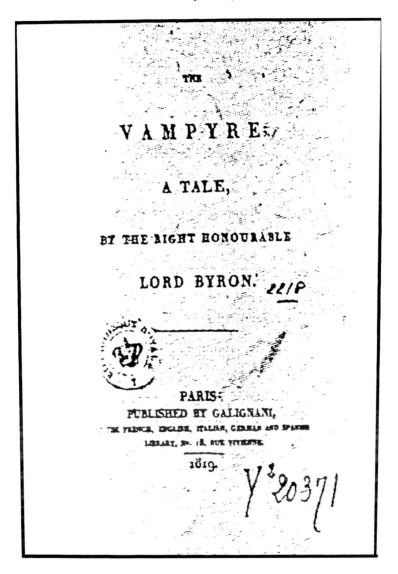

Title page of the first edition of *The Vampyre* published in Paris bearing
Lord Byron's name

C

Calmet, Augustin (1672–1757)

Augustin Calmet, a French Benedictine monk, has been described as the *éminence grise* of vampire lore: a man whose dedication to unearthing and assembling the facts about the undead was second to none. Born at Mesnil-la-Horne in the Lorraine, he was educated at Breuil Priory and in 1688 joined the Benedictine Abbey at Saint Mansuy in Oril. Calmet was subsequently an abbot and teacher at Moyenmoutier, Munster in Alsace and Senones near Saint-Dié. Living in seclusion much of the time, he wrote a number of biblical and historical studies and it was his research that brought him into contact with many unique documents and records concerning vampires which he reprinted and discussed in his pioneering study, *Traité sur les Appirations des Esprits, et sur les Vampires, ou les Revenants de l'Hongrie, de Moravie & etc* which was published in Paris in 1751 and quickly ran through several editions. It was not until a century later, however, that the book was translated into English by Reverend Henry Christmas as *The Phantom World; or, The Philosophy of Spirits and Apparitions* (1850). Many readers found his account of vampires plaguing Europe from the days of Plato to the present century hard to believe – Voltaire, for one, was not sure the book should even have been published – but Calmet's painstaking work has provided a great deal of source material for many subsequent studies. In his book, the abbot, a devout Christian, posed the question as to whether vampires were *really* dead, and if they *were* then their existence must surely be due to the will of God, as only He had the power to ressurect people from the grave. And if this was the case, Calmet said, then what was the *real* purpose of such beings?

Carmilla

Carmilla is the beautiful, sensual young vampire in the story of the same title by the Irish writer, Joseph Sheridan Le Fanu (*q.v.*), which began publication in the *Dark Blue* magazine in December 1871 with superb illustrations by D.H. Friston. It is the earliest tale of its kind to describe the sexual delight to be had from sucking blood from the point of view of the victim and breaks new ground by describing a lesbian entanglement between the heroine, Laura, and Carmilla, whose name is actually an anagram of her real identity, the undead Mircalla, Countess Karnstein. The events occur near the city of Gratz in south-east Austria, an area with a long-standing vampire tradition, and features the first 'vampire hunter' in fiction, Baron Vordenburg, who is actually the latest member of his family to have devoted their lives to pursuing the undead. The Baron is

The vampire Carmilla attacks one of her victims – as visualized by D.H. Friston (1871)

also the author of 'a curious paper devoted to prove that the vampire, on its expulsion from its amphibious existence, is projected into a far more horrible life', and brings this knowledge and his single-minded determination to bear in the ultimate staking, decapitation and cremation of Carmilla. Le Fanu's classic story has been filmed several times, notably as *Vampyr* by the French director Carl Dreyer (*q.v.*) in 1932 starring Sybille Schmitz; again in France in 1960 as *Et Mourir de Plaisir* directed by Roger Vadim with Annette Stroybeg; in 1962 in Spain as *La Maldicion de los Karnsteins* directed by Thomas Miller with Christopher Lee (*q.v.*) as Count Ludwig Karnstein; a Hammer version, *The Vampire Lovers* in 1970 which Peter Sasdy directed featuring Ingrid Pitt (*q.v.*); and the following year as *Vampiros Lesbos*, a joint Spanish–West German adaptation directed by Jesus Franco.

Carradine, John (1906–1988)

Considered by some to be one of the most outrageous ham actors – and by others as a highly skilled character player – the gaunt and saturnine-looking John Carradine, who played a host of eccentrics and villains during his career, is notorious in vampire history for starring in *Billy the Kid vs. Dracula* (1966) a film so poor and unorthodox that it had the undead Count flying about as a bat in broad daylight! The actor himself later said he thought it was the worst part he ever played on the screen. Born in Greenwich Village, New York, Carradine was initially a stage actor, later going to Hollywood where he obtained a number of bit parts before being offered (and turning down) the role of the monster in *Frankenstein* (1931) which made an international star of Boris Karloff (*q.v.*). It was with Karloff in *House of Frankenstein* (1944) that he first played Dracula, giving a memorable performance very different to that of Bela Lugosi (*q.v.*). The success prompted a sequel, *House of Dracula* (1945), during the making of which he said, 'I devised my Count from the description given in the book by Bram Stoker (*q.v.*). I had read *Dracula* in my early teens and I went through it again to be sure my recollections were correct: using a wig of white hair and

Billy The Kid Vs. Dracula starred John Carradine and is considered one of the worst vampire films ever made

moustache, plastic material to create the vampire's aquiline nose, and small red lines to make my eyes look large and the pupils dilated.' Carradine subsequently played Dracula a number of times on the stage and for television; as well as the absurd *Billy the Kid vs. Dracula* in which his reign of terror in the Old West was brought to an end when the outlaw stabbed him with a scalpel; he was a nondescript vampire in the Spanish movie, *Les Vampiras* (1967); a murderous butler in *Blood of Cradula's Castle* made in 1969; and in 1979 filmed *The Vampire Hookers* about which the less said the better. Despite these later aberrations, John Carradine does deserve credit for creating the first faithful screen portrayal of Count Dracula.

Cat, Vampire

Vampire-like creatures in the form of cats have been recorded in the folk traditions of several countries, most notably Japan. There, the

Japanese vampire cats prey on females while they are asleep

animals vary in size from domestic pets to creatures of gigantic proportions and are said to have large, staring eyes and seek blood from the feet and ankles of people rather than the neck. Vampire cats are believed to live in old houses and cemeteries and usually prey on victims who are mentally deranged or in poor health. The anonymous story of 'The Vampire Cat of Nabeshima', about a demonic cat that plagues the royal family of Nabeshima in the sixteenth century, is the best known account of the creature and is reprinted in *Passport to the Supernatural* by Bernhardt J. Hurwood (1972).

Catacano (Rhodes)

This species of vampire is found in remote districts on the beautiful Greek island of Rhodes. It is a particularly terrifying member of the undead with its mouth always split into a wide grin revealing very sharp, white teeth. Before biting, the *Catacano* spits blood onto its victim's skin producing a terrible burn, while at the same time paralysing the person. The most effective barrier to this vampire is salt water, though its long nails are believed to be very inflammable and if set alight will also drive-off the creature. When trapped, the *Catacano* should be decapitated and the head boiled in vinegar, local tradition maintains.

Caul

In many countries of the world, a caul – the membrane found covering the head of some new-born babies – is regarded as a sign of good luck. In Italy, for example, people born with a caul are said to possess special healing powers, while in England their ability to bring good fortune has resulted in them being offered for sale as recently as the nineteenth century (*vide* an advertisement in the *Malvern Advertiser* of March 1872). But in Romania, an old tradition claims that the male child born with a caul will become a vampire forty days after he has been laid in the grave. As Agnes Nurgoci wrote in 'The Vampire in Roumania' in *Folk Lore* (1938): 'It is said that sometimes in Roumania, a man who knows that he was born with a caul will, when he dies, leave instructions to his family to treat his body as that of a vampire and so avert any future danger.'

Ch'iang Shih (China)

In China, the *Ch'iang shih*, or 'Corpse-Spectre', is said to be the most dreaded of all evil spirits. Probably the earliest account of one is to be found in the *Tso Chuan* written in the sixth century BC by Tso Ch'iu Ming, a work of history much admired by Confucius. In this, the author describes a dead body which became a demon when the soul refused to leave the body. Chinese vampires are somewhat similar in appearance and behaviour to those in the West: they have read, staring eyes, claw-like nails, and pale, greenish-white hair all over their bodies which looks like mould or decay. The *Ch'iang shih* can fly and are said to gain their strength from the moon. Not only do they suck blood from living victims, but they will also eat the

The Ch'iang Shih, or 'Corpse Spectre', the vampire of China

flesh of corpses. The best method of putting an end to one of these vampires is to make a circle of rice around its tomb or, if cornered, to set light to the creature, whereupon it emits a terrible, piercing shriek. (A Chinese superstition says that the moon or sun should never be allowed to shine upon an unburied body or an evil soul will gain control of it and seek human blood.) Tradition maintains that the vampires of China can sometimes be created by demon spirits assembling new bodies from a few bones or a skull, alternatively by entering corpses and reanimating them. These undead are prevented from decay by regular infusions of blood. The best stories about the *Ch'iang shih* are to be found in the sixteen volumes of the *Liao Chai* written in the late seventeenth century by P'u Sung-ling, and now held in the same regard by the Chinese as the *Arabian Nights* in the West. The volumes were not printed until 1740 and had to wait many years more before being translated into English. Among the relevant stories now available are 'The Resuscitated Corpse', 'The Corpse at the Inn' and 'The Corpse, the Blood-Drinker' which can be found in *Strange Stories from a Chinese Studio*. Vampires are also discussed in G. Willoughby-Meade's *Chinese Ghouls and Goblins* (1928) in which he writes, 'The malevolence and strength of this monster, and its power of assuming various forms, are manifested between sunset and sunrise; and it is not represented as attacking only the weak-minded or the wicked, but as entirely and gratuitiously hostile to all comers.' Curiously, the *Ch'iang shih* does not turn its victims into vampires like its Western counterpart.

Children

Accounts of vampire children are very rare. In Romania, a tradition is recorded that any child who died before he or she has been baptized is in danger of becoming a vampire seven years after the burial. More curious still, it is held that when a family has seven children of the same sex, the seventh will possess a little tail and is destined to become one of the undead. This is in complete contrast to many other countries where the seventh child is believed to be lucky, while the seventh son of a seventh son will become a powerful healer.

Ciuateto (Mexico)

The name of the Mexican vampire, *Ciuateto*, means 'Honourable Mother' and these members of the undead are said to be the evil spirits of noblewomen who died in childbirth. The creatures are unmistakable with their faces, arms and hands covered in what looks like very white chalk. They are said to be linked to Tezcatlipoca, the most powerful of all the Mexican gods, and have inherited his ability to fly. The *Ciuateto* direct their attacks at children – who lose colour and die within a matter of weeks of being bitten – and are believed to be responsible for the spread of infantile paralysis in Mexico. The creatures first became known in the West following the Spanish conquest and allegedly meet at crossroads to plan their bloodlust missions. Local folklore says they can be stopped by being made to eat bread or pieces of meteorites! Mexico is also the haunt of male and female vampires who have extremely black bodies and a skull in place of a head. They are rather grandly known as *Lord of the Mictlampa* and *Mictecaciuatl* – 'Lady of the Place of Death', but appear to be held in rather less awe by modern men and women who often dress up as them for parties and carnivals.

Clerk-Maxwell, James (1831–1879)

James Clerk-Maxwell was a Scottish physician, born in Edinburgh, who became the first Professor of Experimental Physics at Cambridge in 1871, organised the Cavendish Laboratory and, two years later, published his great work, *Treatise on Electricity and Magnetism*. It was as a 15-year-old schoolboy that Clerk-Maxwell had first demonstrated his prodigious intellect by devising a method for drawing certain oval curves, which was published by the Royal Society of Ediburgh, while in the same year – and in a quite different vein – publishing a notorious piece of juvenilia, an imitation Scottish ballad entitled 'The Vampire'. Written in archaic Scottish dialect, it tells the story of a 'douchty knichte' who fails to recognise that a mysterious woman he meets on his travels is actually a vampire – and when he does, all too late, 'the vampire suckis his gude lyfe blude/She suckis hyum till hee dee.'

Cooke, Thomas Potter (1786–1864)

Actor T.P. Cooke, as he was usually billed, was the first Englishman to play a vampire on the stage in *The Vampyre; or, The Bride of The Isles* by James Robinson Planche (*q.v.*) which opened at the Lyceum Theatre in London on 9 August 1820. Cooke was a former merchant seaman who, at the age of 11, had run away from home to join the navy and served at sea for a number of years before being shipwrecked off Cuxhaven. Thereupon he returned to dry land and in 1804 launched what proved a very successful acting career with the Royal Theatre Company, specializing mainly in seafaring roles: his appearance as the vampire Lord Ruthven (*q.v.*) was unconventional to say the least. Because Planche had set the drama in Scotland, Cooke appeared wearing a plaid kilt, silver breast plate, and a bonnet complete with a spray of feathers. Accounts indicate that the actor played the undead man with 'great gusto', leering malevolently at his victims and the audience. The highlight of the production – which was later transferred to Dublin and Paris – was a specially-created 'Vampire Trap': a stage trap-door, through which Cooke disappeated with spectacular effect. A contemporary description explains,

> A vampire trap consists of two or more flaps, usually India-rubber, through which the sprite can disappear almost instantly, where he falls into a blanket fixed to the under surface of the stage. The trap is secured against accidents by placing another piece or *slide* fitting close beneath when not required and removed when the prompter's bell gives the signal to make ready.

Variations of this mechanism have been in use in stage productions ever since.

Thomas Cooke, the first Englishman to play a vampire on stage

Copper, Basil (1924–)

A former English journalist, Basil Copper, is the author of a long-running series about a Los Angeles private eye, Mike Faraday, as well as a number of excellent vampire short stories and the critically acclaimed study, *The Vampire in Legend, Fact and Art* published in 1973. His knowledge of the undead tradition has been especially evident in the sleeve notes he wrote for the record album, *Dracula* (1974) and short stories such as 'Dr. Porthos' (1968) and 'Reader, I Buried Him!' (1995). 'Reader, I Buried Him!' which first appeared in *The Vampire Omnibus* edited by Peter Haining, drew on the vampire elements in Charlotte Brontë's *Jane Eyre* as well as an extraordinary experience Copper had while making one of his regular visits to France. For while in the remote and mountainous Var district in the autumn of 1993, dozens of sheep were attacked by 'something which crept beneath them and with a sucker-like mouth, drained all their blood', to use his words. Copper adds, 'No creature known to science was responsible – could it have been a vampire? I must confess my hair stood on end!' A possible solution to this mystery may be the *Moribondo* (*q.v.*).

Count Duckula

Count Duckula is a green, vegetarian, cartoon duck who was created for younger TV audiences by Thames Television in 1989. The animated series produced by John Hambley, features the versatile David (*Only Fools and Horses*) Jason as the voice of the broccoli-juice swigging Count Duckula with Jimmy Hibbert, Jack May and Brian Trueman giving vocal life to the other major characters, Doctor Von Goosewing, Igor and Nanny, the maid at Castle Duckula. Additional voices for the popular series have also been provided by the American comedienne, Ruby Wax.

Croglin Grange Vampire

'The Vampire of Croglin Grange' in Cumberland is one of the best-known British cases of the undead and has been thoroughly examined in numerous books and magazine articles. The village of Croglin stands about 20 miles southeast of Carlisle and although there is no trace of a 'Croglin Grange', a house known as Groglin Low Hall fits the first description of the events given in a somewhat guarded account by Augustus Hare in his book, *The Story of My Life* published in 1900. According to Hare, two brothers and two sisters named Fisher were living in Croglin about the year 1858 when, one night, one of the women reported seeing a 'monstrous figure with glaring red eyes' staring through her bedroom window. Too terrified to cry out, she huddled in her bed as the creature scratched at the window and then entered the room. Only when the creature's brown, withered face loomed over her and its teeth began to bite into her throat did she scream – but by the time the other

Croglin Low Hall, location of the best known British vampire case

Fishers had reacted to the shout, the vampire had fled. Nothing further happened at Croglin until the following year when, on a similar night, the woman was again awoken by the same sounds. This time she screamed immediately and her two brothers, who had been sleeping in adjacent rooms ever since the first incident, rushed into the bedroom, one of them having just enough time to fire off a shot at the departing creature, hitting it in the leg. The next morning the Fishers followed an unmistakable trail of blood to the nearby church which led to the vault of a long-extinct family. Inside, all the coffins except one were open, their contents scattered about and mangled. With some trepidation, the two brothers lifted the lid of the undisturbed coffin and found inside the creature that had attacked their sister – the bullet-wound still livid on its leg. Without delay, the Fishers burned the vampire and the curse of Croglin Hall was lifted. Chapters devoted to this remarkable story can be found in *Haunted Houses* by Charles G. Harper (1907) and *The Natural History of the Vampire* by Anthony Masters (1972).

Crucifix

Although many vampire films have shown the use of a crucifix to ward off the undead, there is very little evidence in folklore of their use – or of their having any effect. However, the shape of the cross painted on the doors and windows of houses is a well-known method of protection against vampires in a number of countries. In Scotland, for example, tradition says the cross must be daubed in tar, while on the other side of the world in Siberia, red paint will have the same effect.

Cuntius, Johannes (c.1532–1592)

Johannes Cuntius was an alderman in the town of Pentsch in Silesia who, following his death at the age of 60, returned as a vampire to attack local people – in particular the priest of the parish – until his reign of terror was ended in 1592. His story is told by Dr Henry More (*q.v.*) in his *Antidote Against Atheism* who describes how the visits of the vampire to people's homes was preceded by 'a most grievous stink that spread to every corner' and proved to be the dead man's fetid breath. The priest in the story said he had been awoken several times to find Cuntius leaning over his bed about to sink his teeth into his neck. The attacks continued for about five months, until the evidence that the dead alderman was the source of the trouble resulted in his tomb being opened. The body was found to be bloated with fresh blood and at once beheaded and burned.

Cushing, Peter (1913–1994)

Probably the screen's best-known vampire hunter, Peter Cushing was the star of innumerable horror films, yet his screen image belied his real nature as a kind and gentle man. Born in Kenley in Surrey, the son of a quantity surveyor, he initially worked in the same profession until his passion for acting lead him to train at the Guildhall School of Music and Drama in London. He worked in repertory for four years before deciding to look for work in Hollywood. Cushing got his break in a Laurel and Hardy film, *A Chump at Oxford* (1940) and by the time he returned to the UK was

Peter Cushing, the screen's most famous vampire hunter, in
Brides of Dracula (1960)

rarely to be out of work again in either films or on television where
he made a memorable appearance in a production of George
Orwell's *1984*. It was, though, his association with Hammer Films
(*q.v.*) which began with *The Curse of Frankenstein* (1957), in which
he played Baron Frankenstein to Christopher Lee's monster, that
helped to make him a star. The following year, he made the first of

several appearances as Professor Abraham Van Helsing in *Dracula*, a part he came to understand and regard with affection. 'To me, Van Helsing is the essence of good, pitted against the essence of evil,' he once told the author. 'He is such an intriguing man, dedicated and determined, not to say brave in the face of great danger. I think the Dracula films have the same appeal as the old morality plays with the struggle of good and evil, and good always triumphing in the end.' Peter Cushing also appeared as Van Helsing in *The Brides of Dracula* (1960), *Dracula AD 1972* (1972), *Dracula is Dead and Well and Living in London* (1973) and *The Legend of the Seven Golden Vampires* (1974). He recounted his fascinating life on and off screen in two biographies, *Peter Cushing: An Autobiography* (1986) and *Past Forgetting* (1988).

Dakhanavar

The *Dakhanavar* is the name of the central character in the most famous vampire story of Armenia. The creature once haunted the mountains of Ultmish Altotem, with their vast network of valleys and glaciers, stalking any travellers and sucking them dry of blood, 'from the soles of their feet', according to Baron August von Haxthausen in his book, *Transcaucasia* (1854). Legend says that the vampire was finally outwitted by two men who were mapping the valleys.

> When night came, they lay down to sleep, taking care to place themselves with the feet of one under the head of the other. In the night, the vampyre came, felt as usual, and found a head: then he felt at the other end and found a head there also. 'Well,' cried the monster, 'I have gone through the whole 366 valleys of these mountains and have sucked the blood of people without end, but never yet did I find any one with two heads and no feet!' So saying, he ran away and was never more seen in that country. But ever after the people have known that the mountain has 366 valleys.

Daniels, Les (1943–   )

American writer, composer and author of *Living in Fear: A History of Horror in the Mass Media* (1991), Les Daniels has made a speciality of vampire novels ever since the late 1970s. His series featuring the Spanish vampire, Don Sebastian de Villanueva, has charted the progress of the undead man through various time periods including the Spanish Inquisition, the Spanish arrival in America, the French Revolution and even the present century. The stories are unusual in that Don Sebastian is often horrified by the atrocities committed by ordinary men and women during these violent and bloody periods of history. The vampire made his first appearance in *The Black Castle* (1978), returned in *Silver Skull* (1979) and *Citizen Vampire* (1981), following which he moved to nineteenth-century Britain in *Yellow Fog* (1986), changing his name to Sebastian Newcastle. In *No Blood Spilled* (1991) the scene shifted to India where he confronted the murderous Thuggee killers and a further novel, *White Demon* is expected.

Dark Shadows

In the late 1960s and early 1970s, an ABC TV series, *Dark Shadows*, featuring a 175-year-old vampire named Barnabas Collins, became so popular with American viewers that it was made into a daily soap and attracted audiences often as big as contemporary programmes like *Dallas* and *Hawaii Five-O*. Producer Dan Curtis had taken the Gothic trappings of *Dracula* and grafted them onto a centuries-old New England house, Collinwood, where the mysterious Barnabas Collins lives, provoking fear and trepidation among the residents of the nearby town of Collinsport, Maine. Played by a stylish Shakespearian actor, Jonathan Frid, Collins, with his gaunt features, sallow skin, flowing black cape and cane with a silver top in the shape of a wolf's head, was a mesmerising figure who initially dabbled in black magic and made the occasional attack on young girls. As the series grew in popularity, however, Collins became less villainous and more of a tragic, almost romantic figure cursed to a living dead existence who uses his inside knowledge to wage a one-man-vampire campaign against a host of other diabolical foes who threaten the community. Not surprisingly, he was dubbed by one critic as 'the most unlikely TV soap star of them all.' The success of the series generated five Barnabas Collins Fan Clubs, a series of 32 novelizations written by 'Marilyn Ross' (the pseudonym of prolific Canadian writer, William Edward Daniel Ross) and, in 1970, a full-length movie, *House of Dark Shadows*, and twenty years later a pilot for a short-lived revival *Dark Shadows* (1990) in which Ben Cross replaced Jonathan Frid and horror actress Barbara Steele (*q.v.*) co-starred as a medical researcher who claims she can cure the vampire of his bloodlust.

Jonathan Frid starred as Barnabas Collins in the TV series, *Dark Shadows*

Davanzati, Gioseppe (1665–1755)

The Archbishop of Trani, Gioseppe Davanzati, was the author of another of the landmark studies of vampirism, *Dissertazione Sopra I Vampiri*, published in Naples in 1744 after being widely circulated in manuscript among the church authorities. The author was born at Bari and studied at the college in his native town before going to the University of Naples where he distinguished himself in Science and Mathematics. He spent his early years travelling about Europe before returning to Italy and being made a priest and appointed treasurer of the famous Sanctuary of St Nicholas at Bari, where his great learning was also put to use in researching and writing on a variety of religious subjects. His classic work on vampirism was written at the suggestion of the Bishop of Olmutz and reviewed all the existing material on the subject as well as considering a number of cases that had been brought to the attention of his church. Davanzati devoted several chapters to the powers of vampires and was the first to assemble a wide-ranging list of antidotes for the undead. Montague Summers (*q.v.*) in *The Vampire* (1928) says of the book, 'with all its faults and limitations, the *Dissertazione* is deserving of careful consideration.'

Dead Men of Pest

An anonymous poem of this title was hugely popular with British readers in the nineteenth century and much reprinted in 'Penny Dreadfuls' and collections of verse and fiction such as *Legends of Terror* (1826). The five-page poem was based upon actual events which had occurred in the Hungarian town of Pest in the early 1700s and 'were firmly believed in by villagers and seriously reasoned upon by learned divines and physicians'. It concerns an outbreak of deaths in the town in which all of the dead are found to have been drained of their blood. After dozens of victims have been accounted for, suspicion falls upon a tailor named Vulvius who had died a year earlier, apparently of the fever. When a lumbering figure is spotted entering the room of a young girl and sucking her blood, a priest is summoned and declares that Pest is under siege by a vampire. The narrator of 'The Dead Man of Pest' then goes on to deliver a surprise finale:

> *The churchyards straight were ransacked all throughout*
> *With pickaxe, shovel, mattock, and with spade;*
> *But every corpse that we did dig thereout*
> *Did show like living men in coffins laid.*
>
> *It was these corpses that our churchyards filled*
> *That did at midnight lumber up our stairs;*
> *They sucked our blood, the gory banquet swilled,*
> *And harrowed every soul with hideous fears.*
> *And so was barred with iron bolts the churchyard-pale*
> *To keep them out; but all this would not do;*
> *For when a dead man has learned to draw a nail,*
> *He can also burst an iron bolt in two.*
>
> *At the telling of this terror, I myself arose,*
> *And felt great grief and horror in my breast.*
> *I rode nine leagues before I sought repose,*
> *And never again drew nigh the walls of Pest.*

Deafula

A curiosity among vampire films, *Deafula*, made in 1975, was one of the first full-length movies made especially for the deaf. Written and directed by the two-time Emmy award winner, Peter Wechsberg, who is himself deaf, all the dialogue in the picture was signed with a voice-over translation. Wechsberg himself starred as a young theology student in Oregon who has been infected by Dracula before his birth and later in life finds himself growing fangs and in need of fresh blood. Deafula comes to a spectacular end when he is cornered by police in an ornate church decorated with an array of religious artifacts.

Deane, Hamilton (c.1868–1943)

Actor Hamilton Deane, who apparently made his professional debut with the 'Vacation Company' of Henry Irving (*q.v.*) in 1899,

Hamilton Deane wrote and produced the first stage version of
Dracula in 1924

was the man who wrote and produced the first stage version of *Dracula*. An Irishman by birth, he had at first worked in a London bank before his enthusiasm for the stage and some successful appearances in amateur dramatics convinced him that his future lay in the theatre. Signing up with Irving also brought him into contact with the company's manager, Bram Stoker (*q.v.*), and his novel, *Dracula*. Later, Deane recalled: 'I thought it the most gripping story I had ever read and was thrilled by its wonderful stage possibilities. It seemed to me to have all the material for a perfect melodrama.' It was to be some years – and not until after Stoker's death – that he was able to make the dream come true: having, in the meantime, secured the dramatic rights from Stoker's widow, Florence. In the interim, Deane had also made something of a name for himself on both sides of the Atlantic as a performer of Shakespearian drama and old English comedies. Failing to find a suitable writer to adapt *Dracula*, he tackled the job himself and opened the production at the Grand Theatre in Derby in June 1924. Although he had intended the part of the Count for himself, Deane could find no other member of the company capable of playing the vampire hunter, Van Helsing, so he took the role himself and cast Edmund Blake as the vampire. He was, though, responsible for dressing the vampire in the tuxedo and cape with stand-up collar which subsequently became the Count's trademark in virtually every play and film. *Dracula* was a triumph, transferred to The Little Theatre in London, where the young Raymond Huntley, later to become a leading English stage, film and TV actor, appeared as the Count. Deane himself continued to be associated with the play as an actor and producer for the rest of his life. 'I could do no wrong with *Dracula*,' he said later, 'I simply coined money with it, everywhere.' In October 1927, the play, adapted by the US playwright, John Balderstone, opened with equal success at the Fulton Theatre on Broadway, where the title role was taken by another unknown actor who would become forever identified with the part, Bela Lugosi (*q.v.*).

Dearg Diulai

The name of the traditional Irish vampire, *Dearg Diulai*, means 'red bloodsucker' and accounts of this universally feared creature have been recorded since as early as the sixth century AD. Stories of the *Deamhain fhola* – blood sucking demons – and *Neam mhairbh* – or Un-dead – can also be found in numerous Irish folk legends and folklore, and two typical examples appear in *Ancient Legends, Mystic Charms and Superstitions of Ireland* by Lady Wilde (1888). Irish vampires generally take the form of tall, evil-looking men, but can be beautiful young women or, occasionally, even wolves. According to ancient tradition, the best method of preventing a vampire from being active is to pile large quantities of stones on its presumed tomb. 'Let every one throw a stone on his grave lest perchance he return to earth,' is a familiar phrase in Irish hagiographical lore. In their book, *The Un-Dead: The Legend of Bram Stoker and Dracula* (1997), Peter Haining and Peter Tremayne (*q.v.*) have suggested that Stoker may even have been influenced in the choice of the name for his vampire Count because of its similarity to the Irish word *droch-fhola* (pronounced drok'ola) which means 'bad blood'. A twentieth-century instance of Irish vampirism was reported by R.S. Breene in *The Occult Review*, October 1925, but this unfortunately contains no specific details as to names, dates or location.

Corpses like these in St Michan's Church, Dublin have been compared to the famous Irish vampire, the *Dearg Diulai*

Barbara De Cilly was portrayed by Catherine Mathilde in *The Games of Countess Dolingen of Graz* (1981)

De Cilly, Barbara (c.1451)

Barbara De Cilly, Countess Dolingen, was a noted fifteenth-century beauty who lived in a castle at Gratz in the mountainous regions of Upper Styria, now part of Austria. According to legend, she was the mistress of King Sigismund of Hungary who secretly met her to escape from the machinations of his scheming wife. Suddenly struck down by illness, the Countess was apparently saved from death by the use of a secret ritual devised by Abramerlin the Mage – but the cost of this respite was to become a vampire after her death in 1451. Several authorities have claimed that this beautiful lady was the inspiration for the classic vampire story *Carmilla* (*q.v.*) by Joseph Sheridan Le Fanu (*q.v.*).

De Morìève, Viscount Jacques (c.1798)

The young Viscount, Jacques de Morìève, was one of the few French noblemen who managed to retain his Normandy estates during the French Revolution. He was a very tall, thin man with a high, pointed forehead and protruding teeth. Though outwardly suave and courteous, de Morève had a sadistic streak, and at the end of the Revolution he attempted to get his own back by systematically torturing and occasionally killing his peasant workers. Fearing for their lives, a group of workers living adjacent to the Count's estate took matters into their own hands and assassinated de Morève. According to Jessie Adelaide Middleton, who tells the story in her book, *Another Grey Ghost Book* (1917), 'No sooner had the Viscount been laid in the grave than an appalling number of young children died in the neighbourhood, all of whom bore the vampire's marks at their throats.' These attacks apparently continued intermittently for the next seventy-two years, until de Morève's grandson decided to 'try and lay his horrible ancestor's ghost'. The family vault was opened and all the coffins – bar that of his grandfather – were found to have rotted away. Inside that of the viscount, the body was found to be quite fresh and free from decomposition. Middleton completes the saga: 'The body was removed from the coffin and with a white thorn driven by an expert through the heart of the corpse, with the ghastly result that blood poured forth and the corpse groaned and screamed. Then the remains were buried on the sea-shore [sic] and from that day the child deaths ceased.'

De Turo, Jehan (c.1310)

Jehan de Turo was a Frenchman of mystic powers who was said to have been an initiate of the Temple and died towards the end of the twelfth century. Legend claimed that in the following years he was often seen by people who had known him in life and they came to believe that he must be one of the undead. The terror that surrounded de Turo's name reached such a pitch that in May 1310 at the Council of Troyes, King Philippe listened to petitions from a dozen of his subjects and afterwards ordered that the man's corpse should be exhumed and destroyed by fire, 'on suspicion that he was a vampyre'.

Dhampir (Serbia)

This word *Dhampir* is basically of Serbian origin and means 'vampire's son'. He is, in effect, a vampire hunter and is said to have the ability to 'see' the undead, who in this part of the world go about invisible. Serbian vampires, known as *Vlkoslak*, apparently attack people in much the same way as a poltergeist, hurling objects at their victims in order to stun them and then feed on their blood: only the *Dhampir* can stop them. Great care has to be taken to avoid this species of vampire because according to tradition, they bleed easily, and one drop of blood falling onto a person can lead to madness and death. When visible, the *Vlkoslak* resembles a human being or, alternatively, a serpent. In order to rid a district of such a creature, the *Dhampir* will carry out a ritual rather like a wrestling match – challenging the vampire to a fight during which he gives his audience every impression of tearing the invisible foe to pieces. Naturally, these men expect to be handsomely rewarded for their efforts, and as recently as 1959 a battle was recorded at the village of Vrbrica in Kosovo with the successful vampire hunter being paid a 'fee' of 1,800 dinars.

Dobie, Charles Caldwell (1881–1943)

Although best remembered today as a writer of realistic novels and short stories in the same mould as his fellow countryman, Frank Norris, Charles Caldwell Dobie also wrote the first tale of a native American vampire, 'The Elder Brother' published by *Harper's Magazine* in June 1914. Dobie was born in San Francisco and lived there all his life, becoming very much identified with the city and surviving its devastating earthquake and Great Fire. He worked for some time in an insurance company, before finally managing to sell some of his stories to the popular magazines of the day including the *Smart Set*. The success of his first novel, *The Blood Red Dawn* (1920) made his name, and he drew on the colourful history of his native city for several subsequent bestsellers including *The Arrested Moment* (1927) and *San Fransisco Tales* (1935). Dobie's mother was apparently of Greek origin and inspired his interest in the supernatural which can be seen in occasional examples of his work, like the landmark short story, 'The Elder Brother' which features the sinister and mesmerizing Elena with her 'bright red lips and hair as sleek and shining as the wing of a blackbird.' The story has been reprinted in *The Vampire Omnibus* edited by Peter Haining (1995).

Doyle, Sir Arthur Conan (1858–1930)

World famous as the creator of Sherlock Holmes, Sir Arthur Conan Doyle was also fascinated by the supernatural and he wrote several books about ghosts, spiritualism, fairies and about his own psychic experiences. He was also a friend of Sir Henry Irving (*q.v.*) and his manager, Bram Stoker (*q.v.*), who were responsible for staging his first play, *A Story of Waterloo*, in 1894. The three men met and dined regularly at the Lyceum and it is impossible to believe that the subject of vampirism did not crop up in Conan Doyle's conversations with Stoker. In fact, Conal Doyle's classic tale of psychic vampirism, *The Parasite* (1894), was published in the same series of Acme Library books from Constable in which Stoker's book, *The Watter's Mou'* (1895) appeared. *The Parasite* features Mrs Penlosa, a medium with enormous mesmeric powers, who drains the vitality out of an unfortunate young physiologist, Dr Austin Gilroy, after he rejects her advances at seduction. Another energy draining vampire is featured in Conan Doyle's short story, 'John Barrington Cowles' first published in *Cassell's Saturday Journal*, 12 April 1884. In 'The Adventure of the Sussex Vampire' (1924), Sherlock Holmes declares as 'pure lunacy' the idea that 'walking corpses can only be held in their grave by stakes driven through their hearts' and goes on to solve a case with a much more commonplace explanation. This said, the Sherlockian expert, William Leonard has suggested in an article 'Re: Vampires' in the *Baker Street Journal*, 1957, that Holmes could hardly have failed to know about Dracula and wondered whether the great detective – perhaps disguised as the mysterious Van Helsing – actually participated in the hunt for the vampire? Furthermore, Leonard has speculated on whether Homes' great enemy, Professor James Moriarty, and Count Dracula (*q.v.*) might not have been one and the same person.

Dracula, Count

Count Dracula is the immortal hero of the famous novel by Bram Stoker (*q.v.*). His appearance in the book is rather different to that which has been generally portrayed in the media: the Count is tall, pale and clean-shaven except for a long, white moustache and has peculiarly cruel-looking and sharp white teeth that protrude over his lips which have a great vitality and redness despite his evident old age. His face is strong and aquiline with massive eyebrows that

Count Dracula as originally visualized by Bram Stoker – a French illustration, circa 1920

almost meet across his nose, and he has a lofty, domed forehead with hair growing scantily around his temples, but profusely elsewhere. Dracula has a thin nose with a high bridge 'and peculiarly arched nostrils'. His hands are curiously coarse with squat fingers, though the nails are long and fine and cut to a sharp point. In the centre of his palms grow a few strands of hair. The general impact created by Dracula is a man of great pallor, enhanced by being dressed in black from head to foot without a trace of colour anywhere. He invariably wears a cloak, never an evening dress and flowing cape. He speaks perfect English, although with a strange but charming intonation. A number of popular misconceptions have grown up about the vampire Count which are in direct contradiction to the 'facts' of the novel. In the book, the Count is an old man who grows younger whenever he drinks blood; he is not afraid of sunlight and is several times seen in London by day, although his powers are restricted; and he has the ability to climb walls face down. On the other hand, his creator Bram Stoker was wholly responsible for inventing the idea that Dracula can turn into a bat and that he throws no shadow – for neither ability is mentioned anywhere in vampire lore.

Drakul (Moldavia)

The *Drakul* is the vampire of Moldavia. Human in appearance, tradition says that the creature requires the help of a demon to be able to move around at night and find victims to sustain its blood-lust. Some reports of the *Drakul* say that it never goes anywhere without its coffin, which it can apparently carry on its head. The most successful method of stopping one of these vampires is to part it from this coffin, which must be immediately burned. The *Drakul* is then easier to catch, behead and burn.

Dreyer, Carl Theodor (1889–1968)

The Danish-born film-maker, Carl Dryer's *Vampyr*, made in 1932 and inspired by *Carmilla* (*q.v.*) by Joseph Sheridan Le Fanu (*q.v.*), has been described as one of the true masterpieces of the horror film genre and, according to Lotte Eisner, 'a worthy successor to *Nosferatu* (*q.v.*) bathed in an atmosphere whose magic only the cinema could express'. Dreyer, who first worked as a cafe pianist, book-keeper and sports journalist before becoming a screenwriter, made his début as a director in 1919 with *The President*. With his second picture, *Leaves From Satan's Book* (1920), he started to show the talent which would ultimately see him acknowledged as the greatest creative talent in the history of the Danish cinema. With *The Passion of Joan of Arc* (1928) and then *Vampyr*, he displayed the fantastic attention to detail and atmosphere on which his reputation is built. Dreyer's film version of the Le Fanu story (also known as *The Strange Adventure of David Gray*) was produced in partnership with a wealthy young Dutch baron, Nicolas de Gunzburg who, under the pseudonym of 'Julian West', also starred in the picture, shot mostly on location in a small French mountain village with many of the locals appearing as extras. The movie tells

Dramatic scene from Carl Dreyer's landmark film, *Vampyr* (1932)

the story of David Gray who, while staying at an old inn, is given an ancient book, *Strange Tales of the Vampires*, and begins to suspect the reason why certain local people are wasting away and dying. It takes all his resourcefulness to track down the cause, a bloodsucking old woman (Henriette Gérard), who is staked by a massive iron pole through the heart and dissolves into dust. There are a number of remarkable sequences in the picture – including one in which Gray imagines himself locked in a coffin with the vampire peering in at him – and these were shot by Dreyer and his cinematographer, Rudolph Mate, using gauze over the camera lens to give the film an eerie, ghostly quality. Yet despite this ingenuity and the power of the storyline, *Vampyr* was indifferently received by the critics and proved a commercial failure at the box-office. Only the passage of time has ensured Carl Dreyer's film recognition as a work of genius.

E

Eastbury Vampire

The north wing of what was once a large and splendid Vanbrugh mansion, demolished by its owner almost two hundred years ago near the village of Tarrant Gunville in the Cranbourne Chase district of Dorset, is the last remaining evidence of a curious vampire story. The house was originally built in 1753 for Lord Melcombe who had among his staff a steward named William Doggett to whom he apparently lent large sums of money. When Doggett was unable to replay these loans, he committed suicide by shooting himself, leaving blood stains on the marble floor which legend says could never be erased. Shortly afterwards, reports began to circulate in Tarrant Gunville of Doggett's ghost being seen arriving at Eastbury Park in a coach with a headless driver and horses, followed by the echo of a pistol shot that sounded just like the one that had killed the steward. What convinced eyewitnesses that the man must be Doggett were the knee-breeches tied with yellow ribbons that he had invariably worn during his lifetime and were spotted adorning the eerie figure. These accounts continued until 1845 when the local churchyard was being reorganized and it was decided to remove a number of graves – including that of William Doggett. When his coffin was opened, the steward's body was found to be undecayed and his complexion quite fresh, except for the marks made by the fatal bullet. On his legs, the yellow ribbons glowed as brightly as ever. The local priest had no doubt Doggett was the inspiration for the stories of a vampire in the district and the body was promptly incinerated. Conjecture about Lord Melcombe's reason for demolishing so much of the mansion has continued to this day – with the favoured suggestion being that he may have ordered it because of the terrible event that occurred there and its gruesome sequel.

Easter

In many European nations, Easter is believed to be the time when the powers of vampires are at their height and special precautions should be taken against their attacks. In these countries, measures to safeguard a house or a village are generally put into place during the week preceding the holy weekend. Folklore in several central European countries states that laying branches of thorn on the threshold of houses will keep vampires away, while a cross painted in tar on the door will add to the security. The ringing of church bells at nightfall fulfils another old tradition decreeing that no member of the undead can come within the sound of a church bell. In places such as Bulgaria, Romania and large areas of Russia, bundles of garlic (*q.v.*) in the windows and doorways are advised. Other Easter customs to ward off vampires include placing every cooking utensil upside down, and keeping an unsheathed knife underneath the pillow. Montague Summers (*q.v.*) discusses this element of vampire lore in his book, *The Vampire in Europe* (1929), and adds a word of warning about answering a solitary call at night during the Easter period. 'No one must answer if called by name – at least not until he has been summoned three times – because a vampire may call you once at night, but cannot repeat his request. Therefore if a person waits to hear their name a third time, they may be assured it is not the horrible intruder.'

Eaves, A. Osborn (c.1852–1918)

Osborne Eaves was a Harrogate doctor and writer on the supernatural today best-remembered for his curious work, *Modern*

Vampirism: Its Dangers and How To Avoid Them which he published in 1904. Previous books from his pen had dealt with esoteric subjects such as *The Colour Cure* (1897), *Mastery of Death* (1898) and *The Art of Luck* (1900), but it was his work on 'vampirism', which was described as 'a practical guide to those under threat', that drew the widest attention. It was stated to be aimed at those who did not enjoy 'robust health' as a result of having their energy sapped by 'soul-less human beings, demon lovers – *modern vampires'*. According to Eaves, Sir Arthur Conan Doyle (*q.v.*) had already drawn attention to such people in his work, *The Parasite*, and readers should be in no doubt that Bram Stoker's *Dracula* was a work of *fact* not fiction. He warned his readers,

> With regard to protecting yourself generally, when rising imagine that a shell is forming at the extremity of the aura. Picture a white mist, ovoid, becoming denser every moment. Just as in winter the breath is clearly visible with each exhalation, so as you breathe outwards see in the mind the breath taking form. Use the will in addition and this will have the desired effect. Repeat about midday, or whenever entering a crowd, or a low quarter of a city. At night again form this protective shell before going to sleep, and you are not likely to be troubled with Vampires.

Eaves also explained that as a person's vitality flowed from their extremities, it was possible to avoid it being 'lapped up by vampires' in public places such as railway compartments, trams and the like by 'clasping the hands and placing the left foot over the right, thus forming a complete circuit and preventing any leakage'.

Ekimmu (Babylon)

The *Ekimmu* is the vampire of ancient Babylon and a depiction of one was found in the last century among some Babylonian cylinder seals, complete with a description of its activities. As R. Campbell Thomson who translated the seals explains in his book, *The Devils and Evil Spirits of Babylonia* (1903), 'If it found a luckless man who had wandered far from his fellows into haunted places, it fastened upon him, plaguing and tormenting him until such time as a priest should drive it away with exorcisms.' The word *Ekimmu* translates as 'that which is snatched away' and according to tradition, it is a very dangerous being whose mere presence in a house can lead to the death of those living there. These vampires are said to originate because of people dying in circumstances where a proper burial was not possible – such as drowning, starvation, death in battle, being murdered in an isolated spot, dying of exposure in the desert, or attack by wild animals. Bodies that were buried but not laid to rest with the correct ceremonial could also result in another *Ekimmu*. In all such cases, the outcome was the same: a highly unpredictable vampire, some with cannibalistic tendencies as well as a thirst for blood, and all very difficult to destroy. Assyrian records indicate that many *Ekimmus* attached themselves to people or families who they believed had done them some wrong in life. They could some-times be female, too – women who had died in childbirth, or alter-natively, prostitutes who had become ill and died.

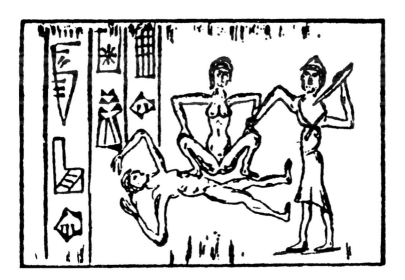

Engraving of an *Ekimmu* discovered on an ancient Babylonian cylinder seal

Elga, Countess

The portrait of 'Countess Elga' by the Austrian painter Hans Makart (1840–1884) is associated with a curious vampire legend. Little is known of the lady beyond the fact she was the daughter of

The eerie portrait of Countess Elga, vampire. Just look into the eyes!

a Romanian nobleman whose castle in the Carpathian Mountains had been burned to the ground by local people because of the belief that he was a vampire and had caused the deaths of a number of their children. However, Makart's picture escaped the conflagration and eventually came into the hands of a cavalry officer in Vienna. He hung the picture in his home until, one after another, guests began to complain of the uncanny effect the portrait had on them whenever they stared too long into the eyes of 'Countess Elga' – a feeling of having all the vitality sucked from their bodies. Events came to a head according to occult writer Dr Franz Hartmann (*q.v.*), in a subsequent report for the *Neues Wiener Journal* in June 1909, when a serving girl 'about to light the fire in the stove, raced from the room screaming after the door opened and she saw the actual figure of the Countess standing there'. According to Hartmann, the owner was now convinced that the portrait somehow provided a 'doorway' into the real world for the dead Countess, and promptly had it removed. The officer was also convinced that it had probably not been the old Count who had been the vampire, but his daughter. A fuller account of this unique case of vampirism appears in *The Occult Review*, September 1909.

The Greek *Lamia* sometimes mistakenly thought to be a vampire

Empusa (Greece)

The *Empusa* is an ancient Greek spirit that is sometimes incorrectly described as a vampire. It is, in fact, a demon with a tangible body, but one that is not composed of human flesh and blood. Another name for this creature is a *Lamia* whose most familiar shape is that of a serpent with the face and breasts of a woman. The famous English poet John Keats (1795–1821) based one of his imaginative works, 'Lamia', on this legendary creature.

Endore, Guy Samuel (1900–1970)

Guy Endore was an American novelist and scriptwriter who learned about the real-life vampire story of the French army sergeant, Francois Bertrand (*q.v.*) and used it as the basis of his bestselling book, *The Werewolf in Paris* (1933), later made into a successful film. Born in New York, Endore's early work portrayed the brash lifestyle of the 1930s, but it was his intelligent biographies of characters obsessed with sex such as Casanova and the Marquis de Sade that brought him to public attention, along with his macabre novels including *The Man From Limbo* (1930) and *Methings The Lady* (1945) about a female Jekyll and Hyde. It was the strong sexual overtones of the Bertrand affair that attracted Endore, and in his novel the central character, Bertrand Caillet, becomes obsessed with the need for blood every time he has sex. Even when he falls in love, he cannot resist slaking his bloodlust on his mistress. Eventually caught and imprisoned in a mental institution, Caillet commits suicide. Years later, his coffin is disinterred and the skeleton of a wolf is found inside. The story was filmed in 1961 as *Curse of the Werewolf* starring Oliver Reed; although Endore was not involved in the making of this picture, he did write scripts for several other fantasy films including the highly acclaimed *Mad Love* (1935) with Peter Lorre. He also translated some of the works of the German author, Hans Heinz Ewers (*q.v.*), and *The Werewolf of Paris* has certain similarities with Ewers' 1922 novel, *The Vampire*, in which the main character's activities are compared to the 'blood madness' of the First World War. *The Werewolf of Paris* is undoubtedly a work of extraordinary power and has been compared to another definitive novel by *The Penguin Encyclopedia of Horror and the Supernatural* (1986): 'It can stand as both an examination of clinical lycanthropy (an actual psychological delusion) and the recognised classic of werewolf fiction, the only example of its type comparable in impact to Stocker's *Dracula*.'

Energy Vampire

The Russian city of Vologda to the north of Moscow has a new form of vampire, the *Energy Vampire*, according to reports which appeared in November 1992 as a result of an opinion poll conducted to discover what strikes most fear into people. Published in the local newspaper, *Rissky Sever*, the answer most frequently given was the 'energy vampire' – a supernatural beast whose mission is to suck the 'life energy' from the people who live in this part of northern Russia. The report added, 'Running vampires a close second on the list of fears were witches and black magic, while third place went to silly bosses and their stupid orders.'

Erotic Vampire

Eroticism has been closely allied to vampirism for centuries. In several of the Mediterranean countries, there are innumerable stories of male vampires returning to have sex with their widows and sometimes raping other women while their husbands or lovers are absent. Lascivious female vampires are also a feature of various South American traditions, and in Mexico it is said that the female undead are worse than their male counterparts at luring unsuspecting lovers from among the living. These instances have led to a conviction that the vampires in question must have been people of great wickedness and lust in their previous lives. The topic of vampires and sexuality has been discussed in several articles in *Time*

Erotic Vampires – a photograph posed by models for *Supernatural* magazine in 1975

magazine (18 May 1985) and *New Scientist* (26 September 1998) and in fiction in the novels of the American writer, Poppy Z. Brite (*q.v.*).

Ewers, Hans Heinz (1872–1943)

A notorious German literary and political figure – he was an early member of the Nazi Party and an associate of Hitler – as well as being the author of a series of highly sensational, sadistic and grotesque novels, Ewers is perhaps best remembered today for *The*

Vampire (1921). Born in Dusseldorf, he trained originally for the law, but instead worked for a time in a vaudeville company before

Illustration by Mahlon Blaine for Hans Heinz Ewers' vampire novel, *Alraune* (1911)

settling on a literary career. His travels took him to America where, during the First World War, he was briefly an undercover agent for Germany before being deported. Despite his association with Hitler and the fact he prepared a biography and script for a film about Horst Wessel, the Nazi storm-trooper 'hero' killed in a street fight with Communists, Ewers fell out of favour during the Second World War: his books were banned and burned, and he died in obscurity. His series of novels featuring the exploits of the mysterious aesthete, Frank Braun – *The Sorcerer's Apprentice* (1907), *Alraune* (1911) and in particular *The Vampire* with its terrifying scenes of vampirism at sea – have won him acknowledgement as one of the great German weird fiction writers, although most of his books have been unobtainable for years. *The Vampire* is said to be partly autobiographical, though whether Ewers ever satisfied a craving for blood by drinking the blood of beautiful women, as Frank Braun does while sailing in a plague-ridden vessel from South America to New York, must now be purely a matter for conjecture.

Eyrbyggia Saga

In this curious Icelandic saga, translated by the great Scottish historical novelist and writer of supernatural stories, Sir Walter Scott (1771–1832), the story is told of a group of vampires who committed dreadful ravages in the country around the year AD 1000. After dozens of people had died – including 18 in a single household – an unusual method of getting rid of the vampires was adopted: a tribunal was set up to institute proceedings against them. According to the *Eyrbyggia Sage*, the undead themselves were called upon to give evidence, and did so, disputing claims they were blood drinkers and maintaining that the deaths had actually been caused by the spread of a contagious disease. The account continues,

> It does not appear that the vampires put themselves on their defence, so that the sentence of ejectment was pronounced against them individually in due and legal form. As they heard their individual sentence, each of the undead left the place

saying something that indicated their unwillingness to depart. A priest afterwards entered with holy water and the celebration of a solemn mass followed. This completed the conquest over the vampires, which had been commenced by the power and authority of the Ielandic law, and they were heard of no more.

Farkaskoldus (Hungary)

According to the learned Jesuit scholar, Gabriel Rzazeynsci, in his *Historia Naturalis Curiosa* (1721), Hungary shared with Greece and what was then Czechoslovakia, the reputation of having been infested for longer than most other countries by some of the ugliest and worst vampires or *Farkaskoldus*. During the years around the turn of the eighteenth century when Rzazeynsci was writing, Hungary suffered a plague of the undead which is recorded in a collection of documents. A typical entry in one reads: 'A *heyduk* named Stanko, a much-respected and important character in his village. He had died six weeks previously at the age of sixty. In the chest and abdomen there was found to be a quantity of rich new blood and the whole body was in the Vampire condition.' The accounts all describe the undead as appearing by night 'in the exact shape and habit of the deceased' whereupon they would 'lay heavily upon their victims and drink the life-blood'. When tracked to their graves, the *Farkaskoldus* were found to be, 'not at all putrid, no ill smell about them, saving the mustiness of the Grave-clothes.' The only way to destroy these vampires was to cut off the head, arms and legs, and *'opening the back'* (my italics) remove the heart and burn everything on a pile of wood. The ashes had then to be carefully put into a sack and tipped into the nearest river. According to tradition, Hungarian vampires can change shape – into a dog, cat or goat – and in some instances a dying *Farkaskoldus* has been seen

90

taking on the features of a werewolf in order, apparently, to continue its existence in a new form.

Farson, Daniel (1927–1997)

Daniel Farson was a prolific writer, photographer and broadcaster, and the great-nephew of Bram Stoker (*q.v.*) about whom he produced a controversial biography, *The Man Who Wrote Dracula* (1975) in which he claimed the author died in poverty and suffering from syphilis. Associated for many years with the bohemian life style of Soho and friend of many leading celebrities including Noel Coward, Graham Sutherland, W. Somerset Maugham, John Osborne and Francis Bacon – about whom he wrote the highly regarded biography, *The Gilded Gutter Life* (1993) – Farson was the son of the famous American foreign correspondent, Negley Farson, and worked for a time as a staff photographer on *Picture Post*, subsequently pioneering 'live' interviews on television in the 1950s. For a number of years he contributed to leading newspapers including *The Sunday Times* and the *Mail on Sunday*, and wrote non-fiction books on subjects as diverse as the music-hall star, Marie Lloyd, and Jack the Ripper. His inspiration to produce the book about his great-uncle was a conviction based on family memories that, 'Bram Stoker was really two people – outwardly bluff and hearty, inwardly he needed release. I would hardly recognise a Freudian symbol if I saw one, but he was obviously disturbed.' Farson believed that Stoker's wife was a cold, frigid woman and that the author sought his 'release' with prostitutes. Although Stoker's death certificate states the cause of death as *locomotor ataxy* and 'exhaustion' this is not sufficient evidence according to contemporary medical expertise to *prove* he was suffering from syphilis. As to the claim he was living in poverty, the probate of Stoker's will – made on 19 March 1912 just a month before he died – shows his estate valued at £5,640, no mean figure at that time. Nonetheless, Farson unearthed much new material about his forebearer and the creation of *Dracula* which makes the biography a valuable source of information.

Fearless Vampire Killers (1967)

The film *Fearless Vampire Killers; or, Pardon Me, But Your Teeth Are In My Neck* was the Polish-born film maker, Roman Polanski's satire on vampire movies. Yet it has been acclaimed by Donald F. Glut in *The Dracula Book* (1975) as 'one of the finest vampire films ever made'. It is also famous for a scene in which a Jewish vampire laughs at the efforts of a victim to ward him off with a crucifix. Written, directed and even co-starring Polanski, the black comedy focuses on the mission of Professor Abronsius (Jack MacGowran) and his assistant, Alfred (Polanski), to rid Transylvania of vampires. The Professor is little more than a buffoon in comparison to the undead Count Von Krolock (Ferdy Mayne), a dignified member of a not altogether evil life-form. Under the Count's spell falls the lovely heroine, Sarah (Sharon Tate who, in real-life, married Polanski and was brutally murdered by Charles Manson in Hollywood in August 1969) and though she is later rescued, nonetheless grows fangs and sinks them into Alfred. In the closing scene, the audience is informed that far from stopping vampirism, Professor Abronsius has actually been responsible for its spread all over the world! (The picture was released in England as *Dance of the Vampires*.)

Femme Fatale

Throughout history, numbers of women possessing the power to lure men into trouble have been compared to vampires – notably Cleopatra and Semiramis who became the pattern for a tyrannical seductress who has each lover killed the morning after they have made love. In art there have been several more examples: notably Leonardo's *Mona Lisa* of whom the critic Walter Pater (1839–1894) said she was 'older than the rocks among which she sits; like a vampire, she has been dead many times and learned the secrets of the grave'; while the faces of the *Mermaids* in the painting by the Austrian, Gustav Klimt, foreshadow the vamps of the twentieth century, notably Theda Bara (*q.v.*) and Marlene Dietrich who has been called 'the screen's ultimate *femme fatale*'.

Fisher, Terence (1904-1980)

London-born, former merchant seaman turned film-maker, Terence Fisher was responsible for directing the landmark Hammer version of *Dracula* in 1958 that turned Christopher Lee (*q.v.*) into an international star. Initially an assistant editor, Fisher made a number of romantic dramas for the Rank Organisation before joining Hammer and becoming identified with its hugely successful series of horror films. In shooting *Dracula*, he employed brilliant camerawork and subtle lighting to present the undead Count as a suave seducer and man of demonic power locked in battle with Peter Cushing's (*q.v.*) single-minded vampire hunter, Van Helsing. The mixture of powerful action and eroticism resulted in the picture being attacked by several critics for pandering to excessive violence and sexual explicitness, yet created a bench-mark for all subsequent vampire movies. To some fans it was – and is – the greatest horror film ever made.

Director Terence Fisher on the set of *Dracula, Prince of Darkness* (1965) with his star, Christopher Lee

Released in America as *The House of Dracula*, it remains Terence Fisher's most powerful and enduring movie – still a favourite at film festivals and on late-night television. He also directed *The Brides of Dracula* (1960) and *Dracula, Prince of Darkness* (1965) with Lee and Cushing, but never quite reached the same heights of Gothic terror as the original.

Flies

In many cultures, the soul is believed to resemble a small insect like a fly or butterfly. The history of witchcraft in particular records many instances where the souls of sleeping witches were said to have left their bodies in insect form, and carried out missions of evil while their owner slumbered. If, however, the soul was not able to find its way back to the mouth, the witch would die. According to Montague Summers (*q.v.*) in *The Vampire in Europe* (1929), a similar tradition exists in vampire lore: 'In many districts of Romania, it is thought that persons are doomed to become vampires and that they cannot escape their destiny. Whilst they lie asleep, their soul comes out of their mouth like a fly. If the body were to be turned around so that the head reposed where the feet had laid the soul would not be able to find its way back and the man dies.' An obsession with flies also overwhelms the character, Renfield in Bram Stoker's *Dracula*. See also *Alp*.

For The Blood Is The Life (1911)

'The blood is life' motif can be found repeated time and again in classical myth, as well as in both the Old and New Testament, where it appears both as an objective statement and psychological truth. Christ himself, of course, exhorted his followers to drink his blood as a way of sharing his power, and the sacrament of communion is based on the transfer of energy through blood. The phrase has also been used frequently in vampire fiction, notably in *For The Blood Is The Life* (1911) undoubtedly one of the best novellas in the genre ever written. The work of Francis Marion Crawford (1854–1909) it tells the story of Cristina who is murdered when she surprises two thieves at work, but returns from the dead to lure the unsuspecting young hero, Angelo, to slake her bloodlust. A mixture of the poetic and the atmospheric, it was one of a number of

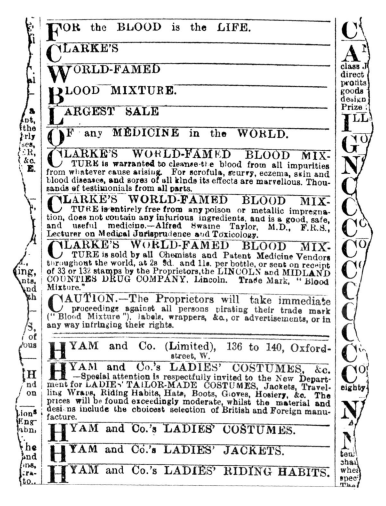

Advertisement for the 'World Famous Blood Mixture' sold during the Victorian era

outstanding supernatural tales written by Crawford including an occult novel, *The Witch of Prague* (1891) and several collections of short stories notably 'The Upper Berth' (1984) and 'Wandering Ghosts' (1911). The author, who was born in America, worked for a time in India, and then settled in Italy for the remainder of his life. Now recognized as an important literary figure, The F. Marion Crawford Memorial Society has been set up in Nashville, USA and publishes a magazine, *The Romantist*, as well as monographs on the author's life and work.

Fright Night

Fright Night was one of the most successful horror movies of the 1980s and inspired an equally impressive sequel – the two pictures representing another landmark in the history of vampire films. Written and directed by Tom Holland, the story concerns a teenager Charley Brewster (William Ragsdale) who spends much of his time watching 'Fright Night Theatre', a series of horror movies hosted by a former star, Peter Vincent (Roddy McDowall). When Charley begins to suspect that his neighbour, played by Christopher Sarandon, is a vampire, he has the utmost difficulty convincing anyone, until he finally manages to enlist the aid of Vincent in destroying the undead. The highlight of the picture was the special effects and its box-office success encouraged Columbia to produce *Fright Night, Part II* which Tommy Lee Wallace directed from his own screenplay based on Tom Holland's characters. Ragsdale returned as Charlie Brewster this time encountering Regine Dandrige (Julie Carmen) who proves to be a seductive vampire, and once more has to call on Vincent (again played by Roddy McDowell) to break her power. Paired together on late-night television, the two *Fright Night* movies make for entertaining if unnerving viewing.

Garlic

Garlic is regarded as a powerful talisman where vampires are concerned because they hate it and cannot stand the smell. A perennial of the *Liliaceae* family, its bulb has a strong odour and flavour; the edible variety, *Allium sativum*, is credited with curative powers for a whole variety of ailments, not to mention having health-giving properties. In many countries where vampires are active it is believed that bundles of garlic hung around windows, over doors, across ceilings and on bed-heads are a good form of protection. A necklace of garlic bulbs is also believed to be very potent. In several central European countries – where it is known as *usturoi* – country folk smear garlic crosses on their window-frames, doorknobs and locks for protection. Many also do the same to their stable doors and on their animals' horns, for it is well known that vampires can do harm to cattle or cause them to lose their milk. Graves can be protected with a lining of garlic and Russians believe that when a vampire is found in its grave, a bulb of it should immediately be stuffed into his mouth. In a tragic example of this idea being reversed, a Polish emigrant living in England in January 1973 who was obsessively afraid of vampires, died from choking on garlic which he had placed in *his* mouth for protection. The man, Demitrious Myiciura, of Stoke-on-Trent in Staffordshire, also had garlic hanging all around the room and stuffed in his bedroom keyhole in addition to salt strewn about the floor and a bag of salt resting on his testicles. Like garlic, salt is also believed to be a vampire repellent. The man's landlady, Mrs Eugizig Rodazichwicz, told the inquest that although Myiciura had come to England 25 years earlier to become a pottery worker, 'He thought vampires were everywhere and used salt, pepper and garlic to keep them away.' The association of garlic and vampires was even raised in a letter to *The Times* of 29 June 1999 by Joseph Sinclair of London who had been surprised to read in an article about the herb that its most important property was not mentioned. 'I have been taking garlic in capsule form for more than 15 years and have not encountered a single vampire in all that time,' he said.

Gaule, John (c.1600–1668)

Reverend John Gaule was an English clergyman and writer who came to prominence during the infamous sixteenth century 'Witch Trials', when the self-professed 'Witchfinder General', Matthew Hopkins (d.1646) was busy torturing and hanging unfortunate old men and women suspected of being in league with the Devil. Gaule was totally opposed to Hopkins and his methods, yet believed in witchcraft as he revealed in his *Select Cases of Conscience Touching Witches and Witchcraft* written in 1646. The book also shows that he was fascinated by vampires and knew all about one particular ability of the undead that few other authors have mentioned. 'It is commonly held that witches, like vampires, may by a process of dematerialization, enter a room through the merest chink. I do believe this to be true where vampires are concerned, but have seen no proof where witchcraft is ascribed.' Gaule also drew on the vampire tradition in his curious later work, *Mysmantia – the Magastromancer* published in London in 1652.

Gautier, Theophile (1811–1872)

Theophile Gautier was a French critic, poet, dramatist, writer of fiction and prolific journalist who also write another of the landmark vampire stories, *Le Morte Amorous* – alternatively known as

'Clarimonde', 'The Beautiful Vampire' and 'The Dead Lover' – first published in the *Chronique de Paris* of 23 and 26 June 1836, when the author was just 24. Although undoubtedly one of the most

Theophile Gautier, author of the vampire classic *Le Morte Amorous* (1936)

important figures in the development of French Romanticism – typified by his novel, *Madamemoiselle De Maupin* (1836) – Gautier is also acknowledged as a master of grotesquely diabolical novels and stories such as *Avatar or the Double Transformation* (1856), *Spirite, A Fantasy* (1877) and the collection, *One of Cleopatra's Nights and Other Fantastic Romances* (1882). The story of the courtesan Clarimonde who seduces a young country priest, Romuald, and is then discovered by the man's superior, the Abbe Serapion, to be a vampire upon whom he sprinkles holy water to cause her to crumble into dust, is an erotic tale of remarkable artistry. Montague Summers (*q.v.*) went even further in *The Vampire* (1928), declaring in a chapter on 'The Vampire in Literature', 'Undoubtedly the vampire tradition has never been treated with such comsummate skill as by Theophile Gautier in his exquisite prose poem . . . nowhere beside has it been so ingeniously moulded with such delicacy of style, with such rich and vivid colouring, with such emotion and such repression.' It is available in a number of anthologies including *The Bedside Book of Strange Stories* edited by Herbert Van Thal (1974).

Gerard, Emily de Laszowska (1867–1928)

The English wife of a Hungarian army officer, Emily Gerard was the author of an authoritative article, 'Transylvanian Superstitions' which appeared in the July 1885 issue of *Nineteenth Century Magazine* – an English publication that Bram Stoker (*q.v.*) read and to which he contributed. The article contained accounts of the myths and legends of the country, and especially its vampire tradition; a subject that caught Stoker's eye while he was researching *Dracula*. Mrs Gerard was one of those intrepid Victorian women explorers who used the opportunity of her husband's posting to Transylvania to investigate local customs. She was, therefore, able to write with authority that the country 'might well be termed the land of superstition', and of all the species of demons that flourished there, 'Most decidedly evil is the vampire, or *Nosferatu*, (*q.v.*) in whom every Roumanian peasant believes as firmly as he does in

Illustration of a group of gipsies from 'Transylvanian Superstitions'
by Emily Gerard

heaven or hell.' Therafter followed page upon page of details that
Stoker enthusiastically adapted for his novel. As all scholars are now
agreed, his debt to Emily Gerard and her article was huge. Three
years later she herself embodied the material as three chapters in her
two-volume book, *The Land Beyond The Forest*: a title derived by
translating the country's name from Latin into English. (Abridged
versions of 'Transylvanian Superstitions' containing the relevant
details can be found in *The Dracula Scrapbook* by Peter Haining,
1975 and *The Origins of Dracula* by Clive Leatherdale, 1987.)

Gierach (Prussia)

Prussia, the former state of Germany bordering the Baltic, which
was abolished by the Allies after the Second World War, had its own
species of vampire, the *Gierach*, sometimes known as a *Stryz*.
Similar in appearance to most other European vampires with fierce
red eyes, long teeth and reeking of the grave, it was most active
during the seventeenth century, although incidences were also
reported during the reign of Frederick the Great (1740–1786)
when the regions of Silesia, East Frisia and West Prussia were

annexed. The Prussian method of getting rid of vampires could be summed up in two words: *confuse them*. Because it was believed that the undead could not resist trying to solve problems they encountered, traditon said that a woollen stocking should be put into the tomb for the creature to unravel, which it would apparently do at the rate of one stitch per year, or alternatively cover it with a fishing net to untangle. Poppy seeds scattered over the grave were also said to put them to sleep for years. A curious vampire legend recorded in Prussian folklore tells the story of a citizen of Egwanschiftz who in 1617 was tormented to death by a vampire. Almost immediately afterwards the vampire was caught and the local population, anxious not to have a repeat of these events, decided to burn the bodies of both the vampire *and* his victim on separate pyres just outside the town.

Giffard, Pierre (c.1858–1932)

The years between th 1880s to the 1930s are generally considered to be the 'Golden Age' of science fiction and fantasy in France, when Jules Verne's novels generically titled *Voyages Extraordinaires* opened the eyes of readers everywhere to the ideas of space travel. Pierre Giffard, a Parisian, was one of a group of writers at this time who fed the public appetite with a long series of novels around the turn of the twentieth century entitled *Les Drames de l'Air* published by Albert Mericant. Giffard was evidently a man of greater imagination than many of his contemporaries and introduced elements of the supernatural, the occult and vampirism into his titles. A bestseller among these was *Les Vampires De L'Ocean* (1907), in which a group of the undead terrorize the shipping lanes of the world. Unlike most vampires, Giffard's undead have no fear of water and apart from sustaining their lives with blood, also plunder the cargoes of all the vessels they attack. This now very collectable work was illustrated by the famous Albert Robida (1848–1926) whose remarkably prophetic drawings of future cities, transport and space machines have earned him the recognition of founding father of science fiction illustration.

Pierre Giffard's *Les Vampires De L'Ocean* (1907) was illustrated
by the great Albert Robida

Glamis Castle

Beautiful Glamis Castle in Angus, Scotland, the seat of the Earls of
Strathmore and Kinghorne, has been a Royal residence since 1372
and was the childhood home of the Queen Mother. Framed by the

majestic Grampian Mountains, it is the legendary setting for Shakespeare's most famous play, *Macbeth*, and has a reputation for being one of the most haunted buildings in the British Isles. Among the ghost stories told about the castle are: the tale of Earl Beardie who played cards with the Devil and now walks the corridors on certain dark nights; the sad figure of the 'White Lady' who glides about in the vicinity of the chapel of St Michael; and the ethereal little black serving-boy who was ill-treated more than two centuries ago and has several times been seen near the Queen Mother's sitting room. But more terrible still is the legend of a vampire that haunts Glamis. Ghost hunter Peter Underwood tells the story in *A Gazetteer of Scottish and Irish Ghosts* (1973): 'A woman servant who was caught in the act of sucking the blood from one of her victims was hustled into a secret room and left to die – but that is not one of the ways to rid the world of a vampire; and legend has it that her secret tomb is still open somewhere in Glamis and her menace still potent.' A variation of this story claims that the Lyons – the Queen Mother's family– have a vampire that was born hundreds of years ago and is kept hidden in a secret room. The creature has, however, escaped on a few occasions and its activities have prompted several of the most sensational legends of Glamis Castle. It has been suggested that it was this 'awful secret' that the 14th Earl of Strathmore was referring to shortly before his death in 1905 when he said, 'If you could guess the nature of this secret you would go down on your knees and thank God *it* were not yours.'

Glass, Philip (1937–)

American composer and pianist Philip Glass was the man responsible for providing the first musical soundtrack for the classic 1931 version of *Dracula* starring Bela Lugosi (*q.v.*) nearly seventy years after the release of the film. The combination of primitive technology and budgetary restraints when the picture was made prevented it from having the now essential element of the horror genre – music – apart from a short episode when Dracula visits a concert hall. This, though, was no more than music within the plot rather than being a device to heighten the emotions. Glass provided a score which simplifies the movie's sinister atmosphere in order to mesmerize audiences as unerringly as Lugosi's stare. Previously, the composer had written music for a number of films including Martin

Philip Glass's 1999 soundtrack for *Dracula* enhanced Bela Lugosi's 'ashen and hypnotic attraction' on the screen, according to critics

Scorses' *Kundun* and Christopher Hampston's *The Secret Agent*, but had virtually pioneered the concept of adding music to classic pictures in 1992 when he provided a score for Jean Cocteau's fifty-year-old masterpiece *Belle Et La Bête* (1946). The first performance of the music at a showing of *Dracula* occurred in London at the Royal Festival Hall in October 1999 when Michael Riesman conducted the Kronos Quartet augmented by Glass himself on piano. The music was hailed by the *Daily Mail* as 'an elegiac tribute' to the movie, the score enhancing Bela Lugosi's 'ashen and hypnotic attraction'.

Gogol, Nikolai Vasilyevitch (1809-1852)

Born in the Ukraine, Gogol who became one of Russia's most famous writers, novelists and playwrights, has also been described by the American critic, Edmund Wilson, 'as the very greatest master of the horror tale'. Among his most notable stories in this genre are 'St John's Eve' about the sacrifice of a child at a witch's sabbat; 'A Terrible Vengeance' in which an evil sorcerer summons the soul of his daughter in order to seduce her; and the classic vampire tale, 'Viy' which again Edmund Wilson has praised as 'one of the most terrific things of its kind ever written'. The story features a philosopher, Khoma Brut, who beats a woman to death and is then haunted by her corpse, which has been transformed into a vampire or *Viy*. Gogal described the creature as 'a squat, thickset, bandy-legged figure, covered all over with black earth'. It has arms and legs that grow out like sinewy roots, treads heavily and stumbles at every step. More awful still are its long eyelids, 'that hung down to the very ground'. Not surprisingly, the hapless man is no match for the undead and is ultimately devoured. In 1960, the story was adapted for the screen by the Italian Galatea-Jolly production team as *La Maschera Del Demonio (The Mask of the Demon)* starring Barbara Steele (*q.v.*) in the dual role of witch and vampire. Directed by Mario Brava, the film was given a succession of titles when released elsewhere: *Die Stunde Wenn Drakula Kommt* ('The Hour When Dracula Comes') in Germany: *Black Sunday* in America; and *Revenge of the Vampire* in Britain.

Nikolai Gogal, author of the much-admired Russian vampire tale, 'Viy'

Gorey, Edward Saint John (1925–2000)

Now a cult figure among American illustrators, Edward Gorey created the stark and majestic sets for the Broadway production of *Dracula* in 1975 starring Frank Langella (*q.v.*). Already popular with readers for his cartoon books of creepy images and grotesque characters set against Victorian of Edwardian backgrounds such as *Nightcrawlers*

(1957), *Amphigorey* (1972) and *Amphigorey Too* (1975), Gorey's designs for the production received as many rave reviews as the cast. One critic referred to him as a 'Master of the Macabre' while another said his costumes and sets had 'a touch of genius' – and they undoubtedly contributed to the success of the production in New York and when it was transferred across the Atlantic to London in 1978 where Terence Stamp took the leading role. A feature of Gorey's designs was a tiny vampire-bat motif with which he wittily decorated everything from the wallpaper to pajama buttons and even tennis shoes. To coincide with the production a collection of his sketches were published in 1976 as *Edward Gorey's Dracula*.

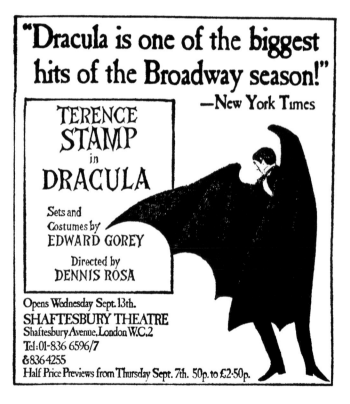

Edward Gorey designed the sets, costumes and posters for the 1975 production of *Dracula*

Goths

Lovers of all things Gothic have become increasingly evident in recent years and at the centre of their various preoccupations runs an abiding interest in vampires and the undead. The Goth subculture began in Britain at the beginning of the 1980s among the followers of doom-laden, post-punk rock bands and has grown to embrace a plethora of diverse groups of young people on both sides of the Atlantic. Goths dress mainly in black – a colour considered extremely intense and emotionally and spiritually powerful – whiten their faces, redden their lips and eyes, and are fascinated by various forms of music, literature, art, concepts and religions that go beyond what they call the 'everyday ideas of normality'. As the anonymous author of 'Concepts of a Gothic Identity' wrote in *The Necroscope* magazine in 1992: 'The label "Goth" should not be restricted to the image because, in its glory, it is a state of mind, a cult. To be Gothic is to escape from the festering, corrupt, vindictive manipulation of humankind, and instead to look beyond the accepted means of emotional therapy. . . . Such things as depression, death and suicide are things of fascination and intrigue, rather than taboo subjects. Graveyards, hearses, death and the desire to look undead, shows a desire to bring the next life (if, how, and as what it exists) from being pushed into the corners of the mind.' In 1988, a leading English Goth, Carole Bohanan, founded *The Vampyre Society* which publishes a quarterly journal, *The Velvet Vampyre*, and has members all over the world. Bohanan has commented, 'It is definitely not a plastic fangs and black cape society – it's more a meeting of minds in that many of us enjoy dying arts like gilding, stone masonry and corsetry. Quite a lot of members have been taunted about vampires – it's a relief for them to meet people with similar interests.' There are numerous websites in Britain and America devoted to explaining the Goth culture, and these came to the defence of followers after they became the subject of a somewhat hysterical national debate as a result of the 'Vampire Murders' in 1996 when a suburban couple in Florida were killed by teenage members of a vampire cult. The gang, it transpired, had no connections with Goth culture and had become involved in vampirism after steeping themselves in a role-playing video game, *Vampire: The Masquerade*. In the UK, there is an annual festival, Vampyria, the first of which, held in 1997 to celebrate the centenary of *Dracula*, drew over 1,000 'vampires' and led to the launch of a quarterly magazine, *Bloodstone* 'for everyone with a passion for the unlife'. The American writer Poppy Z. Brite (*q.v.*) has used her own experiences as a Goth in her increasingly influential novels and short stories.

Gran Chaco

Gran Chaco, a wild and remote region of South America, was the primary location for a French documentary film, *Le Vampire*, shot in 1943 by the French director, Jean Painlève. The film is remarkable for a sequence of scenes in which one of the native vampire-bats (*q.v.*) was captured on camera actually stalking a victim, piercing its skin with its razor-like teeth, and then lapping up the blood. Extracts from *Le Vampire* have been used repeatedly in films about vampire lore and the Dracula legend.

Grey, Elizabeth Caroline (1798–1869)

Elizabeth Grey was a Victorian 'penny dreadful' author who is credited with writing the first vampire serial story, *The Skeleton Count; or, The Vampire Mistress* which was published in weekly parts in a magazine of Gothic stories and morbid poetry called *The Casket* in the autumn of 1828 concluding the following spring. Born in London, Elizabeth Grey initially ran a school for girls before marrying a journalist who worked on the *Morning Chronicle*. This connection lead to her appointment as secretary to Edward Lloyd, London's leading publisher of 'penny dreadfuls' during the Victorian era. Later, she became the editor of his various publications and also found time to write stories herself, both for Lloyd and a number of other periodicals including *The Casket*. Subsequently she produced a number of popular novels including,

The Iron Mask (1847), *The Horrors of Zindorf Castle* (1850) and *Murder Will Out* (1860). Her vampire story, *The Skeleton Count*, focused on the activities of Count Rodolph of Ravensburg who makes a pact with the devil in return for eternal life. The cost is that he becomes a vampire at night and also turns his mistress into one of the undead. In the best tradition of such publications – and in line with vampire lore – the Count is finally cornered by the villagers of Ravensberg who have suffered his atrocities for years and is firmly staked into his coffin. A typical episode of this landmark story is reprinted in *The Vampire Omnibus* edited by Peter Haining (1995).

H

Haarmann, Fritz (1879–1924)

Named 'The Hanover Vampire' by the press, Fritz Haarmann conducted an undetected reign of terror in his home town in the 1920s, during which he lured homeless boys and young men to his home and then killed them by sinking his teeth into their throats. After attending military school – from which he was discharged for offences against children and spent some time in a mental institution – Haarmann managed to get into the Germany army where he served during the First World War, apparently with distinction. On returning to Hanover in 1918 he opened a butcher shop and used it as a front for criminal activities and as a haven to prey on young males. According to a subsequent report in the *News of the World* of 7 December 1924, 'Haarmann would take them to his room and, after a copious meal, would kill them in the manner of a vampire.' He got rid of the evidence in the classic style of Sweeney Todd by turning the victims' bodies into fillings for his meat pies. When finally arrested in the summer of 1924, he was charged with killing 27 men – thought the real total may have been nearer 50 – all between the ages of 12 and 18 years old. In December, Haarmann was tried at the Hanover Assizes, found guilty, and sentenced to be beheaded, which is, of course, one of the traditional methods of destroying a vampire. This was not quite the end of the story, however, for the following year, the London *Daily Express* carried a story on April 17 headlined: VAMPIRE BRAIN TO BE PRESERVED FOR SCIENCE in which it was reported that scientists at Gottingen

University were to examine Haarmann's brain, because of the nature of his crimes: 'it may provide an explanation for the causes of vampirism.' Nothing further, though, was ever heard of this project.

Haigh, John George (1910–1949)

George Haigh was an English mass-murderer who confessed to drinking the blood of nine victims before dissolving their bodies in acid and was consequently referred to by the press of the time as the 'Acid Bath Vampire'. A self-styled engineer, Haigh claimed to have killed a Dr Henderson and his wife, three members of a family named McSwain, three more unknown people, and lastly a wealthy widow, Olive Durand-Deacon, whose disappearance in February 1949 – reported to the police by a suspicious neighbour – eventually led officers to a store room in Crawley, Susex where he had sampled the blood of each of them before placing the corpses in a drum of sulphuric acid. During the course of his trial at Lewes Assizes the following July, Haigh said he had been obsessed with blood ever since having a dream in which a man had emerged from a forest of crucifixes carrying a cup of blood from which he ordered him to drink. As a result, Haigh believed it was his mission to kill and taste the blood of his victims. Of one, he said, 'I fetched a drinking glass and made an incision in the side of her neck and collected a glass of blood which I drank'; and of another, 'I hit him on the head with a cosh, withdrew a glass of blood as before, and drank it.' Although Haigh pleaded not guilty to the charges of murder on the grounds of insanity, he was found guilty and executed at Wandsworth Prison in London on 19 August 1949. A full account of the life and crimes of the 'Acid Bath Vampire' can be found in *John George Haigh: Acid Bath Killer* by Gerald Byrne (1968)

Hamilton, George (1939–   )

A darkly handsome leading man in many Hollywood films and on TV, George Hamilton also played the role of Count Dracula (*q.v.*)

in *Love At First Bite* made in 1979. The script, a spoof on Stoker's original novel, co-starred Susan St James as the girl the Count sets out to win. During filming, Hamilton said of Dracula, 'He is the ultimate romantic – a great male chauvinist.' The star also revealed that in his own desire to remain young, he regularly took doses of an anti-toxin that is claimed to wipe out poison in the blood stream. 'It's like having the oil in a car changed,' he told Brian Wesley of the *Daily Star* in June 1979. 'But afterwards you feel terrific. I know because I've been to every youth doctor there is – even one in deepest Romania the legendary home of Dracula!'

Hammer Films

Founded originally in 1935 by William Hinds (known as Will Hammer) and Enrique Carreras as a distribution company, Hammer Films became one of the most successful British film makers through a cycle of horror movies started in the 1950s in which the figure of Dracula, played by Christopher Lee (*q.v.*), formed a major part. The trademark of all the films were their glorious technicolour *mélange* of blood, gore and eroticism. A tight control of costs and rigid shooting schedules was also very important in this success story. The first *Horror of Dracula* was shot by Terence Fisher (*q.v.*) in six weeks on a budget of £81,413, with the writer (Jimmy Sangster) being paid £1,000 and the whole cast £7,310. The cost of the crowd scenes came in at just £87. Even by 1972 when Hammer was making *Dracula AD 1972*, the total budget was only £220,000. Other vampire movies made by the company were: *The Brides of Dracula* (1960), *Kiss of the Vampire* (1963), *Dracula – Prince of Darkness* (1965), *Dracula Has Risen From the Grave* (1968), *Lust For A Vampire* (1970), *The Vampire Lovers* (1970), *Countess Dracula* (1970), *Scars of Dracula* (1970), *Dracula and the Legend of the Seven Golden Vampires* (1974) and *The Satanic Rites of Dracula* (1978). Michael Carreras, the son of one of the founders who carried on his work, was made a knight for his contributions to the British film industry, and Hammer won a Queen's Award for Industry. The legend has been kept alive by

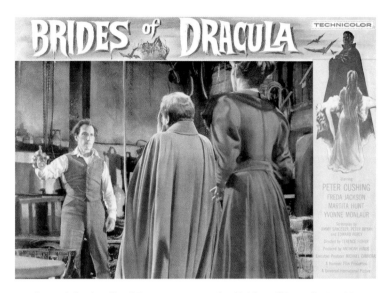

One of the familiar Hammer posters for *Brides of Dracula* (1960)

regular re-showing of the Hammer pictures on late-night television, a BBC TV tribute programme, *Hammer, The Studio That Dripped Blood* (1987), the 12-part series, *Hammer House of Horror* (1979), and the plans of current owner Roy Skeggs to make further stories in the same tradition for both the cinema and television.

Hannya (Japan)

The *Hannya* are the traditional vampires of Japan. These creatures only appear as females, with dark, evil eyes and long, pointed teeth. They are usually dressed in long, flowing robes and scream hellishly when they attack. According to tradition, the *Hannya* are women who have lost children during pregnancies or childbirth resulting in their premature death and they consequently have a tendency to attack young people. There is also an aerial form of vampire known as a *Tengu* which has wings like a bird and a sharp pointed beak and attacks its unsuspecting victims at dusk. A number of accounts of the Japanese undead are to be found in the works of Lafcadio

Hearn (1850–1904), the Irish-born writer of supernatural fiction who spent the last 14 years of his life living and teaching in Japan, notably in the collections, *In Ghostly Japan* (1899) and the posthumous *Fantastics and Other Fancies* (1914)

Hantu (India)

The *Hantu* is a species of vampire that has been reported in India for many centuries. These creatures are human in appearance, generally materialize at dusk, and come in three distinct categories. The *Hantu Saburo* is assisted in his quest for human blood by a pack of huge dogs which chase victims into forests, run them down, and then allow their master to drink the human blood before feasting on the corpse. The *Hantu Dondong* lives in caves and crevices in the rocks, and when unable to find human victims, will kill and eat wild hogs. The third type, the *Hantu Parl*, is particularly feared because it is attracted to any location where fighting has occurred and there it sucks the blood of the dead or dying. There have been several reports this century of *Hantu Parls* creeping into the grounds of rural hospitals to feast on the wounds of injured patients. Occasionally the *Hantu* may be in the company of another dreaded Indian spirit, Siva, as K.W. Barth explains in his *History of Religions* (1906): 'Siva is identified with *Mrityu*, Death, and he is chief of the mischievous spirits, of ghouls and vampires that frequent places of execution and those where the dead are buried, and he prowls about with them at nightfall.'

Hartmann, Franz (1842–1926)

Franz Hartmann was an Austrian physician and writer on the occult who investigated many stories of vampires and the undead as part of his larger enquiry into life after death. Following years of assembling information from all over Europe, he published in 1896 a volume entitled *Premature Burial* containing several accounts of vampirism amidst a whole variety of chilling reports about people buried before they were dead. Hartmann's conclusions were that the medical profession actually knew very little when it came to determining *precisely* whether a patient had passed away. He believed the only way to be sure was to keep the body around for days until decomposition set in! Hartmann catalogued horror after horror story about bodies that had been discovered in tombs and which showed clear signs of a terrible struggle having occurred before death. In consequence, he advocated a scheme for a bottle of chloroform to be placed in every coffin to enable anyone who *did* revive to commit suicide and be spared further suffering! *Premature Burial* also contained several specific accounts of vampires to underline the dangers of not being certain of death. Hartmann also developed what he called an 'astral tumour theory' which defined vampires as 'astral forms living at the expense of a person from whom they draw vitality and strength'. He felt that vampires did not necessarily have to be the result of premature entombment, but could be exteriorized by a healthy agent: 'Consequently the body of the dead in whom a remnant of the astral life exists may vampirize the living and still

'The Resuscitated Corpse', an illustration from Franz Hartmann's important study of *Premature Burial* (1896)

more this may take place among the living themselves.' To corroborate his theory, the author cited a case in which a young suicide became a vampire because of his love for a married woman. Although the affection was mutual, Hartmann said, the woman had discouraged his advances, but the youth's spirit had attached itself to her and even materialized by drawing on her vital forces.

Hawthorn

For centuries, the hawthorn tree (*crataegns oxyacantha*) with its thorny leaves and red berries, which is indigenous to much of Europe, has been considered a powerful weapon in the battle against vampires. A tradition, observed in Britain and as far east in Europe as Bosnia, says that after a person has died, a sprig of hawthorn should be left in the vicinity of the grave. If that person then becomes a vampire – Montague Summers (*q.v.*) states in *The Vampire in Europe* (1929) – then he or she 'will be so busily engaged in picking up the hawthorn that it will not be possible for them to track victims to their homes'.

Highgate Cemetery, London

Highgate Cemetery, with its 45,000 graves, tombs and mausoleums sprawling amidst suburban London, has been the scene of many eerie and curious events over the years, none stranger than the mass 'Vampire Hunt' in March 1970 following claims that had been circulating for some time about a 'tall, dark figure' prowling around the grounds who might be one of the undead. Thereafter the story of the alleged 'Highgate Vampire' became surrounded in controversy, generating innumerable newspaper stories, several television programmes and further searches in the cemetery – one of which led to police action. An account of these events, including details of a ceremony of exorcism carried out in 1975 is given in *The Highgate Vampire* by Sean Manchester (1997). According to a number of literary experts, Lucy Westenra, Count Dracula's first female victim when he comes to England, is buried in the cemetery. However, a closer reading of the text and what Bram Stoker (*q.v.*) refers to as 'Kingstead Cemetery' points to the place actually being nearby Hendon Cemetery, which is located between *Kings*bury and Hamp*stead*. The case for this locality has been made convincingly in 'The Origins of *Dracula*' by Philip Temple in *The Times Literary Supplement*, 4 November 1983 and *The Un-Dead: The Legend of Bram Stoker and Dracula* by Peter Haining and Peter Tremayne (*q.v.*) (1997). Highgate Cemetery was used as a location for the BBC2 two-part version of *Dracula* made in 1977, directed by Philip Saville and starring Louis Jordan as the Count and Frank Finlay as Van Helsing.

Hodgson Memorial

The remains of a metal stake once driven into a grave in the churchyard of St Andrew's at Dent, in Yorkshire, is believed to be the only surviving example of a vampire ceremony carried out in Britain. The tomb is that of a local man, George Hodgson, who died, the object of much fear and trepidation, in 1715. According to a still-current story, the inhabitants of Dent were too scared to open the coffin to prevent Hodgson from returning as one of the undead and, instead of the traditional manner, drove an iron stake through the memorial stone into the body lying below. At the same time, on the chancel steps, a bat was pierced through the heart with a silver pin in an act of sympathetic magic intended to make doubly sure the vampire lay still. Today, the stone containing the tip of the stake which was removed from Hodgson's tomb some years ago can be seen at the porch entrance to St Andrew's.

Hopkins, Sir Anthony (1937–   )

Welsh-born actor, Anthony Hopkins, who came to prominence in the late 1960s playing impressive character roles such as Richard the Lionheart in *The Lion in Winter* (1968) has now become an

Sir Anthony Hopkins as the vampire hunter Van Helsing in
Bram Stoker's Dracula (1993)

international star largely as a result of his performance as the blood-sucking cannibal, Hannibal ('I ate his liver with some fava beans and a nice Chianti') Lecter in *Silence of the Lambs* (1992), for which he received an Oscar. In a quite different mode he was stolidly impressive as Professor Van Helsing in *Bram Stoker's Dracula* (1993) directed by Francis Ford Coppola. Originally tipped to play the leading role, Hopkins said during filming: 'Too obvious – I didn't want to play Dracula after Lecter as it would have been too over the top. I think Van Helsing has been down in the depths, seen the face of terror, and then come out of the other side.' Hopkins himself has lead a turbulent life – including recovering from alcoholism – all of which, he has said, gave him experiences to draw upon when playing the vampire hunter. His knighthood awarded in 1993 has confirmed Anthony Hopkins as one of the greatest contemporary actors. A projected sequel by Coppola entitled *The Van Helsing Chronicles*, with Hopkins repeating his role in an original story told from the vampire hunter's point of view, has been announced but not yet gone into production.

Hubner, Stephen (d.1732)

Stephen Hubner is the subject of one of the best documented cases of vampirism in Czechoslovakia. In the year 1732, reports began to circulate in the area of Treautenua of terrible attacks on people and cattle by a creature who killed his victims and drank their blood. Investigating the incidents, local officials realized that the perpetrator used strangulation to kill both men and beasts. The fatal attacks continued for much of the year, until the wife of a shopkeeper, who had been killed by the mysterious figure, claimed he bore a distinct resemblance to Stephen Hubner – himself a local shop owner, who had died five months earlier. The officials acted on her advice and opened Hubner's coffin where he was discovered quite unchanged. 'All the signs of vampirism were found upon him,' says P. Gengell in his contemporary account of the events. 'The body was decapitated by the common executioner and the remains burned and scattered to the wind. For precaution's sake, the bodies of those near Hubner were exhumed and reverently cremated.'

Illustration from Joris Karl Huysman's controversial novel, *La Bas* (1891)

Huysmans, Joris Karl (1848–1907)

Described as 'the quintessential exponent of decadence in literature' the French author Joris Karl Huysmans has also been deeply influential on the horror story genre with his short stories and two great novels, *A Rebours (Against the Grain)* (1884), a tale of the erotic and the arcane often compared to Oscar Wilde's *The Picture of Dorian Gray*, and *Là-Bas (Down There)* (1891): the latter is generally considered his masterpiece and it certainly played a seminal part in making the general public aware of the black magic and satanism then being practised. Huysman's achievement is all the more remarkable because he was ostensibly a respectable Parisian Civil Servant, but privately he was fascinated by mysticism and the supernatural. *Là-Bas* is largely autobiographical and features a number of people who helped him to learn all about the occult. According to Aubault de la Haulte Chambre in his study, *J.K. Huysmans: Souvenirs* (1924) one of these, who appears as 'Madame Chantelouve', was a vampire. 'Those who personally knew the lady, a Spaniard called by everyone, Dona Sol, declared this to be true. Her presence, her society had the effect of sucking the vitality of those who were with her, and her energies markedly increased, her brilliance shone brighter, as their depression and enervation grew more languid and more tired.'

1

In Search of Dracula (1972)

Christopher Lee (*q.v.*) was the narrator of *In Search of Dracula*, an hour-long documentary film made by Aspekt Films of Sweden and filmed on location in England and Romania in November–December 1971. Lee also appeared in three other guises: as the Hammer Films'

While filming *In Search of Dracula* in 1971, Christopher Lee was struck by his remarkable physical likeness to Vlad Dracula (opposite)

Dracula, as Bram Stoker's (*q.v.*) original concept and as Vlad Tepes (*q.v.*), one of the book's sources of inspiration. The programme, directed by Calvin Floyd, was based on the book, *In Search of Dracula* (1971) by Raymond T. McNally and Radu Florescu, who acted as consultants on the film. Lee visited several of the sites associated with the legend, including Snagov Monastery near Bucharest, the site of Vlad's (now empty) tomb, the ruined castle at Argesh – 'a very eerie ruin on top of a gigantic rock with an atmosphere, Gothic and brooding, exactly as Stoker described it' – and Bran Castle where he appeared in the costume of 'The Impaler'. He commented later, 'Although Vlad Dracula was a cruel and monstrous man, he wasn't a vampire. That was an embellishment on Bram Stoker's part. In the district where he lived, he's still regarded as a folk hero who saved the country from the Turks. I got the biggest surprise when I was shown some wood engravings of his face. He looks exactly like me. The resemblance was really quite uncanny.'

Interview With The Vampire (1995)

After numerous attempts to turn the groundbreaking 1976 novel, *Interview With The Vampire* by Anne Rice (*q.v.*), into a movie, the picture was finally filmed in 1994 by the Irish-born director, Neil Jordan, with Tom Cruise as Lestat (*q.v.*), Brad Pitt as Louis and Kirsten Dunst as the child-woman, Claudia, and became an instantaneous box-office hit. The making of the film was, though, surrounded by controversy – at one stage there were plans to relocate the setting of the story from eighteenth-century New Orleans to Vietnam, and the casting of Cruise provoked a protest from Anne Rice who thought the actor was totally unsuitable as the tall, blond vampire and would have preferred either Rutger Hauer or Jeremy Irons. After seeing the finished picture, Rice dramatically reversed this opinion with a two-page advertisement of unstinted praise for the star and the movie in the *New York Times*. While filming the story, which remained faithful to the book, on location in New Orleans and at Pinewood Studios in England, Jordan said: 'The book is one of the most original pieces of Gothic horror fiction since *Dracula*. It's a vampire story written from the point of view of the vampire which had never been done before and the minute I read it I had to do it.' After completing the five-month shooting schedule, he added, 'I've tried to make a movie that deals with a sort of dysfunctional family, with these three characters, two parents and a child – one is this kind of monstrous parent, the other is like a parent with a soul, and the child is Claudia – and to look at these characters like they were real people.' The dialogue provided several lines which have now entered vampire movie folklore including the moment when Lestat (Cruse) says to the newly vampirized Louis (Pitt), 'God kills indiscriminately and so shall we!' and also when this pair are united with Claudia, and Lestat again exclaims gleefully, 'One happy family!'

Irma Vep

The Mystery of Irma Vep (the anagram is obvious) was a very successful two-man Gothic burlesque melodrama written by the extraordinary American playwright Charles Ludlam (1943–1987) which was first performed in New York in 1984 and subsequently staged all over the world. Ludlam, famous for his 'lunatic extravagence of ideas', according to the London *Times* theatre critic, Benedict Nightingale, was the son of a Long Island plasterer who said he might have become a criminal if he had not become fascinated by *outré* spectacles like freak shows and be inspired to enter the world of the theatre. He joined the Ridiculous Company to play 'Peeping Tom' in a version of *Lady Godiva* and quickly became the moving spirit of the company, turning it, and himself, into a cult. 'Nothing is too far out for me, I want to outrage' Ludlam said, while he wrote, directed and starred in productions like *Conquest of the Universe, When Queen's Collide* and *Eunuchs of the Forbidden,*

Poster for the bizarre *Mystery of Irma Vep* by Charles Ludlam (1984)

culminating in the company's biggest commercial success, *The Mystery of Irma Vep*. The story combined elements of *Dracula* and *Jane Eyre* in a camp drama about Lady Irma, mistress of a fog-shrouded grange, Mandacrest, who is under constant threat from the undead. Ludlam's manifesto for the play in which he starred in New York and Nickolas Grace made his own in London, was, 'To test out a dangerous idea, a theme that threatens to destroy one's whole value system – but treat the material in a madly farcical manner without losing the seriousness of the theme.' He died, aged 44, of pneumonia, which he was reportedly trying to cure by placing live carp on his chest.

Irving, Sir Henry (1838–1905)

Sir Henry Irving was the famous English actor for whom Bram Stoker (*q.v.*) served as business manager from 1878 until his death in 1905 and was clearly one of the models for Count Dracula (*q.v.*). Born in Somerset, Irving worked for a time in London before making his acting debut at the Sunderland Theatre in 1856. After several years appearing in other provincial cities, he opened at the Lyceum Theatre in London in 1874 playing *Hamlet*; and with successive triumphs in *Macbeth* (1875) and *Othello* (1876) gained his reputation as the greatest English actor of his time. After Bram Stoker had joined Irving at the Lyceum and begun his years of devoted and often thankless service, the actor starred in a notable production of Goethe's *Faust* (1885). His saturnine costume, dark make-up and the dramatic gestures of his performance – not to mention his peculiarly striking face and long, grey hair thrown back – stuck in Stoker's mind and later found their way into the character of Dracula. In 1895, Irving became the first actor to receive a knighthood, but three years later tragedy struck when the Lyceum was gutted by fire and was forced to sell the lease. Sir Henry saw nothing of the subsequent fame of his friend's novel. Indeed, when Stoker staged a single, four-hour reading of the novel on 18 May 1897, a month prior to its book publication to establish theatrical copyright, Irving dismissed it and the actor playing Dracula for the very first time and remembered only as 'Mr Jones' with one word, 'Dreadful!' He was quite oblivious, of course, that it would play a significant part in his own immortality.

Sir Henry Irving, a source of inspiration for Count Dracula,
appearing in *Faust* (1885)

J

James, Henry (1843–1916)

Henry James was an American novelist, short story writer and essayist, best remembered for his classic ghost story, *The Turn of the Screw* (1898) as well as a series of novels about the relationships between Americans and Europeans including *The Portrait of a Lady* (1881), *The Spoils of Poynton* (1897) and *The Ambassadors* (1903) which considerably influenced the direction of twentieth-century fiction. Less well known is the fact that he played a major role in the development of the 'Psychic Vampire' theme (*q.v.*) in which men and women prey on unsuspecting victims, draining the energy and vitality from their bodies. This particular 'Jamesian formula', as it has been described, was also employed by a number of other writers, and the three short stories and novel of this kind which he produced have continued to be influential as well as frequently reprinted to the present day. James began the sequence when he was just 25 with 'De Grey: A romance' all about Margared Aldis, a penniless servant who marries the heir to the De Grey fortune and drains his vitality, eventually causing his death. The story appeared in the *Atlantic Monthly* of July 1868 and undoubtedly startled a number of the magazine's more staid readers. He followed it with 'Longstaffe's Marriage' (*Scribner's Monthly*, August 1878), 'Maud-Evelyn' (also for the *Atlantic Monthly*, April 1900) and then, the following year, with a novel, *The Sacred Fount*. In this, a woman decides to save her husband's sacred fount – the energy exchange between interacting humans – by taking a lover who she can 'live off', in a vampiric fashion. James B. Twitchell in

The 'vampire husband' in 'Longstaffe's Marriage' by
Henry James (1878)

The Living Dead: A Study of the Vampire in Romantic Literature (1981) has commented, 'By the time Henry James came to tell his own vampire stories, the myth had been worn almost to the bone ... what he did was to combine the traditions of the vampire as noctural terrifier and the other as psychological analogy to produce truly dangerous but believable characters.'

James, Montgue Rhodes (1862–1936)

Although M.R. James is generally considered to be one of the finest of all English ghost-story writers, he was also a distinguished scholar and spent a considerable amount of time researching ancient documents and medieval manuscripts which gave him a more than passing interest in vampires. Born in Suffolk, the son of a clergyman, he studied at Eton and Cambridge, and then settled for the life of an academic, ultimately becoming Provost of Eton. What began as an annual task of writing a ghost story to tell a group of friends at Christmas, ultimately led to his acclaim as a writer of brilliant supernatural tales when they were published for general consumption in volumes like *Ghost Stories of an Antiquary* (1904), *A Thin Ghost* (1919) and *A Warning To The Curious* (1926). James came across stories of vampires both during his researches and also while travelling abroad with friends. One visit to Scandinavia – ostensibly on a 'Troll Hunt' – was particularly rewarding and resulted in the outstanding story 'Count Magus' (1904) in which a tourist visiting the tomb of the evil seventeenth-century Count Magus de la Gardie wishes he could see the monster of wickedness – and does. Another story, 'An Episode of Cathedral History (1919) contains a chilling description of a vampire much closer to home in England at Southminster. This time it is the widow of the former verger in Southminster Church who sees something flitting out of the building and disappearing into nearby houses. The narrative continues: 'She could see nothing of it, she said, but that it was a moving form; only she had an impression that when it returned to the church, it turned its head; and then, she could not tell why, but she thought it had red eyes.' James also found two allegedly true

M.R. James the scholarly English ghost-story writer was also fascinated by vampires

vampire stories among a collection of twelve medieval ghost stories during his researches among old documents in the British Museum in 1922, written in Latin apparently by a monk at Byland Abbey in Yorkshire around the beginning of the thirteenth century. James published them with copious footnotes in the *English Historical Review* of July 1922 and they were not translated into English until

1979 when they appeared in *M.R. James – Book of the Supernatural* by Peter Haining. M.R. James also wrote a number of articles about supernatural fiction including 'Some Remarks on Ghost Stories' for *The Bookman* in December 1929, in which he discussed *Dracula*, declaring that it 'suffers by excess' and made this extraordinary claim: 'I fancy, by the way, that it must be based on a story in the fourth volume of Chamber's *Repository* issued in the [Eighteen] Fifties.' No other writer has advanced this claim, although there are certainly elements in the story to which he refers, 'The Vampire of Kring', in the 14 November 1856 issue that bear comparison with the classic novel. There is, however, no written evidence to show that Stoker had read the story, but readers interested in investigating this mystery will also find the complete text in *M.R. James – Book of the Supernatural*.

Jaracara (Brazil)

The Brazilian vampire or *Jaracara* has the ability to turn itself into a snake when seeking victims. It is particularly intent on attacking mothers when they are suckling their babies. The creature brutally snatches the child away, puts its own tail into the infant's mouth like some kind of hideous baby's dummy, and then itself feeds from the terrified mother's breast. According to Brazilian tradition, the *Jaracara* regards milk as an equal life-supporting fluid to blood.

Jelf-Petit, Louis (1844–1913)

According to his grandson, F.H. Tate, Louis Jelf-Petit was a friend of Bram Stoker (*q.v.*) when both were young men, and Tate has claimed there is an alternative version as to how *Dracula* was created. In a letter to the London *Times* in December 1971, Tate outlined what Jelf-Petit had told him: 'The story was that Bram Stoker and a friend entered into a wager as to which could write a more horrible and frightening story. When the time limit for the wager had expired and the tales were submitted to the adjudicator, it was decided that Bram Stoker had lost his bet. The other story has never been published!' Despite appeals by F.H. Tate for any further information, this intriguing claim has never been substantiated.

Jewett Vampires

The story of the 'Vampire Brothers' of the little town of Jewett near Norwich in New England, is among the most curious in America and has been recorded in several vampire studies. The facts are these: in 1846, a man named Horace Ray who lived close to Jewett with his wife and five children, including three sons, died of consumption. Shortly afterwards, two of the sons, both young men, developed the same disease and died in 1851. The following year, the third and last of the Ray boys fell victim to the same disease. At this point – so the account which appeared in the *Norwich Courier* in 1854 stated – some of the local people 'resolved to exhume the bodies of the two brothers and cremate them because the dead were supposed to feed upon the living and so long as the dead bodies in the grave remained entire the surviving members of the family must continue to furnish vital substance upon which these could feed.' The account in the *Courier* added: 'Wholly convinced that this was the case, the family and friends of the deceased on 8 June proceeded to the burial ground, exhumed the bodies of the deceased brothers, and having erected a great pyre, burned them there on the spot.'

Jonathan, Vampire Sterben Nicht (1970)

The German scriptwriter and director, Hans W. Geissendorfer, was the mastermind behind *Jonathan, Vampire Sterben Nicht*, filmed in 1970. An outrageously erotic film, it was loosely based on Bram Stoker's novel, although the central character, Jonathan, played by Hans Engelmann, uses his vampiric powers to establish himself as a kind of fascist dictator. Colourful and gory, the movie has become something of an underground classic with younger audiences in Germany and several European countries as well as a late night television favourite in Japan.

K

Kallicantzaros (Crete)

There are several species of vampires to be found among the Greek islands, with the *Kallicantzaros* of Crete being 'the most extraordinary and horrible of all', according to Robert Pashley, a fellow of Trinity College, Cambridge, writing in his *Travels in Crete* published in 1837. These undead creatures are extremely gaunt in appearance and have tremendous strength. They have black, distorted faces, glaring red eyes, huge ears, and gaping mouths with a slobbering red tongue and sharp, gleaming white teeth. Greek tradition says there is another similar type known as a *Katakhanas* which is smaller and stunted and at first glance can appear like a grotesquely deformed child. According to local folklore, both types of vampire are unwitting members of the undead, having been born on Christmas Day, and this is the punishment for their mothers having conceived and given birth on the same days as the Virgin Mary. In his personal account of the vampire tradition in this part of the world, Robert Pashley has witten:

> In the islands of the Archipelago, where the belief in vampires is generally prevalent, if a man has committed a great crime or dies excommunicated by a priest or bishop, the earth will not receive him and he therefore rambles about all night, spending only the daytime in his tomb. Many believe that, even in the day time, it is only once a week, on the Saturday, that he is allowed to occupy his burial-place. When it is discovered that such a crea-

ture is about, the people go, on the Saturday, and open his tomb, where they always find his body just as it was buried and entirely undecomposed. The priest by whom they are accompanied reads certain parts of a ritual, supposed to be of peculiar efficacy for putting a stop to every restless Vampire's wanderings, and sometimes this course suffices to restore the neighbourhood to peace and quiet. Whenever this ordinary religious ceremony is found inefficacious, the people go to the tomb on a Saturday, take out the body and consume it with fire: an operation which nothing but extreme necessity would ever make Greeks consent to perform, on account of their religious horror of burning a body on which the holy oil has been poured by the priest when performing the last rite of his religion over the dying man.

Another tradition suggests boiling the head of the *Kallicantaros* in vinegar!

Kaplan, Stephen (1942–   )

The founder of the Vampire Research Centre based in New York, Dr Stephen Kaplan has been described as 'one of the world's leading vampirologists.' He set up the centre in 1972 because he wanted to discover whether vampires still existed and placed advertisements in a variety of publications. The response, Kaplan says, included many hoaxes, but as a result of this and three world-wide censuses, he now believes that there are almost a thousand vampires alive in the world: the largest number – over 600 – in America, with Germany topping the European nations with 25 vampires. Kaplan defines a vampire as someone who must drink human blood, not as a psychological manifestation but as a physiological need. He explains, 'Real vampires drink ounces of blood, not gallons. They drink two or three times a week, not daily.' According to Kaplan, real vampires do not have fangs, do not kill their victims, are not immortal – although some may live to 150 to 200 years old – do not necessarily sleep in coffins, can be photographed, are sensitive to garlic because of an antibacterial ingredient, and tend to be very dominating, sexually.

They are not people who dress up like Bela Lugosi (*q.v.*) or Christopher Lee (*q.v.*), but are generally articulate, good-looking and merge with the crowd. According to Kaplan, vampirism is a genetic syndrome: 'But it can skip several generations and manifest itself later, especially during puberty, when there is a dramatic drop in the red blood cell count, triggering the need to drink human blood. The habit of inflicting love-bites, bringing blood to the surface of the skin, may be a sign of latent vampirism or vampire ancestry.'

Karloff, Boris (1887–1969)

The actor born William Henry Pratt in Camberwell, South London, is today regarded as one of the immortals of the screen for his performance as the 'monstrous creation' in the 1931 production of *Frankenstein*. The son of a Civil Servant, Karloff (to use the name he adopted after one of his mother's ancestors and Boris because he liked it) was intended for a career in the diplomatic service, but instead emigrated to Canada where he worked briefly as a farm-hand before joining a touring theatrical company. From there he moved to Hollywood and found work as an extra before the director James Whale cast him in *Frankenstein* and his career was transformed. Curiously, Karloff got the role of the monster because Bela Lugosi (*q.v.*) fresh from his triumph in *Dracula*, turned it down; the previous year the roles might have been reversed when Karloff was short-listed for the vampire film which was given to Lugosi. Despite his long and successful career playing a variety of supernatural creatures, Karloff only appeared in two vampire pictures. The first was *House of Frankenstein* (1944) in which he played Dr Gustav Niemann, a scientist who discoveres the skeleton of Count Dracula (*q.v.*) in a 'Chamber of Horrors' and revives him. The Count was played by John Carradine (*q.v.*). In the second, made some twenty years later, he was actually one of the undead playing a Serbian vampire, a *Vourdalak* (*q.v.*) in *Black Sabbath* (1965) based on a short story 'The Family of the Vourdalak' (1847) by the Russian poet and historical novelist, Alexis Tolstoi (1817–1875). Tolstoi had a life-long interest in folklore and had earlier written a novel, *Upyr*

(Vampire, 1841) published under the pseudonym 'A. Krassnyrogski' which dealt with both diabolism and vampirism. In the film, directed by Mario Brava, Karloff was a peasant, Gorca, whose family are being terrorized by a vampire which, after a long pursuit, he manages to corner and decapitate – taking the head back home in a sack. But out of triumph comes disaster when Gorca becomes a *Vourdalak* himself and destroys the family he had tried to protect. Karloff also narrated the story and felt it was one of the best variations on the vampire theme he had seen during his lifetime. In the year of his death, aged 82, he was given the Ann Radcliffe Award by the Dracula Society for his contribution to horror films.

Portrait of Boris Karloff who played a merciless *Vourdalak* in
Black Sabbath (1965)

King's Road Vampire, The

'The King's Road Vampire' was the name given to an unnamed woman who led a Vampire Secret Society in London in the 1930s. Her story is told by the ghost hunter, Elliot O'Donnell (1872–1965) in his book *Strange Cults and Secret Societies* (1934) in which he claimed to have been present at one of the meetings of the cult. He wrote, 'I smiled when Miss Hester Stanhope told me that there were vampires and witches in both Chelsea and Brixton; but I did not smile when I saw the woman she called "The King's Road Vampire"; I was both horrified and disgusted.' O'Donnell discovered that the woman and her followers met in blood-red rooms in a number of London houses to discuss vampirism. They also ate special white flowers as part of a ritual to *become* vampires. O'Donnell explained: 'These flowers came from the Balkans and are known among the natives as "vampire flowers". If eaten shortly before midnight, to the accompaniment of certain incantations, they are deemed sufficient in themselves to develop vampire tendencies. The development is much quicker and certain if a vampire girdle is worn at the same time. This girdle, so I was informed, is made of the bark of a *stichimonious* tree, growing in a notoriously vampirous district in Hungary, encased in a goat skin and soaked in the blood of someone who has been murdered.' Once this ritual has been completed, O'Donnell said, the members were able to project themselves by separating their immaterial from their material body and in 'spirit vampire' form visit those from whom they wished to suck vitality like blood. 'The woman who told me this was quite serious and I felt sure she believed it herself,' the author concluded. 'And, perhaps, it was true.'

Kinski, Klaus (1926–1991)

Klaus Kinski was the Polish-born actor with an alarming, unforgettable face and an ability to project gloomy intensity on the screen – all of which made him a natural for playing sinister characters. This was especially true in *Nosferatu, The Vampyre* (1979) (*q.v.*) a remake of the earlier, unauthorized *Nosferatu* filmed by F.W. Murnau in 1921. Born Nicolaus Gunther Nakszynski in Danzig – now Gdansk – Kinski was moved by his pharmacist father to Berlin where the family took German citizenship. He served briefly in the Wehrmacht, but while on a training exercise with his unit in Holland they were overrun by advancing British forces and he spent the rest of the war in a British POW camp. It was there he got his first stage experience in a camp show. After the war, Kinski worked in the struggling German theatre and also got small roles in various B-movies playing lunatics or thugs, before meeting up with the German director Werner Hertzog who made him an international star as the mad conquistador in *Aguirre, Wrath of God* (1972) and the eccentric hero of *Fitzcarraldo* (1976). In the winter of 1978, Hertzog offered him the starring role in *Nosferatu*. 'From the minute he told me about it, I felt the vampire growing inside me,' Kinski said later. He was not, though, entirely unfamiliar with the vampire legend, having appeared in the 1970 Spanish film, *El Conde Dracula* directed by Jess Franco with Christopher Lee (*q.v.*) in the lead. Kinski played Renfield with 'extreme restraint' according to one critic evidently aware of the actor's incendiary reputation both on camera and off. Before appearing as Nosferatu, Kinski spent five hours having special white Japanese Kabuki make-up applied to achieve a walking-dead appearance. 'The shaven head, the long nails and the teeth placed centrally because there is no animal that sucks blood with fangs wide apart, were all my idea – I thought Dracula was something that was not human, but not a monster either.' The result was a critically acclaimed film in which Kinski was described as 'the epitome of suffering – a Dracula we are meant to feel sorry for despite his grotesque appearance,' according to the *Observer*. In 1988, several years after he had moved to Hollywood, he reprised the role of Nosferatu in *Vampire in Venice*, a joint Italian–American production directed by Augusto Caminito. In this, the vampire went to Venice in search of love and death during the famous annual Carnival but only encountered a Van Helsing-type adversary played by Christopher Plummer. The poor script and confusing storyline condemned the picture despite another energetic performance from Kinski. The actor's final years

Klaus Kinski starred in the 1979 remake of *Nosferatu, The Vampyre*

were marred by constant disputes with producers – he was, for example, offered the lead in *Indiana Jones* but turned it down as 'a yawn-making, boring pile of shit' – as well as a damaging feud with his actress daughter, Nastassia Kinski, that took up his time rather than furthering his career. On 24 November 1991 he was found dead in his California home.

Kipling, Joseph Rudyard (1865–1936)

The English-born author, Rudyard Kipling, famous for the two *Jungle Books* (1894–1895), *Kim* (1901) and the children's classic, *Just So Stories* (1902), all inspired by his early career as a journalist in India, is also highly regarded for his horror tales including 'The Phantom Rickshaw' (1888) and 'The Mark of the Beast' (1891). Less well known is the fact that he played a major part in the creation of the cinema's first 'vamp' and 'It' girls. In 1914 he wrote a poem, 'The Vampire' which, the following year, was filmed in Hollywood as *A Fool There Was*, turning the star Theda Bara (*q.v.*) into an international sensation and launching the phenomenon of the 'vamp'. In Britain the film was considered 'too offensive' and banned from cinemas for years. The story is about a businessman who abandons his family for drink and drugs after being seduced by a *demi-monde*. The background to the creation of Kipling's poem has been uncovered by Andrew Lycett, the most recent of Kipling's biographers, who explained in an interview in *The Sunday Times* in August 1999, 'Kipling wrote the original poem about his cousin, Philip Burne-Jones, an artist who had loved and been spurned by Mrs Patrick Campbell, a famous actress of the time. Kipling felt sorry for Burne-Jones – who depicted himself in one of his paintings as a miserable youth, lying on a bed straddled suggestively by a wild-eyed woman – and he was inspired to pen "The Vampire" in revenge.' The origin of the 'It' girl, made famous in the 'Roaring Twenties' films of the American actress, Clara Bow (1905–1965), also came from one of Kipling's stories, 'Mrs Bathhurst' (1904) set in South Africa and featuring a barmaid who has what the author describes euphemistically as 'just "It" ' – 'a special quality some women have that stays in a man's memory once they walk down a street'.

Kolchak, Carl

Carl Kolchak was ostensibly a crime reporter with the Independent News Service in Chicago, but whereas most other reporters had to contend with criminals and killers, he was forever being confronted with vampires and other supernatural creatures. He was the leading character in an American TV series *Kolchak: The Night Stalker* which was first shown in the mid 1970s and repeated in the UK in the mid 1980s. Introduced in an hour-long special in 1972, Kolchak, played by Darren McGavin, tracked down a vampire amidst the glitz and high rolling gamblers of Las Vegas. The superb acting of Barry Atwater as the ominous Eastern European vampire, Janos Skorzeny, was another factor in the show's instant appeal to viewers. (Atwater also made another memorable appearance in a short promotion film for Christopher Lee's *Dracula* AD *1972* in which he played the Count and declared, 'Dracula is back because you have called him!') Such was the popularity of the TV series that at one point *Night Stalker* was achieving ratings figures of 75 million people – one third of all American viewers – a record which stood unchallenged for more than a decade. Despite his success in defeating the undead, Kolchak invariably found, when he returned to the newspaper office with his story, it was spiked by his highly sceptical boss Tony Vincenzo (Simon Oakland). The series was created by Jeff Rice (1944–) a former Las Vegas newspaperman who had a citation as 'Outstanding Young Journalist of Nevada' in 1968. Moving to Hollywood, he appeared in and scripted a number of movies before creating Kolchak which is still acknowledged today as a unique cult series.

Kostartsa Plague

Kostartsa in Hungary was the scene of a notorious plague of vampires in the early years of the eighteenth century. According to the records of three Hungarian army surgeons, Johann Baumgartner, Johannes Flickinger and Isaac Siedel, during the winter of 1731–2, a number of people died in the town of Kostartsa from loss of blood, 'their bodies in a terribly anaemic and attenuated condition'. The officers immediately suspected vampirism, and ordered a search to be made in the local cemetery for any graves that looked suspicious and for them to be opened. The result was extraordinary, for over a dozen bodies of men, women and even two teenage boys were found to be free of decomposition and showing signs that they had been stirring in their coffins. All of the vampires had rosy complexions, their nails had grown long and when their chests were pierced with stakes, fresh blood poured forth. The report of the outbreak complete with details of the medical findings was contained in an account signed by the three officers and dated 7 January 1732 – the same day, history shows, on which all the bodies were burned and the Kostartsa Plague came to an end.

Kronos, Captain

Captain Kronos is a nineteenth-century Nordic knight and self-styled vampire hunter. A man with a mysterious past who composes himself for this battles with the undead by meditating, he was created in 1973 by Hammer film writer/director Brian Clemens, for what it was hoped would be a series of films to capitalize on the popularity of the company's Dracula movies. In *Captain Kronos – Vampire Hunter* which starred Horst Janson and his faithful companion, Professor Gorst (John Carter), the vampire hunter finds that the vampires terrorizing a mid-European village are immune to stakes and crosses and has to forge a sword made of silver to complete the task. To date there have been no further adventures of Captain Kronos.

Krvoijac (Bulgaria)

The *Krvoijac* is the vampire of Bulgaria – sometimes called a *Vepir* – a person who is said to have led a very evil life, although in some accounts it has been suggested this species become undead by drinking wine and smoking during Lent! They are indistinguishable from the living, except that they possess only one nostril, providing a means of identifying them when found in the grave. Bulgarian tradition says that it is possible to locate the tomb of a *Krvoijac* by having a teenage girl – who must be naked and a virgin – ride a black foal into a cemetery and step over all the graves. Any spot that the foal refuses to cross is where one of the undead lies. Local folklore maintains that any person suspected of returning as a *Krvoijac* may be prevented from doing so by being garlanded with wild roses before burial.

Kukuthi (Albania)

The *Kukuthii* of Albania is another much-feared vampire which preys on small communities and is believed to be the undead body of a person who has been buried in unconsecrated ground. The vampire may even have been a man or woman murdered and buried secretly and thus compelled to search for human blood to preserve its existence. The *Kukuthi* is cunning and strong, and attempts to catch one and burn the body in the traditional way have not always been successful, according to local folklore. A curious legend says that wolves have no fear of these vampires, and if one catches a *Kukuthi* and eats off a leg, the undead must crawl back to its grave and will rise no more.

Kurten, Peter (1883–1931)

Described in the press in the early 1930s as 'The Vampire of Dusseldorf', Peter Kurten was a mild-mannered factory worker who for several years led a double-life as a mass murderer revelling in the sight and taste of blood. Born in Kóln-Mulheim, one of 13 children ill-treated and abused by their violent, drunken father, Kurten ran away from home when he was a teenager and apparently discovered his lust for blood while living with a prostitute who enjoyed being ill-treated. Moving to

The mild-looking Peter Kurten, 'The Vampire of Dusseldorf'

Dusseldorf, he found a factory job and soon after married another of the employees. His bloody career began in 1929 when he committed his first murder of a 9-year-old girl. In the next two years, the city became gripped with fear as killing followed killing: in all of which the female victims were found to have been sexually abused and their blood sucked. A panic which mirrored that in

London during the era of Jack the Ripper grew up around the activities of the mysterious killer, until the complaint of a young girl who had managed to resist Kurten's attempt to rape her, finally brought the police to his door. Kurten's wife expressed total disbelief at the idea her apparently hard-working, loving, church-going husband could be the monster everyone had been seeking. At his trial in April 1931, Kurten was charged with nine murders and entered a plea of insanity which was rejected. He was sentenced to death and guillotined at Cologne's Klingelputz Prison on 2 July 1931. The last request of 'The Vampire of Dusseldorf' was very much in keeping with his reputation: 'I wish to hear the blood gurgle as my head is cut off.'

Kuzlak (Dalmatia)

The *Kuzlak*, a vampire unique to Dalmatia, the region lying alongside the eastern shore of the Adriatic in Croatia, has been described as being a violent creature that often announces its intent to prey on a lonely household by shifting about wood and other objects lying outside the building. According to Ornella Volta in *The Vampire* (1965), it is believed in Dalmatia that any child taken away from its mother before it has finished suckling will become a *Kuzlak*, 'the taste for milk naturally enough becoming transformed into the taste for blood'. In contrast, the milk of three nursing mothers used in the making of bread will provide an effective antidote against these vampires. Perhaps more certain is to stake the creature with a hawthorn bough (*q.v.*) that has been especially picked in the region's mountainous interior and sharpened to a point.

L

Langella, Frank (1940–   )

The American actor, Frank Langella, has played Dracula on both the stage and screen – 400 times in the 1977 Broadway production designed by Edward Gorey (*q.v.*) and then in the 1979 film version directed in England by John Badham. Langella, the son of a New Jersey businessman, capitalized on his elegant, darkly handsome good looks to make an almost immediate impact in the theatre and on television in the late 1960s, thereafter breaking into films. It was his stylish performance in the play *Dracula* that convinced film producer Walter Mirisch to cast him in the movie along with Kate Nelligan and Laurence Olivier (*q.v.*) who played Van Helsing. Whilst researching his role, Langella said he first began to understand the Count through his *humour* – 'If you had been lying in a box all day you would need a little light relief at night,' he explained – and also what he saw as Dracula's vulnerability, sensitivity and even fear.

> I've always felt that he's the kind of man, if he has lived for 500 years and experienced different times and different cultures and different peoples, he's bound to have gained a certain amount of philosophy about life, so that he doesn't spend all his time lurking and looking for blood. He needs blood to survive, but when he gets it, he has another ten or twelve hours to pass. He can enjoy the company of other people, he can find himself more attracted to one woman than another, it doesn't have to be purely indiscriminate blood-letting.

Frank Langella as a dexterous Count Dracula climbing *down* a wall
in the 1979 *Dracula*

The result was a vulnerable, slightly melancholic and highly sensual
vampire who female audiences found so appealing that Langella
actually heard sighing and swooning while he was playing the part
on Broadway: 'The way to a woman's heart is through her neck,' he
joked. For both the stage and on screen Langella wore the Count's
traditional cape, but resisted all suggestions that he should have
fangs. Although his two performances earned him the accolade of
being 'the sexiest Dracula of them all', the picture with its ground-
breaking special effects – particularly the Count walking down
walls – was a failure at the box-office.

Langsuir (Malaysia)

The *Langsuir* – sometimes spelt *Langsuyar* – is the Malaysian
species of vampire and appears in the shape of a beautiful lady

wearing a flowing green robe. She has long, sharp nails and jet black hair that reaches down to her feet and this covers the hole in the back of her neck which she uses to feed on her victims, mainly young children. The tradition behind this undead spirit has been recorded by Sir William Maxwell in the *Journal of the Straits Branch of the Royal Asiatic Society* (1899): 'If a woman dies in childbirth before delivery or after the birth of a child, and before the forty days of uncleanness have expired, she is popularly supposed to become a *Langsuir*. To prevent this, a quantity of glass beads are put in the mouth of the corpse, a hen's egg is put under each armpit, and needles are placed in the palms of the hands. It is believed that if this is done, the dead woman cannot become a *Langsuir*, as she cannot open her mouth to shriek or wave her arms as wings or open and shut her hands to assist her flight.' To destroy one of these vampires, W.W. Skeat explains in *Malay Magic* (1900), her nails and hair must be cut short and the hair stuffed into the hole in her neck, 'after which she will become quite tame and behave as an ordinary woman'.

Lavater, Louis (1527–1586)

In the sixteenth century, the Swiss cleric Louis Lavater wrote what is now recognized as the most exhaustive study of ghosts, vampires and other deadly spirits to have appeared up to that period in time. Entitled *De Spectris, Lemuribus, et magnisatque insolitis Fragoribus*, this massive work was initially published in Geneva in 1575 and several years later translated into English as *Of Ghostes and Sprites Walking by Night*. Lavater was born in Kyburg, in the canton of Zurich, and became a Protestant minister in the same district. He also devoted a great deal of time to writing theological and expository tracts, of which *De Spectris* is the most famous. Lavater believed implicitly in what he described as 'vampyre ghostes', citing as his evidence,

> Many honest and credible persons, as well men as women, of whom some are living and some already departed, which have

and do affirm that they have some times in the night seen and heard these spirits. Some men goeth to bed and laieth down to rest, and by and by there is some thing pinching him or sometimes sitting on him. These have been many times seen, being of a fierce shape, and known unto divers men as persons which died not long before.

Lee, Christopher (1922–   )

Although he is recognized as probably the screen's most famous Dracula, Christopher Lee has, in fact, only played the Count in seven films during a career in which he has appeared in around 300 movies: *Dracula* (1958), *Dracula Has Risen From The Grave* (1968), *Taste The Blood of Dracula* (1969), *Count Dracula* (1970), *The Scars of Dracula* (1971), *Dracula* AD *72* (1972) and the drama-documentary, *In Search of Dracula* (1975). Born in Belgravia, London, Lee's father was a Colonel in the 60th King's Royal Rifles and his mother an Italian contessa. He attended Wellington School and Eton where he met the famous ghost story writer, M.R. James (*q.v.*). Despite his undoubted acting talents and command of languages, Lee's height of 6ft 4ins initially confined him to bit-parts in films until his breakthrough came in 1957 playing the bandage-swathed monster in Hammer Films' (*q.v.*) *The Curse of Frankenstein*. The following year he became an international star in the same company's new version of *Dracula (aka Horror of Dracula)* for which he received a fee of £750. During the making of several sequels, Lee became increasingly disenchanted as the scripts deviated ever further away from his concept of Dracula: 'He is either a reincarnation or he has never died. He is a superman image with erotic appeal for women who find him totally alluring. In many ways he is everything people would like to be – the anti-hero or heroic villain – and, like the much maligned Rasputin, he is part saint, part sinner. Men also find him irresistible because they cannot stop him.' Lee's identification with the role has persisted to his well-documented irritation, and has sometimes re-emerged in the most unlikely places. Once, when driving back from a holiday in

Italy, his car blew a tyre, and he knocked on the door of a nearby house to get help. By his own admission he was muddy and bloodstained from wrestling with the car's wheel, and found the door being opened by a man who screamed in Italian, 'It's him!' and

'Back – this man belongs to me!' Christopher Lee in his favourite interpretation of Dracula in the Spanish-made film, *Count Dracula* (1970)

fainted. The man had, it transpired, being watching *Dracula* on television the previous evening. Christopher Lee wrote his autobiography, *Tall, Dark and Gruesome* in 1977 and subsequently spent ten years living in Hollywood where his versatility enabled him to play a variety of roles from historical dramas to comedy. A short while ago he delivered this verdict on the role which made him a household name,

> It was in the first Hammer version of *Dracula* that I think I came closest to Stoker's dramatic conception of the Count, although in a Spanish version, *Count Dracula* made in 1970, I did present him exactly as the author described him physically – as an old man with white hair and moustache, who grew steadily younger. I don't think I would want to play him again, unless I could make a film which mirrored in every aspect the book that Stoker wrote.

Lee, Tanith (1947–)

A prolific English writer, Tanith Lee, began her literary career writing fantasy stories for children, but has developed into a skilled and imaginative author of horror and science fiction. Vampires of various types have appeared in her work, notably in the stories of Sabella, a human vampire colonist on a planet called Novo Mars who feeds on the blood of the males she seduces. The two novels, *Sabella, or The Bloodstone* (1980) and its sequel, *Kill The Dead* (1980), have been published in a single volume as *Sometimes After Sunset*. Among Tanith Lee's most interesting short stories on the vampire theme are 'Red As Blood' (1979), 'The Vampire Lover' (1984) and 'Quatt-Sup' (1985).

Le Fanu, Joseph Sheridan (1814–1873)

The serial story, *Carmilla* (*q.v.*) by Joseph Sheridan Le Fanu, which originally appeared in *The Dark Blue* magazine in 1871–2, has been

Joseph Sheridan Le Fanu – Irish author of the classic, 'Carmilla'.

widely hailed as one of the best vampire stories of all time. It certainly helped to establish the vampire tale in the higher levels of English literature and there is no doubt of its influence upon Bram Stoker (*q.v.*) in the creation of *Dracula* – a fact which the author acknowledged. Like Stoker, Le Fanu was born into a middle-class family in Dublin and after graduating from Trinity College – where he wrote his first pieces of fiction – became a journalist and editor of several journals including the prestigious *Dublin University Magazine*. His love of Irish folklore and supernatural traditions, not the least of them concerned with vampires, became evident in his early short stories and novels including *Ghost Stories and Tales of Mystery* (1851), *The House by the Churchyard* (1863) and *Uncle Silas* (1864) which one critic called 'a masterpiece of alarm'. After the sudden and tragic death of his wife, Le Fanu became a virtual recluse, working much of the time in bed, and was found dead there of a heart attack on 7 February 1873.

Lemora, Lady Dracula

Lemora is a sensual vampiress, allegedly a relative of the infamous Count, who has settled in Georgia during the Depression era of the 1920s. There she lures young children to her home and turns them into vampires who become her devoted followers. The creation of American scriptwriters, Richard Blackburn and Robert Fern, the story of *Lemora, the Lady Dracula* – sometimes shortened to *Lady Dracula* – was filmed in 1973, directed by Blackburn and starred Leslie Gilb as the voluptuous member of the undead. On its release, the movie became notorious when it was given a 'Condemned' rating by the American Catholic Film Board.

Lerici Vampire

In April 1970, an olive grove near the village of Lerici, at La Spezia in Italy was claimed by the villagers to be the haunt of a vampire. Several Italian newspapers carried eyewitness accounts of the marauding figure who was described as wearing a long black cloak and having a thin, pale face. One terrified worker in the olive grove fled into the village one night after working there until dusk, claiming that the vampire had approached him, snarled, and revealed two long, protruding teeth. On 28 April, the London *Times* carried a further report that the local cemetery had been searched for any signs of a vampire on the loose, but no evidence of the tombs being disturbed was found. Although there were no further signs of the 'Lerici Vampire', as it became known that year, the figure has apparently been reported three times since, in 1976, 1984 and 1992, and the mystery would seem to be no nearer to a solution.

Lesbos Vampire

In the spring of 1995, the coffin of a man believed to have been a vampire was unearthed in a nineteenth-century Muslim cemetery on the popular Greek island and became famous in newspaper stories as the 'Lesbos Vampire'. The remains, nailed through with eight-inch-long iron spikes, were found by a team of archaeologists led by Professor Hector Williams of the University of British Columbia during excavations carried out in a stone-lined crypt hollowed out of the city wall at the town of Mylitene. Williams told newspapers in April 1995: 'The middle aged man had been nailed through his neck, pelvis and ankles. According to eighteenth and nineteenth century travellers, suspected vampires were nailed to their caskets. That a Muslim would be buried this way is of particular interest, since such burials were predominantly a Christian practise.'

Lestat De Lioncourt

Lestat is a blond, blue-eyed, angel-faced vampire who quotes Shakespeare and is the single most important character in the series of novels by Anne Rice (*q.v.*) known collectively as *The Vampire Chronicles*. Apparently born in France, the seventh son of an indigent marquis, Lestat originally wanted to be a monk, but thwarted in this desire by his father, ran away to Paris where he joined a theatre group, Renaud's House of Thespians, and was there turned into a vampire by the shadowy figure of Magnus – a character inspired by the short story 'Count Magnus' by M.R. James (*q.v.*). Although Lestat lives according to his own rules – 'My strength, my

Lestat, the vampire hero of Anne Rice's classic modern novel
of the undead

will, my refusal to give up, those are the only components of my heart and soul which I can truly identify' – he wants to use his evil image to do good and in his attempts to redeem himself, feeds on those mortals who commit the most evil against their own kind – serial killers. As Annie Rice has commented, 'Lestat is the bloodthirsty, wolf-killing, violent person who aspires to be something infinitely good and can't be.' Introduced in *Interview With The Vampire* as the vampire who was responsible for turning the narrator of the book, Louis de Pointe du Lac, into a vampire, he is, again according to Rice, 'the man of action, the person who cannot be paralysed with guilt.' Lestat has several houses in New Orleans, including a favourite in the Garden District which is said to be full of books on arcane subjects and the corpses of animals from which he has drunk blood. Among his capabilities, Lestat can fly, move or turn objects telepathically, live in sunlight and although he craves blood, does not need it for his continued survival. His two greatest convictions are that no human being can resist the urge to become one of the undead and all vampires desire to be human again. According to Katherine Ramsland in her guide to the series, *The Vampire Companion* (1993), 'Lestat is the vampire Anne Rice would want to be if she were given the opportunity.' Such is his popularity with readers that there is now a 'Vampire Lestat Fan Club' based in New Orleans which holds regular meetings and parties for members.

Les Vampires

Les Vampires was a film serial first screened in Paris in 1915 which effectively introduced the vampire theme into the cinema. Made by the great French film maker Louis Feuillade (1873–1925), it starred one of the great sex icons of the era, Musidora (Jeanne Rogues, 1889–1957) as the fiendish Irma Vep (*q.v.*), the central figure in a sequence of mysterious crimes, robberies, murders and supernatural occurrences. With her huge, lustrous eyes and voluptuous figure daringly displayed in a black leotard, Musidora instantly became the most piquant sex icon of the age and the French cinema's first *femme fatale* (*q.v.*). So quickly did the film gain a reputation for notoriety that the French police tried to ban it after only two episodes had been

LES VAMPIRES

Advertisement for the first vampire serial film, *Les Vampires*, shown in Paris in 1915

screened. According to legend, Musidora appeared at the prefecture dressed in her costume and beguiled the poor inspectorate into dropping their plans. Legend has it, too, that Feuillade improvised much of the plot as he filmed, switching from moments of almost dream-like fantasy to the brutal decapitation of a corpse – all done at such speed as to keep his audiences breathless with anticipation. Another major character in the story was the mysterious Dr Nox (Jean Ayme) who lived in a mysterious mansion and was ultimately revealed to be the Grand Vampire of Paris. Rumours from the set at the time claimed that Ayme was notoriously unpunctual for his scenes, and so irritated did Feuillade become that one morning he handed Musidora a gun and instructed her to shoot the actor. Fortunately, it was fitted with blanks – but Ayme was never late again. *Les Vampires* continued to exert its fascination over packed cinema audiences for 24 weeks before reaching a catastrophic finale in which the Grand Vampire and his cronies were all buried alive in the catacombs of Paris. Rightly regarded as a masterpiece among French horror films, the picture was brilliantly restored in 1986 and has since been reshown in France, Britain, America and several other countries.

Loango (Africa)

The *Loango* is the African vampire which has been feared by the people of the continent for centuries. According to tradition, these undead were all sorcerers or wizards during their lives and have sustained their existence by secret rituals and drinking human blood. They are said to be particularly active during the times when the moon is at its fullest and have the ability to turn themselves into winged creatures. A *Loango* can be detected in its coffin by the fact that its eyes are open. The most effective way of getting rid of one of these vampires is to fix it in the ground with a large nail or, better still, to burn the body on a night when there is no moon. As this is being carried out, the creature apparently emits a long moan. African folklore insists that every bit of the *Loango* must be burned, as the vampire can regenerate itself from even the smallest fragment.

Lobishomen (Brazil)

One of the world's most curious vampires, the *Lobishomen* is a tiny, hunchbacked creature that at first glance rather resembles a monkey. But this stumpy member of the undead with its yellow features, bushy beard, bloodless lips and black teeth has murderous intentions towards women, its primary target. According to local belief, after drawing blood from females the vampire turns them into nymphomaniacs. However, it is the bloodlust of the *Lobishomeni* that can be its undoing. For if it takes too much blood from a victim it begins to act as if drunk and can be easily caught. The creature must then be crucified on a tree and stabbed repeatedly to finally put it to death.

London

Several areas of London including Hampstead Heath, Bermondsey and Fenchurch Street are featured in *Dracula* where, of course, Bram Stoker (*q.v.*) lived and worked for many years as manager to Sir Henry Irving (*q.v.*). One particular location in which the Count 'resided' has been identified and may well soon enjoy similar status to that of 221b, the Baker Street 'home' of Sherlock Holmes. In Stoker's novel, the Count's address is given as 347, Piccadilly – a number which does not exist. But as Peter Haining revealed in his book, *The Dracula Centenary Book* (1988), the description of the building and its surroundings are sufficiently detailed enough to conclude that the property Bram Stoker had in mind is 137, Piccadilly. The house has the same type of balcony and ironwork, is adjacent to a 'big, white church' (Christ Church in Down Street) and not far from the Junior Constitutional Club at 105, Piccadilly – all of which are specifically referred to in the text. By one of those curious twists of fate, this building, where Dracula keeps nine coffin-shaped boxes of earth until he returns hastily to Transylvania, is now occupied by Universal Pictures who made the original *Dracula* in 1931! The house where Stoker himself lived during the writing of much of *Dracula* is not far away at 18, St Leonard's Terrace in Chelsea, a small terraced building facing towards the River Thames, and now marked with a blue plaque to commemorate his residency.

Loogaroo (West Indies)

The *Loogaroo* have the appearance of being extremely aged vampires, resembling old ladies with wrinkled faces, loose, fleshy lips and pointed teeth. The largest number have been reported on the island of Grenada where they are said to have long ago signed a pact with the Devil. It was he who gave them the power to shed their skins at night and, changing into a blob of light, set out to drink the blood of their victims. A requirement of the Devil's pact is that some of this blood must be given to him. The *Loogaroo* apparently leave their skins in silk cotton trees and the way to kill them is to find this flesh and burn it. Some experts have suggested that this tradition may have originated in the Congo where many African slaves came from, although there is no dispute that the name *Loogaroo* derives from the French for werewolf: *loup garou*. A few years ago, a travel writer, H.J. Bell commented, 'Even today visitors to Grenada have been called out of doors by servants to see the *Loogaroos*, and their attention is directed to any solitary light which happens to flash through the darkness. Until dawn the

Loogaroos are at work, and any person who feels tired and languid upon awaking will swear that the vampire sucked his blood. Doors and shutters are no barrier to the creature who can slip through the tiniest chink.'

Lory, Robert Edward (1936–   )

Robert Lory is an American public relations adviser and writer who had created a series of novels in which Dracula is revealed to have originated in the lost world of Atlantis before making his home on 'Dracula Mountain' in Transylvania. There, the undead Count ventures out to impose his will on a variety of supernatural foes who have ranged from zombies and witches to a reincarnated Elizabeth Bathory (*q.v.*) – curiously, Robert Lory's Dracula can choose whether those whose blood he drinks will become vampires or not! The books in the series, which have been published in the US, Britain and several European countries are: *Dracula Returns!* (1973), *The Hand of Dracula* (1973), *Dracula's Brother* (1973), *Dracula's Gold* (1973), *Drums of Dracula* (1974), *The Witching of Dracula* (1974), *Dracula's Lost World* (1974), *Dracula's Disciple* (1975) and *Challenge to Dracula* (1975).

Lovecraft, Howard Phillips (1870–1937)

The American writer, H.P. Lovecraft, who created the *Cthulhu Mythos* series of stories about grotesque extra-terrestrials, is now considered one of the most important authors of horror fiction of the twentieth century. Lovecraft in fact contributed most of his work to the legendary pulp magazine, *Weird Tales*, and very little of it achieved book publication until after his death. Today his novels such as *The Shadow Over Innsmouth* (1936), *Beyond The Wall of Sleep* (1943) and *The Dunwich Horror* (1963) are acknowledged as classics of their kind. Perhaps surprisingly because he lived for much of his life in New England with its strong vampire tradition, the bloodsucking undead do not feature very often in his work – the most notable instance being in 'The Shunned House' (1924) which refers to the case of Mercy Brown (*q.v.*) on Rhode Island – but his name is connected with an extraordinary rumour about the creation of *Dracula*. According to Raymond McNally and Radu Florescu's *The Essential Dracula* (1975), 'One prominent story is that H.P. Lovecraft claimed an acquaintance who had been contacted about the job of revising Stoker's hopelessly unpublishable novel. Another imaginative concept claims that *Dracula* is actually a cryptic novelization of the Jack the Ripper case, based on certain secrets known only to Stoker and a close circle of friends.'

Illustration from *Weird Tales* for H.P. Lovecraft's vampire story, 'The Shunned House' (1924)

Ludlam, Harry (1927–   )

Harry Ludlam is a former journalist and historian who wrote the first book about Bram Stoker (*q.v.*), *A Biography of Dracula: The Life Story of Bram Stoker* published in 1962. He had read the vampire novel as a schoolboy under his bedsheets at night and, 'It so scared me I just couldn't finish it,' he said. It was not until years later, when he was working as a young reporter, that he happened to buy a worn and faded first edition of the book for a few pence at a church fete and began to wonder about its author and what kind of man he might have been to have written such a horror story. For seven years he researched Stoker's life and work, consulting old newspapers, magazines and literary archives and finally making contact with the author's son, Noel, who gave him access to the family's private letters, diaries and photographs. Though subsequent research has added considerably to Ludlam's findings – as well as calling into question others – it remains an important pioneering book in the Stoker/Dracula legend.

Lugosi, Bela (1882–1956)

Bela Lugosi was the first internationally famous screen vampire and his thick, Hungarian accent announcing himself, 'I – am – Dracu – la' in the 1931 Universal pictures *Dracula* remains one of the most familiar and often imitated lines of dialogue in the history of the cinema. The actor was born Bela Blasko on 20 October 1882 in Lugos, the son of a banker, and trained for the stage at the Budapest Academy of Theatrical Arts. After playing a variety of leading roles on the Hungarian stage, he became embroiled in politics and was responsible for forming an actors union which, when the Communists came to power in 1919, caused him to flee the country to Germany. There he appeared on the stage and in a few films, before emigrating to America in 1921. Lugosi made his US stage debut in *The Red Poppy* in 1922 and the following year filmed *The Silent Command*. But it was in 1927 when he was offered the leading role in *Dracula, The Vampire* on Broadway that his fame was

Informal photograph of Bela Lugosi with his wife, Lillian, and son, Bela jnr, looking through his 'Dracula Scrapbook' in 1953

assured. The play was an adaptation of the version by the English actor-producer, Hamilton Deane (*q.v.*) rewritten by an American, John L. Balderston, and it gave full reign to Lugosi's Hungarian accent and histrionic acting skill. The success of the adaptation led naturally to the film version in which he created one of the most enduring images of Count Dracula. The *New York Times* critic wrote after the opening, 'Mr Lugosi succeeds in revealing the man-vampire as a hideous creature, one that few would like to encounter within the moss-covered walls of an old English abbey.' The actor himself said in an article in *Film Weekly* of 26 July 1935, 'I do not say that I personally take seriously vampires as such – I am saying that one must take them seriously when one is portraying them. In playing Dracula, I have to work myself up into believing that he is real, to ascribe to myself the motives and emotions that such a character would feel. For a time I become Dracula – not merely an actor playing at being a vampire.' He believed that the success of *Dracula* was also because 'women are interested in terror for the sake of terror' and they find the Count's magnetic power sexually attractive. Unfortunately, Lugosi allowed the vampire image to become part of his life – giving interviews while lying in a coffin, for example – and then accepting roles in which he increasingly parodied himself. From the high points of his vampire roles in *Mark of the Vampire* (1935) and *The Return of the Vampire* (1943) he descended to appearing as Dracula in comedies like *Abbott and Costello Meet Frankenstein* (1948) and *Mother Riley Meets The Vampire* (1952). Money and marriage problems also overwhelmed Lugosi and he became a drug addict. Plans that he nurtured to star in a TV series, *Dr Alucard*, and to remake *Dracula* in both colour and 3D came to nothing and he died on 15 August 1956 with the script for a B-movie by the director Ed Wood in his hands. Lugosi was buried in Holy Cross Cemetery in Los Angeles wearing the cape he had worn as the vampire Count and, although the closing years of his life had proved such an anti-climax, his fame was safe and his features have remained instantly recognizable in every corner of the world. In 1979, the heirs of Bela Lugosi went to the California Supreme Court in order to gain exclusive rights to the commercial exploitation of the actor's portrayal of the Count, but the verdict ruled in favour of Universal Pictures.

Lumley, Brian (1937–   )

The English writer Brian Lumley is the author of two innovative series of books about vampires which combine the traditional elements of horror with a high-tech future: the five *Necroscope* novels and the *Vampire World* trilogy. Lumley found his inspiration reading the works of the American author, H.P. Lovecraft (*q.v.*) and his earliest stories are very much in the same style. His readership grew with a sequence of novels featuring an occult detective, Titus Crow, subsequently issued as *The Compleat Crow* in 1987. But it was the appearance of *Necroscope* (1986) with its account of diabolical enemies in league with vampires from another dimension that established his reputation. The four subsequent books in the series are: *Vamphyri!* (1988), *The Source* (1989), *Deadspeak* (1990) and *Deadspawn* (1991). Lumley then produced a spin-off trilogy, *Vampire World*, beginning in 1992 with *Blood Brothers* and followed by *The Last Aerie* (1993) and *Bloodwars* (1994). Among his notable vampire short stories are 'Haggopian' (1973), 'Problem Child' (1974) and 'Necros' (1986).

ℳ

Map, Walter (c.1140–1210)

Famous during his lifetime for his poetry, Walter Map – known also as Gualteri Mapes – is best remembered today for an exceptional collection of history, folklore, superstition and rumour, *De Nugis Curialium*, still in manuscript at the time of his death and from which generations of writers have subsequently borrowed. Among those scholars who have edited versions of the book is M.R. James (*q.v.*) who did so in 1915. Born in Herefordshire of Welsh parents, Map studied in Paris and in 1162 became a clerk in the household of Henry II. Later he was sent on an ecclesiastical mission to Rome and on his return in 1197, he was made Archdeacon of Oxford. Map's insatiable curiosity and love of gossip inspired him to keep a diary from which *De Nugis Curialium* evolved. Among the items to be found in the book are several dealing with the Anglo-Saxon belief in beings that feed on human blood – including an account of a vampire in his native Wales and another about a creature that terrorized the house of a famous knight. The first concerns 'a Welshman of evil life' who returned after death to drink the blood of his neighbours. Despite several attempts to kill the vampire, his depredations were not stopped until an English nobleman, William Laudun, pursued the undead to his coffin and, according to Map, 'cleave his head to the neck'. The knight – who is not named – had lost three new-born children in succession, each being found in their cradle drained of blood. Keeping watch after the birth of a fourth, the family nurse was discovered bending over the child and

Woodcut from an early edition of Walter Mao's *De Nugis Curialium*

revealed to be 'not a woman, but a vampire in disguise'. At this, says Walter Map, 'a key to the nearby church was fetched, pressed against her face, branding her with its holy impression,' whereupon the woman fled howling and screeching from the house never to be seen again.

Mara (Denmark)

The *Mara* is a beguiling and particularly dangerous female vampire found in the country districts of Denmark. The creature can leave her resting place by day or night to go looking for blood, and because she has the ability to make herself invisible, the *Mara*'s victims are sometimes only aware of her presence when they begin to feel as if they are being suffocated or strangled around the neck by some primaeval force. According to Anthony Masters in *The Natural History of the Vampire* (1972), the only method of protection against this type of vampire is for a person to lie flat on their back holding a knife on their chest with the blade pointing upwards. 'When the *Mara* then adopts a human form the point of the knife will prick her and she will be frightened away.'

Marschner, Heinrich (1795–1861)

The German composer Heinrich Marschner was responsible for one of the earliest operas to feature the theme of the living dead, *The Vampire*, which was first performed in Leipzig in 1828. With a libretto by Wilhelm August Wohlbruck apparently inspired by the story of John Polidori (*q.v.*), the opera mixed romance, comedy, supernatural drama and souls in torment set against a Hungarian background. Born in Zittau, Marschner came under the influence of Carl Weber (1786–1826) – famous for the masterpiece, *Oberon* (1826) – to whom he was assistant before becoming music director at, successively, Dresden, Leipzig and Hanover. Marschner is probably best remembered for the opera, *Hans Heiling*, although *The Vampire*, which displays its creator's splendid feeling for ensemble writing and gift for dramatic timing, has been occasionally revived: notably in 1992 by BBC TV as *The Vampyr: A Soap Opera*. Produced by Janet Street-Porter, the setting was updated to London's Docklands with the vampire (opera star Omar Ebrahim) now a cut-throat stockbroker with a mission to seduce and vampirize three beautiful young women (singers, Fiona O'Neil, Willemijn Van Gent and Sally-Ann Shepherdson) in order to preserve his life. Critics enjoyed the analogy between vampires and yuppie property developers, *The Times* describing the production as 'a clever, fascinating curio', while the *Mail on Sunday* declared, 'It's *Dynasty* meets *Dracula*, but the dialogue is sung, and sung beautifully, by trained opera singers.'

Marshall, William (1924–   )

A noted American Shakespearian actor, William Marshall was also the first black man to play Dracula on the screen in 1972 in an ingenious if deliberately exploitive version entitled, *Blacula*. The film was made at the time when the market in the US for black performers was rapidly developing and the 6ft 5in former understudy made a hugely impressive vampire. Born in Gary, Indiania, Marshall progressed to Hollywood after years on the American stage and created a little bit of vampire history when he took the lead in *Blacula*. He played an African leader, Prince Mamuwalde who, in 1815, visits the Balkans during a tour of Europe and at a dinner in Count Dracula's Castle is turned into a vampire. One hundred and fifty years later, the prince is revived in present day Los Angeles, thirsting for blood. Speaking about the role, Marshall said, 'I took

William Marshall, the first black actor to play Dracula, in the 1972 movie, *Blacula*

a crash course in *Dracula* and vampires. And not just any vampire: but how would an African Prince of the early nineteenth century feel about being taken captive in Transylvania and doomed to live out eternity hungering for human blood? Another interesting thing I discovered was that the effective vampire movie must be flooded with urgent emotions of anguish, yearning, terror and, ultimately, relief.' While filming a scene in the streets of Los Angeles, Marshall had a bizarre encounter with a woman who said she wanted to be a vampire. When he asked why, she replied: 'Because vampires live forever. There's really no way to kill them. If you pull the stake out of their hearts, they revive. They can't really be hurt, no matter what happens.' Marshall has never forgotten the experience. *Blacula* proved a hit with audiences – one critic calling it, 'the most horrifying film of the decade' – and a sequel *Scream, Blacula, Scream*, in which the vampire Count tangled with a voodoo cult, followed in 1973. However, it failed to match the success of its predecessor and plans for the series to continue were dropped, although William Marshall has indicated he would be prepared to play the role again.

Matheson, Richard Burton (1926–   )

Highly regarded as a story-teller with a penchant for fantasy, Richard Matheson has also enjoyed a successful career as a scriptwriter for films and television. His association with the vampire theme goes back to childhood when he read *Dracula* and this found its fullest expression in his novel, *I Am Legend* (1954), about a world full of vampires in which just one human being has survived. Born in Allendale, New York, Matheson began writing fiction shortly after leaving college, and earned instant notoriety with his tale of a child mutant 'Born of Man and Woman' published in the *Magazine of Fantasy and Science Fiction* in 1950, and which later became the title of his first collection. The following year he wrote another little gem, 'Drink My Red Blood' for the April 1951 issue of *Imagination* magazine about a young boy obsessed with vampires whose one great desire – ultimately fulfilled – is to meet Dracula. *I Am Legend* is regarded as a landmark in vampire literature and has been filmed twice: in 1964 as *The Last Man on Earth* starring Vincent Price, and in 1971 retitled *The Omega Man* with Charlton Heston in the leading role. In 1973, Matheson scripted a full-length feature version of *Dracula* for MGM, which was filmed in England and Yugoslavia, starring Jack Palance (*q.v.*): 'I followed the novel as closely as possible and I think it's more faithful to it than most of the films have been,' he says. Richard Matheson also adapted his short story, 'The Funeral' about Dracula and another vampire attending a third vampire's belated funeral, for Rod Serling's famous *Night Gallery* series in 1973. Two other notable vampire short stories by Matheson are 'Dress of White Silk' (1951) and the deceptively entitled, 'No Such Thing As A Vampire' (1959).

Mayo, Herbert (1796–1852)

Dr Herbert Mayo was a distinguished Victorian surgeon and neurologist who spent years studying the link between superstition and the symptoms of vampire victims in an attempt to rationalize the subject in purely medical terms, instead of being a contagion spread by the bite of undead creatures. Born the son of a prominent London physician, he trained to become a surgeon and practised at the Middlesex Hospital; taught anatomy for a number of years at Kings College; and ultimately became one of the leading figures of his time at the Royal College of Surgeons. It was Mayo's special interest in brain disorders that led to his fascination with vampirism and the publication in 1851 of his remarkable book, *On The Truth Contained in Popular Superstitions*. In this he explained how he had reached his 'Vampyr-theorem' as a result of examining the links between superstitious auto-suggestion and the reported physical symptoms of alleged vampire victims. The death-like trance into which those bitten by vampires fell and their terrible anaemia could, Mayo stated, have a joint psychological explanation. He wrote:

> There is no reason why death-trance should not, in certain seasons and places, be epidemic. Then the persons most liable to it would be those of weak and irritable nervous systems. Again a

first effect of the epidemic might be further to shake the nerves of weaker subjects. These are exactly the persons who are likely to be infected with imaginary terrors, and to dream, or even to fancy, they have seen Mr or Mrs such a one, the last victim of the epidemic. The dream of impression upon the senses might again recur, and the sickening patients have already talked about it to their neighbours before they themselves were seized with a death-trance. On this supposition, the Vampyr visit would sink into the subordinate rank of a mere premonitory symptom.

Melrose Abbey, Scotland

The beautiful ruins of Melrose Abbey in Roxburghshire about 35 miles south of Edinburgh, which have been immortalized by Sir Walter Scott, were once the haunt of a vampire. The Abbey, founded in 1136 and said to contain the heart of Robert Bruce near the east window, was home to a flourishing monastic community for years. However, one of the monks broke his vows, lived a life of debauchery and vice, and finally committed suicide. When the man returned as a vampire, his purpose, it seems, was to force his attentions upon a neighbouring abbess – as historian Eric Maple has colourfully related in *The Realm of Ghosts* (1964):

> However much the saintly woman might have aprpeciated a monk in the flesh, she clearly regarded these diabolical over-tures with distaste. The problem was solved somewhat drasti-cally, for one night as the demon monk emerged from his coffin for another orgy of lust or blood, he was felled with a battle axe by another monk and dispatched to the Hellish regions whence he came.

Merimee, Prosper (1803–1870)

The French novelist and short story writer, Prosper Merimee, is probably best remembered for *Carmen* (1845) the story which gave

The French novelist Prosper Merimee described the attack of a vampire in 1816

the composer Georges Bizet, the basic plot for his famous opera. Born in Paris, Merimee held positions in several ministries while developing the knowledge of human nature and powers of observation, the hallmarks of all his writing. Among his varied body of work he produced two popular novels of the supernatural, *The Venus of Ille* (1837) and *Lokis* (1869) in which the heroine, Ioulka, is found dead in bed with her throat torn by a man who is ultimately revealed to have the power to turn into a beast. It has been suggested that the inspiration for this story may well have been a real event that happened to Merimee while he was staying with some friends at Varbeska in Yugoslavia in 1816 and recorded in his *Lettres à un Inconnu* (1875). While the group were at dinner, he explained, a vampire appeared at an upstairs window of the house, broke into the room, and bit the neck of a young girl named Khava who was asleep. The girl awoke just as the creature was raising himself up from her bed and, despite her fear, she recognised him as a man named Vieczany who had died a year before. At this, the family and friends lit torches and went to the village cemetery where the man was buried. Vieczany's coffin was opened and his body was found to be unblemished. Merimee adds, 'Although the vampire was destroyed, his victim passed away 18 days later.'

Mjertovjec (Russia)

The *Mjertovjec*, sometimes spelt *Myertovets*, is a species of vampire found in what was formerly the eastern areas of Russia. The creature is human in appearance with an extremely purple face, and pointed, canine-like teeth. It invariably selects its victims in isolated houses and rises from the grave at midnight, to which it must return by cock-crow. Russian folklore claims the *Mjertovjec* was the offspring of a witch or evil magician, and to be destroyed it must be found in its grave, spiked through the heart with a large nail, and the corpse burned to ashes.

More, Henry (1614–1687)

Known as the 'Cambridge Platonist', Dr Henry More was probably the first English historian to record cases of vampires since the chroniclers of the twelfth century. These appeared, carefully annotated, in his curiously titled book, *An Antidote against Atheism: or, An Appeal to the Natural Faculties of the Mind of Man, whether there be not a God* published in 1653. More was educated at Eton and Christ's College, Cambridge where he remained as an academic for the rest of his life. He devoted himself entirely to philosophy – especially to Plato and the Neoplatonists – producing an interesting volume of *Philosophicall Poems* and a collection, *Divine Dialogues*, before his early rationality gradually gave way to an obsession with mysticism and theosophy. In *An Antidote*, More describes a number of interesting vampire cases in Europe – most of which have subsequently been repeated by other authorities – and in all of which the undead, invariably men or women who had denied God, were despatched by having their limbs cut off and their hearts torn out. Their remains were then either burned or thrown into water, as the different traditions decreed. Totally convinced of the reality of vampires, More summed up, 'I must confess, I am so slow-witted myself that I cannot so much as imagine what the *Atheist* will excogitate for a subterfuge or hiding place from so plain and evident Convictions.'

Moribondo (France)

The *Moribondo* is a species of vampire found in the Brittany area of France. Reported in folklore and local histories for several centuries, the creature has made a speciality of attacking cattle and sucking their blood. The *Moribondo* is human in shape, though it

Underground vaults in Paris are believed to be one of the lairs of the French vampire, the *Moribondo*

sometimes appears to run on its hands and feet like an animal. It has staring eyes and sharp, white teeth. According to local tradition, the way to protect a herd that is being plagued by this type of vampire is to pass the cattle, one at a time, through a circle of fire. A recent attack on a herd of sheep in the Var district of France investigated by English writer Basil Copper (*q.v.*) bears striking similarities to that of a *Moribondo*.

Mulo (Europe)

The *Mulo* is the traditional name given by gypsies to their vampires and means 'one who is dead'. The creature is believed to have a great desire for women and will come after nightfall to the homes of young virgins, divorcees or widows to attempt intercourse. Rarely do these vampires suck blood. Some gypsies believe that the *Mulo* can make a woman pregnant and the children from such a union are known as *Vampijerovic* or 'little vampire'. The gypsies of the Balkan states believe these offspring are invariably boys, and there are stories in Yugoslavian folklore of whole villages consisting of the descendants of vampires known as *Lampijerovices*. The gypsies say that the *Mulo* has no bones in his body and the middle fingers of both hands are missing, as the creature has to always leave these in his tomb. The nature of this particular vampire is explained by Jean-Paul Clebert in his definitive work, *The Gypsies* (1963): 'His dwelling place is the grave or tomb of the deceased. But he is not firmly attached to the body. Death has liberated him and he can wander, travel, go to and from his base. He is not the corpse; he is the man himself in the form of his double. He must return to his grave at dawn.'

Muronul (Romania)

The *Muronul*, or live' vampire, is one of three types of the creature to be found in Romania (*q.v.*), the other two being the *Strigoiul* (*q.v.*), a reanimated corpse, and the mythical *Varcolaci* or 'sun eater'. According to tradition, the *Muronul* is the illegitimate child of parents who were themselves born out of wedlock and will be turned into a vampire by a *Strigoiul* that he encounters at some stage in his life. The *Muronul* is cunning and sly and the only way to kill one is to drive a nail through the forehead or a stake through its heart.

N

Nachtzehrer (Germany)

The *Nachtzehrer* is a species of German vampire, most commonly reported in Bavaria, with very peculiar habits. When discovered in the tomb, it always has its left eye open and holds the thumb of one hand with the other. According to legend, the *Nachtzehrer* eats its own shroud immediately after burial and will then gnaw parts of its own body if it cannot satisfy its bloodlust on nightly forays. *Nachtzehrers* are said to be either people born with a second skin or the undead corpses of those who have drowned. Because a lack of anything to chew drives these vampires out at night, they can be stopped by putting a stone or coin in the mouth or else by binding the jaws tightly together with linen: more certain still is to cut off the head with an axe. Writing about this aspect of the creature in his *Vampires and Vampirism* (1924) Dudley Wright has noted: 'In Diesdorf, it is believed that if money is not placed in the mouth of a dead person at burial, or his name is not cut from his shirt, he will, in all probability, become a *Nachtzehrer*. Another preventative of such a calamity is to break the neck of the dead body.' Some authorities have suggested the creature's name may be a variation of the more familiar *Nosferatu* (*q.v.*).

Neuntoter (Saxony)

There are a number of similarities between the *Neuntoter* of Saxony and its German neighbour, the *Nachtzehrer* (*q.v.*). This vampire is also the undead body of someone who died an accidental or violent death, and in the grave it has been known to gnaw part of its own body when unable to obtain fresh blood. According to local tradition, the creature targets women and children and is said to watch from its grave for the burial of suitable victims. Unlike the *Nachtzehrer*, which requires a stone or coin to be stopped, this species can apparently be banished by placing a lemon in its mouth.

New England

In America, the state of New England has probably the strongest vampire tradition. Here folklore says that anyone who dies of consumption is likely to return from the dead to feed on the blood of relatives and similarly cause them to waste away. This fact was noted by the essayist and poet Henry David Thoreau (1817–1862), 'The Hermit of Walden', in his journal for 26 September 1859, while the subject as a whole generated a very significant half page article entitled 'Vampires in New England' in the *New York World* newspaper of 2 February 1896: significant because a copy was found among Bram Stoker's working papers for *Dracula* and it was obviously influential in his research. The newspaper stated,

> Recent ethnological research has discovered something very extraordinary in Rhode Island. It appears that the ancient vampire superstition still survives in that State, and within the last few years many people have been digging up the dead bodies of their relatives for the purposes of burning their hearts. Near Newport, scores of such exhumations have been made, the purpose being to prevent the dead from preying on the living. The discovery of the survival in highly educated New England of a superstition dating back to the days of Nebuchadnezzar has been made by George R. Stotson, a ethnologist of repute. He has found it rampant in a district which includes the towns of Exeter, Foster, Kingstown, East Greenwich and many scattered hamlets. There is one small village distant fifteen miles from Newport where within the last few years there have been at least half a dozen resurrections

on this account. The most recent was made two years ago in a family where the mother and four children had already succumbed to consumption. The last of these children was exhumed and the heart was burned. . . .

VAMPIRES IN NEW ENGLAND

Dead Bodies Dug Up and Their Hearts Burned to Prevent Disease.

STRANGE SUPERSTITION OF LONG AGO.

The Old Belief Was that Ghostly Monsters Sucked the Blood of Their Living Relatives.

RECENT ethnological research has disclosed something very extraordinary in Rhode Island. It appears that the ancient vampire superstition still survives in that State, and within the last few years many people have been digging up the dead bodies of relatives for the purpose of burning their hearts.

Near Newport scores of such exhumations have been made, the purpose being to prevent the dead from preying upon the living. The belief entertained is that a person who has died of consumption is likely to rise from the grave at night and suck the blood of

was driven through the chest, and the heart, being taken out, was either burned or chopped into small pieces. For in this way only could a vampire be deprived of power to do mischief. In one case a man who was unburied sat up in his coffin, with fresh blood on his lips. The official in charge of the ceremonies held a crucifix before his face and, saying, "Do you recognise your Saviour?" chopped the unfortunate's head off. This person presumably had been buried alive in a cataleptic trance.

WERE THEY BURIED ALIVE?

How is the phenomenon to be accounted for? Nobody can say with certainty, but it may be that the fright into which people were thrown by the epidemic had the effect of predisposing nervous persons to catalepsy. In a word, people were buried alive in a condition where the vital functions being suspended, they remained as it were dead for a while. It is a common thing for a cataleptic to bleed at the mouth just before returning to consciousness. According to the popular superstition, the vampire left his or her body in the grave while engaged in nocturnal prowls.

The epidemic prevailed all over southeastern Europe, being at its worst in Hungary and Servia. It is supposed to have originated in Greece, where a belief was entertained to the effect that Latin Christians buried in that country could not decay in their graves, being under the ban of the Greek Church. The cheerful notion was that they got out of their graves at night and pursued the occupation of ghouls. The superstition as to ghouls is very ancient and undoubtedly of Oriental origin. Generally speaking, however, a ghoul is just the opposite of a vampire, being a living person who preys on dead bodies, while a vampire is a dead person that feeds on the blood of the living. If you had your choice, which would you rather be, a vampire or a ghoul?

One of the most familiar of the stories of the Arabian Nights tells of a woman who annoyed her husband very much by refusing food. Nothing more than a few grains of rice would she eat at meals. He discovered that she was in the habit of stealing away from his side in the night, and, following her on one such occasion, he found her engaged in digging up and devouring a corpse.

Among the numerous folk tales about vampires is one relating to a fiend named Dakanavar, who dwelt in a cave in Armenia. He would not permit anybody to penetrate into the mountains of

Report from the *New York World* of 2 February 1896 found among Bram Stoker's working papers for *Dracula*

As recently as 1990, archaeological evidence of this custom was found when two children playing in a gravel pit at Griswald, Connecticut, found a human skull. Investigations lead by forensic anthropologist, Paul Sledzik, brought to light 29 skeletons and pointed to the fact that the pit had been the site of the nineteenth-century Walton family cemetery. Among these was the corpse of a man aged between 50 and 55 in a coffin bearing the initials 'J.B.' When the stone-lined grave was opened, the man's skull and thigh-bones were found in a skull-and-crossbones pattern on his ribcage, with the ribs and vertebrae disarranged. There were also lesions on the ribs – indicating that the man had a tuberculosis infection – and he had a hunched and crooked shoulder from an improperly healed collar-bone break, four front teeth missing, a crippled leg and what had probably been an open and festering wound on his foot. Commented Paul Sledzik, 'In life, "J.B." must have been a frightening figure.'

Niven, David (1909–1983)

The urbane English actor David Niven played a Count Dracula (*q.v.*) who oozed with charm in the comedy film, *Vampira (aka Old Dracula)* made in 1973. A former professional soldier who by his own account 'drifted' into films while travelling through America, Niven had a lot of experience of comedy, but very little of vampires when he filmed the story set in 1970s London. His Count, with large fangs, moustache and a widow's peak, was now running a 'horror castle' to which he lured beautiful young women in the hope of finding a rare blood type to revive his dead wife. But when he did succeed in his mission, the blood turned them both *black*. Directed by Jack Wiener, the picture co-starred Teresa Graves as Vampira, Dracula's countess, and was described by one US critic as 'one of the worst Dracula films ever made'.

Nodier, Charles (1780–1844)

The French author, Charles Nodier, was the man primarily

responsible for generating a 'Vampire Craze' in France in 1820 when he wrote a two-volume novel, *The Vampyre*, full of high drama and bloodthirsty deeds. The success of the book resulted in a play that the author wrote in association with two playwrights, Achille de Jouffray and T.F.A. Carmouche. The production opened at the Theatre de Porte-Saint-Martin, Paris on 13 June 1820, with a musical score by the Italian composer, Niccola Piccinni, and ran with full houses for over a year. Nodier, who until then had been a librarian at the 'Bibliotheque de l'Arsenal', enjoyed great commercial success with both the book and play. Later he was to be a strong influence on the Romanticists and in 1833 was elected to the Royal Academy. The theme of *The Vampire* was undoubtedly inspired by the notoriety surrounding the 1819 novel of the same title attributed to Lord Byron (*q.v.*), but actually written by his physician and travelling companion, John William Polidori (*q.v.*), although Nodier only acknowledged help from another novelist, Cyprien Berard. Nonetheless, the success of *Vampyr* inspired many imitations in France during the next decade and it was unashamedly copied in several other European countries including Italy, Germany and even England.

Nosferatu

Nosferatu is a generic name for vampires throughout Eastern Europe and comes from the Romanian meaning 'not dead'. It is a word that has become familiar in vampire lore as well as in literature, art and films all over the world. The *Nosferatu* is an emaciated figure, quite small of stature, with huge eyes, vicious teeth and long fingernails, and its very name is said to spread terror. In his book, *Roumanian Superstitions* (1861), the distinguished historian, Heinrich von Wlislocki has provided probably the definitive statement on its activities: 'The *Nosferatu* not only sucks the blood of sleeping people, but also does mischief as an Incubus or Succubus. It is the stillborn, illegitimate child of two people who are similarly illegitimate. It is hardly put under the earth before it awakes to life and leaves its grave never to return. It visits people by night and when its sex is male, it visits women; when female, men.' To be stopped, the *Nosferatu* must be decapitated and its body burned.

Nosferatu, Eine Symphonie Des Grausens (1922)

The first full-length vampire movie, *Nosferatu*, made in 1922 by the young German expressionist director, Friedrich W. Murnau (1888–1931), enjoys a fame and notoriety that has endured the passage of time. Its fame is such that it inspired a faithful remake half a century later; while its notoriety is due to the fact that it was ruled to be an unauthorized adaptation of *Dracula*, one which Bram Stoker's widow successfully got banned. Friedrich Murnau, who learned his profession filming propaganda footage during the First World War, made his debut in horror pictures in 1920 filming *Der Januskopf* based on Robert Louis Stevenson's *Dr Jekyll and Mr Hyde*. Searching for a follow-up, he discovered Bram Stoker's novel, which, unlike the Stevenson classic, was still in copyright, and with the aid of his screenwriter, Henrik Galeen, made a few not-alto-gether subtle alterations to the story. The title was changed; the location was switched to Germany in the year 1838; while Dracula himself became Count Graf Orlock. However, the plot was almost identical. Unlike other silent German expressionist films of the time, Murnau opted to film the picture on real loctions in Westphalia and on the Baltic coast instead of using highly-stylized studio sets. With the skeletal-looking actor, Max Schreck (*q.v.*) in the lead role, the picture won huge critical acclaim on its release in Germany – but also attracted the attention of Florence Stoker who instituted a court case for plagiarism. In July 1925, Murnau was ordered to destroy all the negatives and prints of the film – and save for a handful of copies that were spirited out of Germany, that might have been the last anyone ever saw of *Nosferatu, eine Symphonie des Grauens*. In the early 1980s, however, Enno Patalas of the Munich Film Museum, painstakingly tracked down the illegal copies and restored the film, rediscovering in the process 28 shots and 31 of the original 115 captions which had been left out. He also found to his surprise that Murnau's director of photography, Fritz Arno Wagner, had tinted

Max Schreck in the original *Nosferatu, eine Symphonie des Grauens* (1922)

the original black and white print in blues, browns and yellows to enhance the day and night effects. When screened for the first time at the Berlin Film Festival in 1984, the movie – now with due acknowledgement to Bram Stoker (*q.v.*) – was acclaimed a masterpiece, and it has since been shown all over the world.

Nosferatu – Phantom Der Nacht (1978)

In 1978, the young German producer-director, Werner Herzog (1942–) remade *Nosferatu* because, in his words, 'it was the most important film in the entire history of the German cinema', as well as a landmark in vampire pictures. Already praised for his films, *The Mystery of Kasper Hauser* (1974) and *Heart of Glass* (1976), Herzog believed the original to be 'a visionary picture which prophesied the rise of Nazism by showing the invasion of Germany by Dracula and his plague-bearing rats'. This was not the only element of controversy to attach itself to the film – for while shooting the arrival of the Count on board a ship in the Dutch city of Delft, Herzog released thousands of rats into the streets much to the horror of the residents! The film's script remained faithful to the Stoker original in several respects, although Herzog believed it to be 'a bad novel, more an accumulation, a gathering of all the vampire stories and subjects floating about'. The picture was shot in colour entirely on location in Germany, Holland, Czechoslovakia and Mexico and starred the eccentric Klaus Kinski (*q.v.*) who gave a stunning recreation of Max Schreck's original Count Orlock, plus Isabelle Adjani as Lucy Harker and Bruno Ganz as her husband, Jonathan, who in this version becomes a vampire himself and rides away to spread the cult all over the world. The movie, also known as *Nosferatu, the Vampyre*, is widely acknowledged to be a fitting tribute to the original as well as one of Werner Herzog's finest pictures.

The German director, Werner Herzog, releasing rats in Delft, Holland, while filming his version of *Nosferatu* in 1978

Oakville Vampire

The events which occurred in the little community of Oakville on the Savannah River in Georgia in 1891 are among the most bizarre in vampire history. In the last week of October of that year, a family named Walsingham moved into a small house and within days were being disturbed every night by sounds of shouting and yelling followed by 'the most hideous laughter and a wailing cry of peculiar horror', to quote an account of the events which subsequently appeared in the *Atlanta Examiner* of 29 November 1891. Initially, the family wondered if they might be the object of practical jokes being played by their neighbours, but such thoughts were quickly dispelled when one of the young daughters, sitting in front of a mirror, felt a hand laid roughly on her shoulder. To her horror, there was no reflection in the mirror, although the pain from her shoulder was intense. The following night, while the Walsinghams were seated at dinner entertaining some friends, a sticky red liquid began to drip from the ceiling onto the table-top. The drips looked just like blood to the diners, but when Mr Walsingham and a friend went up to the room directly above to investigate, they found nothing. The following day a chemist confirmed that the liquid was, indeed, blood. At this, the family decided to quit the house until the cause of the horror could be established. A young Oakville man who volunteered to spend a night in the 'haunted' house was found unconscious the following morning, 'his throat black with the marks of long, thin fingernails', according to the *Examiner*. 'He lay prostrate for many weeks, confined to bed, and the doctors expressed themselves unable to account for the extraordinary anaemic condition of his body, although he was a young man of a particularly full-blooded habit.' At this news, Mr Walsingham decided to take drastic action, the newspaper adds: 'It is said that no explanation of these horrors was forthcoming, but it seems very clear that the house was being visited by a vampire. Shortly thereafter it was burned to the ground on the owner's instructions as being the only way to rid the place of such a dangerous manifestation.'

Oath

The Greeks are the only people in the world who claim to have an oath that will prevent a vampire from attacking a victim. The English writer Montague Summers (*q.v.*), who spent some time in Greece researching the vampire legend, was told by an old shepherd that the undead would not approach anyone who threw up their arms and shouted out four times: 'By my winding-sheet begone!'

'By my winding-sheet begone!' – the Greek oath to drive off vampires

Obayifu (Africa)

The *Obayifu* is a violent species of vampire found living in the depths of the forests in western parts of Africa. Its name derives from *bayi* or sorcery, and according to tradition, the creature is the undead corpse of a person who had died brutally. The *Obayifu* can appear either as a man or woman, and especially likes to prey on the blood of small children. The vampire has sharp, shifty eyes and razor-sharp teeth and when prowling about at night, emits a phosphorescent light. Writing about the *Obayifu* in his book, *Ashanti Proverbs*, R. Sutherland Rattray says, 'Besides sucking the blood of their victims, they are supposed to be able to extract the sap and the juices of crops, and cases of coco blight have been ascribed to the work of the *Obayifu*.'

Obours (Bulgaria)

The Bulgarian vampire, or *Obours*, is said to have been responsible for many deaths in remote districts of the country, and during some of the worst periods of its attacks whole communities have been forced to spend nights on end in churches to protect themselves. Human in shape, it has fungoid-like flesh, hypnotic eyes and rises from its tomb 40 days after being interred. According to tradition, the *Obours* announces its presence by casting a shadow on the wall – which will be larger and denser the older the creature is – and then emits a series of sparks. Before seizing its victims, this vampire creates a disturbance in the house and will spit blood onto the floor. In their book, *Studies in Bulgaria* (1877), S.G.B. St Clair and Charles A. Brophy state that the *Obours* is known to have a particularly disgusting taste for human excrement and it is possible to prevent one from leaving its tomb by blocking the entrance with excrement mixed with a selection of poisonous herbs.

O'Donnell, Elliott (1872–1965)

During the first half of the twentieth century, Elliott O'Donnell was Britain's busiest 'ghost hunter' and wrote dozens of books based on his own experiences and those of people whom he met. Such were the number of these titles that some authorities doubted whether one man could possibly have had so many supernatural experiences! For a period of time O'Donnell lived in St Leonard's Terrace in London where one of his neighbours was Bram Stoker (*q.v.*) – a fact which has caused some speculation as to whether he might have helped the author of *Dracula* with his research. Born in Bristol of an Irish family steeped in folklore and legend, O'Donnell was a journalist for some years before the popularity of his books – and his evident skill as a public speaker – enabled him to concentrate on collecting the material that would fill volumes such as *Haunted Places of England* (1919), *Confessions of a Ghost Hunter* (1928) and *Haunted Britain* (1948). He was also interested in vampirism and recorded several classic cases in his book, *Werewolves* (1912), as well as a number of instances of 'psychic vampirism' in *Strange Cults and Secret Societies* (1934) including the bizarre story of the 'King's Road Vampire' (*q.v.*).

Ogoljen (Bohemia)

The historic kingdom of Bohemia in Central Europe, which was for centuries fought over with bloody ferocity by the Poles and the Czechs, is the locality of a rapacious vampire known as the *Ogoljen*. The creature was particularly to be found in the densely wooded Bohemian Forest and among the Sudeten Mountains where it attacked travellers. According to legend, there was another similar kind of vampire in Bohemia known as the *Mura* that sought blood from young women. Folklore says that the only way to ensure the death of either an *Oguljen* or a *Mura* is to bury it at a crossroads with an iron spike through the heart.

Ogulin Vampires

The village of Ogulin in Croatia has a reputation for being plagued by vampires that dates back to the Middle Ages. Not far from the village rises Klek Mountain which, from a distance, looks rather like a sleeping man. According to tradition, Ogulin was once terrorized by a giant, blood-drinking ogre who so frightened the population that they prayed for help and an archangel appeared who turned the monster into the stone mountain. (*Klek* in Croatian means 'scream'.) Notwithstanding this, stories of the undead attacking families in Ogulin occurred throughout the following centuries and right up to the 1950s, when a series of murders in the district again raised the spectre of a vampire on the loose. Each victim had been killed on the night of a full moon and the bodies totally drained of blood. The US historian Professor Stefan Vuglen – whose predecessors come from the district of Klek Mountain – has taken a particular interest in these still unsolved murders and wrote recently in *Fate* magazine, 'The police investigated and could not find a single clue or footprint at the scene of the crime. It is as if the killer attacked and then just flew away without leaving one material clue or even one drop of blood.'

Oldman, Gary (1961–   )

The British actor Gary Oldman has a reputation for playing tortured characters. He was the doomed assassin Lee Harvey Oswald in *JFK* (1991), the punk rocker Sid Vicious in *Sid and Nancy* (1992) and he added a new dimension to Dracula when he starred in the Francis Ford Coppola version, *Bram Stoker's Dracula*, in 1992. Born in New Cross, London, Oldman had a troubled childhood – his father left home when he was seven – and for a time he was a member of a street gang. Inspired to become an actor after seeing the Lindsay Anderson film, *If* (1968), he was rejected by RADA, but instead studied at the Rose Bruford College of Speech and Drama and began his career at the Royal Court before breaking into movies. It was the involvement of the American director Francis Ford Coppola that persuaded Oldman to take the role of Dracula; if the picture had been made in England, he said later, he would probably have been cast as the madman, Renfield. To play the 'aged' Dracula in a number of scenes, he had to spend more than 100 hours in make-up and was almost paralysed with prosthesis and blinded by contact lens. He commented, 'It was unbearable sometimes wearing all that for up to 17 hours. Although I enjoyed playing Dracula, there were days when it was simply work and I thought I've just got to battle through this.' Oldman also spent time with a singing coach to lower his voice an octave in order to produce the convincing Romanian accent, and there is no doubt that his performance, which mixed eroticism with horror, helped to make the picture a box-office success all over the world.

Olivier, Sir Laurence (1907–1989)

One of the great Shakespearian actors of the twentieth century, Lord Olivier also played a variety of screen character roles including

Sir Laurence Olivier as Van Helsing in *Dracula* (1979)

a memorable appearance as Dracula's nemesis, Professor Van Helsing, in the 1979 version fo *Dracula* starring Frank Langella (*q.v.*). In a career which spanned an appearance as a fifteen-year-old in *Taming of the Shrew* to co-starring with Marilyn Monroe in *The Prince and the Showgirl*, which he also directed in 1957, and an unforgettable performance as the fading music-hall star in John Osborne's *The Entertainer* (1960), the role of the vampire hunter remained long in his memory. He recalled later, 'It was the strangest part I had played in a long time – Langella had the funny lines and it was up to my character to keep matters under control and more or less on a straight line.' Although over 70, Olivier played as many of the physical scenes as he could while on location in Cornwall and in doing so gave Van Helsing a shrewdness, energy and sense of purpose that had critics and fans describing it as among the best interpretations of the intrepid vampire hunter. Aged 82, he died on 11 July 1989.

P

Palance, Jack (1919–   )

The American actor Jack Palance survived a terrible plane crash while piloting a bomber during the Second World War and this resulted in him requiring extensive plastic surgery which gave him the gaunt features and taut-skinned look that he turned to such electrifying effect when he took up an acting career in the 1950s. Although Hollywood cast him relentlessly as a sinister heavy, Palance was nominated for an Oscar in 1952 for *Sudden Fear* and the following year for *Shane*. His unmistakable looks also made him ideal casting as Dracula, a role he was offered by MGM in 1973 in a version of the novel scripted by Richard Matheson (*q.v.*). Palance's role as Attila the Hun in *Sign of the Pagan* (1954) had demonstrated how well he could play men of enormous power, and a feature of the vampire picture directed by Dan Curtis was the way he moved with death-like rigidity at one moment and in the next with awesome power and ferocity, hurling people about with almost nonchalant ease. Palance commented on his role, 'I had seen Lugosi on the screen, but my Dracula is more of a victim of his fate forced to carry out bloodthirsty acts over which he has no control. It's a scowl he wears on his face every time he sinks his fangs into someone's throat, not a look of relish.' Co-starring with him in what is regarded as one of the more faithful adaptations of Stoker's novel were the British actors Nigel Davenport playing Van Helsing, and Simon Ward as Arthur Holmwood. Dan Curtis made good use of locations to add authenticity to the film, and several crucial

Jack Palance filming the 1973 version of *Dracula* in the grounds of
Oakley Court in Berkshire

scenes were filmed at Oakley Court at Bray in Berkshire. This
Gothic-looking building has had a reputation for 'strange happen-
ings' ever since November 1972 when the body of an old woman
was found in one of the rooms where she had laid dead for a week.
Another story claims that mysterious figures 'wearing hoods' have
also been seen in the grounds – which gave an added *frisson* to the
scenes whenever Jack Palance's Dracula was seen stalking the
grounds.

Paole, Arnod (d.1732)

Arnod Paole was a Hungarian soldier who became the subject of
one of the most famous vampire cases in the eighteenth century.
Little is known of Paole's childhood beyond the fact he grew up in
the village of Meduegna near Belgrade and as a young man joined

the Army and was for several years stationed at Kosovo on the frontier of Turkish Serbia. When Paole eventually returned home, he bought a small farm and made plans to marry a local girl. Tragically, before this could happen, he was killed when a cart-load of hay fell on him. Thirty days later, four local people had died with all the blood drained from their bodies, and Paole's fiancée came forward with a terrible confession. She told the local authorities that some time before his death, her fiancé had confided to her that he had been molested by a vampire while on duty – but afterwards he had successfully located the creature's grave and destroyed it, so she need not worry. On hearing this story, the local governor immediately ordered Paole's grave to be opened and inside the body was found to be 'flushed, his hair, nails and beard had all grown and his veins full of blood which had splashed all over his winding-sheet'. The body was at once staked – at which it let out a 'fearful shriek' – and the head cut off before the body was cremated. Arnod Paole's four victims were similarly dealt with: but this was not the end of the matter. Two years later, there was another outbreak of suspected vampirism in Meduegna and a group of medical experts were sent from Belgrade to investigate. In all, fourteen corpses were examined, although of these only two were seen as possible victims of a vampire. As far as the rest were concerned, their contorted faces and bloodstained hands pointed more to them being the tragic result of premature burial. There have been numerous retellings of the story of Arnod Paole, notably in *Chronicles of the Vampire* by Manuela Dunn-Mascetti (1991).

Papabawas (Zanzibar)

The *Papabawas* is the species of vampire found in Zanzibar where they are believed to have the ability to become invisible or change their shape. The creatures are said to be corpses inhabited by the spirits of people who practised magic or led depraved lives. They seek out human victims at night, but according to local tradition, are not always intent on sucking blood – they may just be interested in sex! In 1998, Zanzibar was once again alive with rumours of a trio of *Papabawas* who were terrorizing the island. As a result, an unfortunate inmate from a mental institution on the run was captured and beaten to death in the belief that he was one of the undead, while an old woman who announced she had actually captured a *Papabawas* and took it to a police station in a cage, was told that what she actually caught was an African bat.

Papas, Angela (1938–1959)

The events surrounding the gruesome death of a young Greek girl, Angela Papas, made news around the world as a 'Vampire Killing' in April 1959. The girl was burned to death for allegedly being a vampire in a small fishing village on one of the Greek islands. Angela had apparently claimed to have been attacked by one of the undead and as a result had acquired a lust for human blood. According to a despatch about the events from *Associated Press*, one of her victims was a teenager, Angelo Gregor, who had in turn become a vampire and gone seeking his own victims. The report continued: 'Angelo was caught in a young wife's bedroom by her husband. The villagers, enraged that Angela Papas had brought the vampire plague to their village, seized hold of her, tied her to a stake and set her on fire.'

Passion of Dracula

Passion of Dracula which was first staged on Broadway in 1977, is regarded as one of the most successful of the 'comic' stage versions of Bram Stoker's novel, albeit that the events are confined to a mansion adjoining Dr Seward's sanatorium in Essex. Directed by Clifford Williams from a script by Bob Hall and David Richmond, the play featured the American actor/dancer, George Chakiris (1933–), famous for his role as Bernado in *West Side Story* (1961), who played Dracula very much in the style of Bela Lugosi (*q.v.*). Critics on both sides of the Atlantic enjoyed the production (it transferred to the UK the following year) and shared the view of

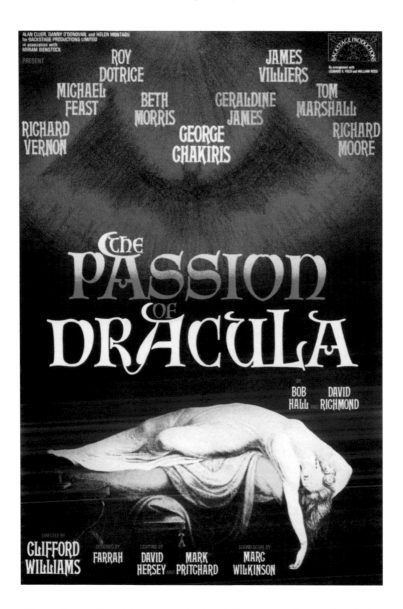

Poster for the 'comic' stage production, *The Passion of Dracula*, which ran on Broadway and in London during the 1970s

Ned Chaillet in *The Times* of 24 August 1978 that it was 'full of happy horrors, where the grotesque pleasures of vampirism are lightened by laughter and the fearsome prospect of bloodstained teeth is eased by the comic lines which may cross over them'. A feature of *Passion of Dracula* was the number of special effects, including a huge bat fluttering against a window, fog billowing into the audience and a fire blazing against the background of a plague of rats.

Pembury Vampire's Tomb

In the churchyard at Pembury Green not far from Tunbridge Wells in Kent stands an impressive stone grave referred to locally as 'The Vampire's Tomb'. The legend behind the edifice dates back to the year 1803 and the death of a young Mrs Ann West of Great Bayhall Manor House, less than a mile from Pembury Green. Mrs West suffered from poor health, says Egon Jameson in his account of the events in *Curiosities of Britain* (1937), and in her late 20s fell into a coma during which she was mistaken for dead and nearly buried alive. To prevent a recurrence of this, the young lady commissioned an undertaker to prepare a coffin for her with a safety device. Jameson writes:

> Well, in 1803 she really did die, but for all that, at midnight every night, she rang her signal bell to the alarm of the cemetery keeper who, they say, used to let her out to prowl around her native village for a few hours during the night. The tomb has a grating to it and she was buried in an open coffin. Ever after, the manor was said to be haunted by the deceased and terrible noises were heard by crowds of people who visited the place at night. Finally, it fell into ruins and became the perfect picture of a haunted house.

Penanggalen (Malaysia)

The *Penanggalen* of Malaysia has been called one of the most repulsive vampires in the world resembling a flying head with trailing

Models of Malaysia's two species of vampire: the gruesome *Penanggalen* (left) and the long-haired female, the *Langsuir* (right)

intestines! One description of the creature appears in *The Golden Chersonese* (1883), a study of Malaysia by Isabella L. Bird which Bram Stoker (*q.v.*) may well have read. The books states, 'A vile fiend called the *Penanggalen* takes possession of the forms of women, turns them into witches, and compels them to quit the greater part of their bodies, and fly away by night to gratify a vampire craving for human blood.' According to Malay legend, this vampire was once a woman who devoted herself to the study of black magic and had for her tutor a devil who taught her everything she wished to know. When her studies were finally complete, she had learned how to separate her head from her body at will and fly about seeking victims to slake her bloodlust. It is also believed that after the *Penanggalen* has satisfied this need, her intestines have become so bloated and distended that she must return to her resting place and soak these entrails in a large jar of vinegar so that they will fit properly when the head and body are reunited. The sight of this monstrous head and dangling stomach is said to be enough to cause panic among even the bravest folk and as the vampire often targets children – particularly new-born infants – the Malay people take special precautions at the time of birth. Thorns hung up around doors and windows are said to be especially effective as they catch onto the *Penanggalen*'s intestines and entangle the creature before she can do any harm. It is also important not to get near this vampire, for a drop of her blood spilled onto anyone can cause terrible sores.

Philostratus (c. AD 170–245)

Philostratus was a Greek sophist who established himself at Rome and was then sent off to travel the known world as the 'companion' of Julia Domna, the second wife of the Emperor Septimius Severus. While on this journey he apparently had a number of strange experiences which he wrote about in his works including the *Hericon* and the *Imagines*, as well as in his idealized *Life of Apollonius of Tyana*. Apollonius was said to be a man with a miraculous power to summon spirits, perform feats of magic, and predict the future – but died an even more mysterious death. Philostratus added to the mystery by hinting that his subject might even have become one of the undead by quoting a source that included the phrase, 'if he did die'. Philostrastus was quite obviously fascinated by such ideas as is further evidenced in the *Life of Apollonius* where he tells the story of an *Empusa* – which translates into English as 'vampire'. This concerns a handsome young Lycian youth, Menippus, who is blinded by the beauty of a 'foreign woman' until told the terrible truth about her: 'She was a vampire, fattening him up with pleasures before devouring his body; for it was her habit to feed upon young and beautiful bodies, because their blood is pure and strong.'

Pijavika (Croatia)

The Croatian species of vampire, the *Pijavika*, is a gruesome-looking creature with bloodshot eyes, sharp teeth and a spring-like way of walking that enables it to pounce on victims with great speed. It is also very strong and has been known to attack more than one person at a time. According to tradition, this vampire is created by a man having incest with his mother and the only way to stop a *Pijavika*, once its grave has been found, is to cut off the head and put this between the creature's legs. Sometimes in the past, the vampire's arms have also been staked with iron nails into the base of the coffin.

Pisco Vampire

In 1993, the town of Pisco, 125 miles south of Lima in Peru, became the focus of world-wide media attention concerning an Englishwoman, buried alive as a vampire years before, who had vowed to return and seek revenge, and was now about to fulfil the prophecy. The story had begun on 9 June 1913, when Sarah Helen Roberts of Blackburn, Lancashire, was shut up alive inside a lead coffin, accused by the authorities of practising witchcraft. With her last cry she had vowed to return in 80 years to exact retribution. According to a report from Reuters News Agency, 'For the next four years, the relatives of Sarah Roberts reportedly tried to find a country that would receive her body for burial, but were turned away everywhere until they reached Peru. Now, eighty years later, on 9 June 1993, the people of Pisco are preparing themselves with festoons of garlic, crucifixes, wooden stakes and prayer services around the tomb, for her return.' Although hundreds of sightseers gathered in the town, nothing stirred in the graveyard that night. But the legend still put another town firmly on the vampire map.

Pitt, Ingrid (1937–)

Frequently referred to as 'the sex symbol of motion picture vampires', Ingrid Pitt was born Natasha Petrovana, on a train from

Ingrid Pitt – sex-symbol and vampire-movie star

Berlin to Gdansk, while her parents, an Oxford-educated Prussian scientist and his young Lithuanian Jewish wife, were fleeing Nazi Germany. The family were trying to reach England, but got no further than Poland where they were arrested, and mother and daughter spent the rest of the war years in the Stuttof concentration camp. The horrors that Ingrid Pitt experienced there had a profound effect upon her, and she has always found it a difficult period of her life to discuss. Settling later in America, she was determined to become an actress and managed to get a number of bit-parts in films before landing a role as a barmaid-cum-spy in *Where Eagles Dare* (1969) which starred Richard Burton and Clint Eastwood. An introduction to James Carreras of Hammer Films (*q.v.*) led to the three vampire roles which have ensured her fame: *The Vampire Lovers* (1970), appearing as the voluptuous Macilla (aka Carmilla) who ends up staked and beheaded; *The House That Dripped Blood* (1970) playing Carla, an actress turned into a vampire by her leading man; and *Countess Dracula* (1971) in which she starred as Countess Elizabeth Bathory (*q.v.*) the real-life vampire who bathed in the blood of young girls in the belief that it would restore her youth. She is unashamed about her appeal in all three: 'It was simple, they just made me bare my fangs and my breasts – gorgeous, weren't they?' Today a cult favourite with generations of fans, Ingrid Pitt is a popular guest at horror film festivals and the author of two books: an autobiography, *Life's A Scream* (1998) and an anthology, *The Ingrid Pitt Bedside Companion for Vampire Lovers* (1999).

Planche, James Robinson (1796–1880)

James Robinson Planche was one of the most prolific dramatists of his age and he was responsible for adapting the story of *The Vampyre* – attributed at the time to Lord Byron (*q.v.*), but actually written by John William Polidori (*q.v.*) – for the London stage as a two-act 'Romantic Melo-drama' in 1820. This production, at the Theatre Royal starring T.P. Cooke (*q.v.*) with music by Joseph Binns Hart, was one of a dozen that Planche had already prepared for theatres in the capital in the two years since he had become a writer – including *The Merchant's Wedding, The Mason of Buda* and *The Brigand* – but it has remained the one for which he is best remembered. Planche later stated in his *Recollections and Reflections* (1871) that he wanted to set the play in Eastern Europe, but was overruled by the theatre manager, Mr Samuel James Arnold. 'He had his heart set on Scotch music and dresses –

the latter, by the way, were in stock – laughed at my scruples, assured me that the public would neither know nor care – and in those days they certainly did not – and therefore there was nothing left for me but to do my best with it and the result was most satisfactory to the management.' During his career, Planche was responsible for introducing a number of innovations into the theatre, including historical accuracy in settings and costumes and the creation of a new form of trap-door, the 'Vampire Trap', to allow for spectacular appearances by the main character. He also wrote the English librettos for a number of operas including Weber's *Oberon, The Magic Flute* and *William Tell*, and in 1831 created *Giovanni the Vampire* – 'a treatment of the same subject in a manner much more satisfactory to myself', though it proved nothing like as successful as its predecessor. Planche fought a long campaign against the 'bloodsuckers' who stole material from other dramatists, helping to ensure copyright protection for playwrights. His knowledge of costume inspired him to write a *History of British Costume* which was published in 1834 and remained the standard work for many years.

Plogosovitz, Peter (d.1725)

The case of Peter Plogosovitz, a farm worker from the village of Kisilova in the Rham District of Yugoslavia, who returned as a vampire in 1725, owes its fame to a colourful account of his activities written by the unknown doctor who attended the events. The man's report is also notable for its description of the vampire's nose 'somewhat fallen in', a condition brought about by an old practise in Europe of burying those who it was feared might become vampires, face down in their coffins. The doctor's account explains:

> After P. Plogosovitz had been interred a few days, several persons at once fell ill and, within eight days, nine people had died. All these on their deathbeds protested that the said Plogosovitz was the sole cause of their deaths, because he had come by night as they slept, had seized them by their throats,

and sucked their blood. In order to put an end to this general calamity in the village, it was determined to open the grave where, to the astonishment of all the spectators, the body, although it had lain three weeks in the grave, gave forth not the slightest odour of death and, except that his nose was somewhat fallen, the whole was perfectly fresh and sound. They took the body out of the grave, sharpened a stake, and drove it through the heart of the vampire, upon which fresh blood gushed from the mouth and ears. They then burnt the body and turned him, thus pierced through, to dust and ashes.

Poe, Edgar Allan (1809–1849)

The American writer Edgar Allan Poe has been rightly described as the 'father' of modern horror fiction, and also played a major role in the development of the detective story and science fiction. A brilliantly imaginative if unstable and depressive character – Poe was expelled from university and dismissed from the West Point military academy before he found his niche as a writer – he explored the theme of vampirism in a number of his stories and poems. What has been described as his 'variations on the lover-as-vampire theme' can be found in stories such as 'Ligeia' (from the *American Museum*, 1838) about the spirit of a dead woman trying to take possession of a living soul, and 'The Oval Portrait' (*Broadway Journal*, April 1845) in which an incredibly lifelike painting sucks the life out of an artist's wife. An ambiguous female vampire also appears in the story of 'Morella' (*Southern Literary Messenger*, April 1835) while a number of critics have pointed to what they regard as elements of vampirism in the extraordinary tale of 'The Fall of the House of Usher' (*Burton's Gentleman's Magazine*, September 1839). A number of vampire movies have been ostensibly based on Poe's stories: in particular *The Tomb of Ligeia* filmed by Roger Corman in 1964 starring Vincent Price, and *Tale of a Vampire* made by the Japanese screenwriter/director, Shimako Sato in 1992, with Julian Sands as a vampire searching

Edgar Allan Poe featured vampires in several of his stories and poems

for his centuries-dead lover in contemporary London. According to the credits, the picture was 'inspired by Edgar Allan Poe's poems, "Annabel Lee" '.

Polidori, John William (1795–1821)

Dr John Polidori was the author of *The Vampyre*, written in 1818, and the first vampire story in the English language. It was composed during a visit to Switzerland that year with Lord Byron (*q.v.*), to whom he was travelling companion and physician, but not published until the following spring in London in the *New Monthly Magazine* issue of April 1819, where it was wrongly credited to Byron. Polidori was the son of an Italian scholar and English mother, educated at the Roman Catholic College of Ampleforth in Yorkshire and Edinburgh University where he obtained his degree and became an MD in 1815 at the age of 19. The following year he was selected to be Lord Byron's personal doctor – just after the poet had separated from his wife – and accompanied him to Switzerland where they stayed at the Villa Diodati on Lake Geneva, spending much time with their neighbours, England's other famous poet, Percy Bysshe Shelley (1792–1822) and his mistress, Mary Wollstonecraft Godwin (1797–1851), later to become Mrs Shelley. On a dark and stormy night after reading extracts from a collection of supernatural tales, *Fantasmagoriana*, the quartet challenged each other to write ghost stories – the result being Mary Shelley's classic *Frankenstein* (1818), a fragment by Byron entitled 'The Burial' which dealt with vampirism in Greece, and from Polidori a story about 'a skull headed lady'. This he abandoned and a few days later decided to write a vampire story of his own featuring a certain Lord Ruthven (*q.v.*). The result, *The Vampyre*, was the second horror classic from that Swiss summer – a story that a number of authorities have credited with inspiring the 'Vampire-mania' that soon afterwards swept Europe in the form of plays, operas and stories. Historian Russel Ash, in his introduction to the 1974 edition of *The Vampyre*, has this to say on the authorship debate:

Polidori had no qualms about having taken Byron's plot and writing his own story around it. It is likely, in fact, that more than just the story line was derived from the poet. Polidori was ambivalent in his attitude towards Byron – honoured to be associated with him, and yet jealous of his literary success and noble birth.

In fact, Polidari was dismissed at the end of that summer and on his return to England only wrote fitfully, struggled to make a success of a practice in Norwich, and on a trip to London was injured in a carriage accident which lead to his death on 27 August 1821. He was aged just 25. A rumour that John Polidori committed suicide by drinking prussic acid to avoid gambling debts is unsubstantiated: but the sad fact remains that he did not live long enough to receive full recognition as the author of one of the greatest classics of vampire fiction.

Dr John William Polidori author of the first vampire story
in English, *The Vampyre* (1818)

Poppysma

Poppysma is the word that has been coined to describe the hissing sound a vampire makes in the moment before sinking its teeth into a victim. According to Peter Thryaeus De Neuss, a nineteenth-century German writer on vampires, when one of the undead satisfies its craving for blood, the pupils of the eyes contract, the skin becomes moist, the breath grows hot and they emit a soft hissing sound. In earlier times it was suggested that vampires only made this sound *while* they were sucking, but De Neuss maintains that performing the two acts at once is actually impossible.

Porphyria

In 1985, Dr David Dolphin of the University of British Columbia advanced a theory that vampires may actually be people suffering from a rare genetic disease known as Porphyria. Victims of this disease, he explained, suffer from a deficiency of the enzyme that helps to synthesize heme, which is a component of hemoglobin in the blood's oxygen-carrying cells, and this, triggered by stressful situations, can result in their bodies becoming grotesquely disfigured and their skin made extraordinarily sensitive to sunlight. Dolphin, a biochemist, said, 'Even mild exposure leads to disfigurement like scarring and sores, and in the advanced stage the nose, fingers and eyelids may fall off. The skin of the lips and gums also gets stretched into a grisly rictus exposing discoloured, reddish, fang-like teeth.' Because exposure to sunlight is so appalling for sufferers, he argued, it is only safe for them to venture into the open at night, and in his view they may have to instinctively seek out blood by biting other humans in order to get healthy hemoglobin into their systems. An injection of a blood production, heme, could make the disease treatable, he said, although a cure has still not been discovered. The paper on Porphyria that Dr Dolphin gave to the American Association for the Advancement of Science in Los Angeles attracted international attention and a variety of headlines ranging from the predictable, DRACULA LEGENDS MAY CONTAIN A DROP

OF TRUTH (*Washington Post*) to the more restrained DID DISEASE TRIGGER VAMPIRES' BLOOD THIRST (*Weekly Reader*). The biochemist also suggested during his lecture that the practice of using garlic to ward off vampires might have a rational explanation: the plant contains a chemical that can irritate the open sores of a Porphryia sufferer. Dolphin claimed that his research has shown that the disease tends to run in families – with the worst incidences being in Sweden and Switzerland where small gene pools are prevalent – and while the symptoms generally lay dormant, the shock of a bite from an open carrier of the disease could start up dormant vampire characteristics in a close relative like a sibling. 'If someone drank a lot of your blood, that would certainly be stressful,' he added.

Victorian concept of a 'Psychic Vampire' draining the vitality
of his lover

Psychic Vampirism

'Psychic Vampirism' was a term coined in the late Victorian era to describe the ability possessed by some people to drain the energy and vitality out of others. The concept was examined by a number of writers in France, England and America, notably the British occultist 'Dion Fortune' (Violet Mary Firth, 1890–1946) in her *Psychic Self Defense* (1930), a do-it-yourself manual to thwart energy predators. 'Physic Vampirism' also formed the basis of a number of popular novels and short stories notably *The Parasite* (1894) by Sir Arthur Conan Doyle (*q.v.*), in which a professor outwits a soul-sucking vampire; *The Vampire* (1912), Reginald Hodder's tale of a psychic vampire battling against loss of virility; and Algernon Blackwood's classic short story 'The Transfer' (*Country Life*, December 1911) in which one of the characters describes a psychic vampire in these words, 'I watched his hard, bleak face; I noticed how thin he was, and the curious oily brightness of his steady eyes. And everything he said or did announced what I may dare to call the suction of his presence.'

Queen Mary (Princess Mary Claudine Agnes of Teck) (1875–1953)

The wife of George V (1865–1936), Queen Mary was much loved by the people of Britain as a regal and in many ways highly individual lady with a keen sense of duty, who devoted much of her time to the interests of women and children. Her family also had a direct link with the homeland of Count Dracula (*q.v.*) according to *Debrett's Peerage*. Queen Mary's grandmother, after whom she was named, Claudine, Countess Rhedy, was born and lived in a castle on the slopes of a mountain in Transylvania. Countess Claudine fell in love with a cavalry officer, Prince Alexander of Wurtemberg, at a court ball in Vienna and married him morganatically in 1835. Six years later she was thrown from her horse and died on the spot, but their son, Francis, Duke of Teck, grew up to become Queen Mary's father. *Debrett's* also notes that the castle in which Countess Claudine was brought up was called Erdo Szent Gyorgy – meaning St George – which was 'proof against dragons if not vampires'.

Quinn, Seabury Grandin (1889–1969)

Despite a roster of writers that included H.P. Lovecraft (*q.v.*), Ray Bradbury (*q.v.*), Robert Bloch (*q.v.*) and many more, the undisputed most popular contributor to the legendary American pulp magazine, *Weird Tales* (1923–1954), was Seabury Quinn. His enormous

Vampire Kith and Kin

BY SEABURY QUINN

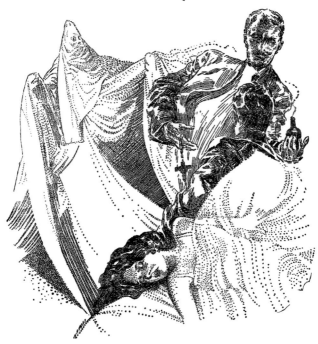

American author Seabury Quinn created the vampire hunter, Jules de
Grandin, and his assistant, Dr Trowbridge, in the pages of *Weird Tales*

popularity was founded on the creation of one of the strangest vampire hunters in fiction, Jules de Grandin, an egotistical if courteous French-born investigator who lives in Harrisonville, New Jersey and pursues the undead across the length and breadth of America in a series of cases 'chronicled' by his long-suffering Watson-like assistant, Dr Trowbridge. Quinn said of his creation, 'One day, thinking up an idea for a yarn, I picked up my pen, started to write – and de Grandin materialized. Jules de Grandin is entirely a synthetic character, as is the locale, Harrisonville. Grandin is my middle name, and I gave him the first French name that popped into my head – Jules. I never dreamed de Grandin would last more than one issue.' In fact, he appeared in 93 cases and the best dealing specifically with vampires are 'The Man Who Cast No Shadow' (1927), 'The Silver Countess' (1929) and 'Vampire Kith and Kin' (1949). Many of the readers of these stories would probably have been surprised to learn that the author was actually a practising attorney and, in between his law work and writing stories for *Weird Tales*, he was also the editor of a trade journal for undertakers with the title of *Casket and Sunnyside!* Quinn was always very circumspect about the number of ideas he got for his horror tales from editing this publication, but did admit that the inspiration for the vampire stories had been reading *Dracula* when he was nineteen. In all of de Grandin's battles with the undead he invariably gets the better of any vampire by traditional methods such as using large quantities of garlic or the quick application of a stake. Several collections of Quinn's stories were published in hardcovers during his lifetime – including *The Phantom Fighter* (1966) – and there has recently been a revival of interest in his work resulting in several paperback collections of the unique little Frenchman's cases, notably *The Horror Chamber of Jules de Grandin* (1977).

R

Rakshasa (India)

The *Rakshasa* is the vampire of rural India, a much feared creature who can change shape and preys especially on solitary travellers and new-born babies. This species of the undead is often very tall, has long arms and fingers, sharp, projecting teeth and probably only one eye or ear. According to a description in William Crooke's *Introduction to the Popular Religion and Folklore of Northern India* (1894), 'The *Rakshasa* also goes about at night, haunts cemeteries, disturbs sacrifices and is generally hostile to the human race. He is emphatically a devourer of raw flesh.' This particular vampire uses its long nails to gouge its victims before drinking their blood, and if it kills someone, they may well return as one of the undead. It has the power to animate dead bodies and can escape capture by assuming a different shape: anything from a humpbacked old man to a virile youth. The *Rakshasa* can only be killed by fire.

Revenant

Sometimes confused by writers as being a vampire, the *Revenant* is actually the *victim* of one of the undead. It is someone who has died from loss of blood or else the shock of a vampire's attack which causes it to return as a wandering soul. Like the vampire, the *Revenant* needs to sustain itself with blood – usually biting the chest in the area of the heart rather than on the neck – but this does not prevent the body continuing to decompose, and these creatures are invariably hideous sights with their flesh peeling away to reveal the bones beneath. According to several authorities, this species also transforms its victims into *Revenants* and it is they who have been responsible for causing some of the terrible epidemics ascribed to vampires. Because of their putrefying state, which gradually slows down their movements, these creatures are easier to catch and destroy. Historian Wilhelm Hertz writing in 1862 refers to a belief that *Revenants* have two hearts, 'one of which is dedicated to the destruction of humanity'. The most famous story of one of these creatures is *Lenore* written in 1773 by the wild and extravagant German poet, Gottfied August Burger (1747–1794) with its famous line, 'We and the dead ride fast.' It recounts the return of young Wilhelm from the Crusades to claim his bride only for the hapless Lenore to discover that he is now a *Revenant*. The poem proved very influential on the English Romantic poets, and following an adaptation in 1796 by Sir Walter Scott (1771–1832) was also endlessly imitated and parodied in periodicals throughout Europe.

Engraving of a Revenant from *Les Loups Ravissants*
by Robert Gobin (c. 1505)

Rice, Anne (1941–   )

Anne Rice is the most popular and successful contemporary writer of vampire fiction, and her series, *The Vampire Chronicles*, featuring the Vampire Lestat (*q.v.*), have been bestsellers all over the world and translated into many languages. The publication of the first of Rice's books, *Interview With the Vampire* in 1976 signalled the arrival of a major new talent – one critic compared her to Henry Hames (*q.v.*) – and a new era in vampire literature. The series has, with some justification been described as the most important vampire fiction produced since Stoker's *Dracula* (*q.v.*). As Raymond T. McNally and Radu Florescu have written in their study, *In Search of Dracula* (1994): 'She has revolutionized the genre. Her vampire world is much like our own. Garlic, crucifixes, mirrors and stakes do not frighten them any more. Some vampires are good and trustworthy; they even join together to protect humans from other bad vampires. The good vampires are the heroes; men are the villains. The vampires are also bisexual.' Anne Rice was born and brought up in New Orleans, USA, one of four daughters of an Irish Catholic post-office worker, and a devoted mother who delighted in telling her ghost stories, but died of alcoholism when Anne was 15. Rice began writing her stories out of a simple desire: to try and find out what it was like to be a vampire. Her first effort, a short story about a reporter interrogating one of the undead was called 'Interview With the Vampire' and from this developed her début novel in which she revealed a strong interest in literary and philosophical themes in recounting the history of the vampire Louis and how he had been turned into a vampire by Lestat. Rice has explained: 'Myths fascinate me – I feel like I'm going into them. For example, when I was trying to discover a plausible origin to the vampires, I happened upon the Osirian myth and thought, "That's it – it's perfect." I see myself exploring the relationship between popular vampire fiction and the gods of ancient times. I feel like I amplified the connection.' She has also said that her characters all represent longings and aspirations in herself: the first book echoing her grief at losing a daughter, Michele, of leukemia, while the rest trace her spiritual quests. A feature of all *The Vampire Chronicles* has been the author's use of real locations, notably in New Orleans and San Francisco, and the background to the whole series is explained in painstaking detail in Katherine Ramsland's *The Vampire Companion* (1993). The initial novel was followed by *The Vampire Lestat* (1985), in which Lestat becomes a rock superstar; *Queen of the Damned* (1988) tracing the origins of the vampire to ancient Egypt; *The Tales of the Body Thief* (1992), in which Lestat makes a doomed body-swap with James Raglan who can jolt souls out of bodies; and most recently *The Vampire Armand* (1998). Anne Rice still lives in New Orleans with her husband, Stan, a poet, whom she met at a high school journalism class (and is said to be the physical model for Lestat) and their son, Christopher. Her home in the Garden District has become something of a mecca for fans of her books, and each year in the city a 'Gathering of the Coven' is held on Hallowe'en which attracts thousands of admirers from all over the world. Curiously, Anne Rice has admitted, 'I don't believe in vampires – I never have. I *do* believe in ghosts and that there may even be a devil.'

Riva, James (1960–   )

The extraordinary trial of James P. Riva II of Brockton, Massachusetts, who declared himself to be a 'living vampire', took place in 1981 and represents the first time in history that 'vampirism' was used as a *defence* plea. Riva was charged with 'shooting his grandmother twice and sucking the blood out of the bullet holes because he believed a vampire told him that was what he had to do', according to his defence lawyer, John T. Spinale, quoted in the *New York Times* of 23 October. Despite the objections of the assistant District Attorney, Henry A. Cashman, to the defence's plea of 'vampirism', the judge, Peter F. Brady, overruled this and allowed the jury to hear the evidence. According to the newspaper report, the strategy of Riva's counsel was that *if* they could prove the young man believed he was a vampire, there were grounds for a plea of insanity. During the trial by jury, a statement was read by Riva's mother who said that her son believed he had been a vampire for years and needed human and animal blood. A physician, Dr Robert Moore, also testified that in 1978 the accused had killed a cat and sucked its blood and the following year struck a horse on the head with a fence post and drunk its blood mixed with biscuits. Riva was found guilty of the murder of his grand-mother and confined to a mental institution.

Romania

In Romania there is an old folk-tale which says, 'There was once a time when vampires were as common as blades of grass, or berries in a pail, and they never kept still, but wandered round at night among the people.' Montague Summers (*q.v.*) in *The Vampire in Europe* (1929) underlines this fact in more specific terms when he writes, 'The vampire tradition in Romania extends back far into the centuries, and there is perhaps no supernatural belief which is so strongly prevalent both in city and market town as in the village and remoter country districts.' There is little doubt that vampire lore is deeply entrenched in the country and no other area is more instantly associated with the undead than its northernmost state of Transylvania. There are, in fact, three types of vampire in Romania: the *Strigoiul* (*q.v.*), or dead vampire, a reanimated body that has been made to live again by the return of the soul; the *Muronul* (*q.v.*), or live vampire, a person destined to become one of the undead and will, while still alive, meet with the *Strigoiul*; and, thirdly, the *Varcolaci*, a mythical vampire who is apparently able to eat the sun and cause eclipses. Details of all of these can be found in Anthony Master's *The Natural History of the Vampire* (1972). The history of Romania is full of stories of vampires: one of the worst outbreaks anywhere in the world occurred as recently as 1889 in Crassova where several dozen men, women and children were discovered to be slowly dying from bite marks on their necks and loss of blood. In a concerted effort by the local people, a total of 30 corpses were disinterred in local graveyards and all were pierced with stakes before the attacks ceased. A few years later in the village of Prejam in the Vilcea district the youngest-ever vampire was reported – a 13-year-old child who had recently died was reported to be attacking other infants as they slept. The solution was provided by staking the child in its coffin after removing the head. A Romanian inventor in the eighteenth century devised an ingenious implement intended to stop any vampire before it could cause harm. The machine consisted of several sharpened stakes driven into the grave of anyone suspected of being one of the

One of the worst outbreaks of vampirism occurred in
Crassova, Romania, in 1889

undead so that as soon as the creature began to rise it would automatically kill itself! For tourists visiting Romania today, the places associated with the legend of Dracula that are well worth visiting are: the island monastery at Snagov where Dracula's tomb is located; the ruins of his main palace at Targoviste; and the edifice of Castle Dracula at Argef. Each of these can be reached in a day's drive from the capital of Bucharest.

Rose, William (d.1894)

William Rose was a well-known inhabitant of the village of Placedale on Rhode Island, and featured in a well-documented case of suspected vampirism in 1874. Rose, a local merchant and elder of the Placedale Community Church, was a strongly committed Christian who believed in vampires. His bookshelves contained several works dealing with the subject, and it was rumoured that one of his ancestors had taken part in the staking of a suspected vampire on Rhode Island. According to the *Providence Journal*, which carried details of the subsequent events, during the early 1870s Rose became increasingly convinced that the lack of energy and general lassitude that had struck him and members of his family – a wife, two sons and two daughters – was due to them being attacked at night by a vampire. Explained the *Journal*: 'Some years earlier, one of the family, a daughter, had died of consumption and lay in the Placedale graveyard. Thus, in his anxiety, William Rose dug up the body of his daughter and burned her heart, acting under the belief that she was exhausting the vitality of the remaining members of the family.'

Rousseau, Jean Jacques (1712–1778)

The Swiss-born political philosopher, educationist and essayist, Jean Jacques Rousseau is credited with one of the most compelling statements about the reality of vampires. A footloose young man, Rousseau mixed his education with amorous adventures before composing his opera, *Les Muses Galantes*, which led to correspondence with Voltaire, an association with Diderot, and being lionized in Paris. In 1762 he wrote his masterpiece, *Du Contrat Social*, with its slogan, 'Liberty, Equality, Fratenity' that became the bible of the French Revolution. Later, Rousseau settled in England, at Wootton Hall, near Ashbourne, where he wrote most of his *Confessions*, published in 1781. It was in 1763 that he made his remark about the undead in a letter of Christophe de Beaumont, the Archbishop of Paris: 'If there is in the world one attested story it is that of the Vampires. Nothing is missing: *procès-verbaux*, certificates from Notabilities, Surgeons, Priests and Magistrates. The judicial proof is most complete. With all this, who believes in Vampires? Shall we all be damned for not having believed?' Ultimately, persecution mania forced Rousseau to return to Paris where he eked out a living writing 'half-insane dialogues' before dying of a sudden attack of thrombosis on 2 July 1778.

Ruthven, Lord

The English nobleman and vampire, Lord Ruthven, with his 'dead grey eyes and deadly hue of face' who appears in *The Vampyre* by John William Polidori (*q.v.*), is believed to have been based by the author on his one-time benefactor and friend, Lord Byron (*q.v.*). Indeed critics have pointed to the obvious parallels between the relationship of the two men and the characters in the story. Ruthven, who lives in London, is seemingly emotionless, yet a fine conversationalist, and with his alleged licentious habits and powers of seduction, he is irresistible to beautiful mature women – although he prefers young, inexperienced girls of fine breeding. His skill at manipulating the affections of females already loved by others has brought death threats from their menfolk. Ruthven is undeniably capable of corrupting all those with whom he comes into contact, and during the course of the narrative takes a talented and handsome young gentleman, Aubrey, on a 'Grand Tour of Europe' where he suffers the same fate. Although it seems evident that the name Ruthven was taken from the character of that name in the novel, *Glenarvon* (1816) by Lady Caroline Lamb (1785–1828) – notorious for her devotion to

Byron and her obvious modelling of the hero of her story on him – it is also that of an infamous old Scottish family who dabbled in alchemy, witchcraft and necromancy. In any event, Ruthven was perfectly suited for Polidori's character: a vampire destined to inspire the genre as no other literary character had done before.

Lord Byron was the model for Lord Ruthven in Polidori's
The Vampyre (1818)

S

St Osyth Vampire

The small village of St Osyth on the bleak Essex coast of England is famous as a haunt of smugglers and has a tradition of witchcraft. In 1921 a skeleton was found in the back-garden of one of the houses that immediately led to the suggestion a vampire might also once have terrorized the neighbourhood. Examination showed that the body was probably that of a female, but what made the find so unusual was the clear signs that the limbs were bound together with rope and large iron nails had been driven through the thigh-bones to prevent the corpse from rising from the grave. Conjecture has surrounded the discovery to this day and is discussed in Eric Maple's history of the supernatural in East Anglia, *The Realm of Ghosts* (1964).

Saberhagen, Frederick Thomas (1930–)

The American author and editor, Fred Saberhagen is another writer who has made significant changes to the vampire story genre with a series of novels featuring Dracula which are told from the Count's point of view. The books also attempt to 'correct' what are perceived as mistakes in the original version of the story by Bram Stoker(*q.v.*). For example, Dracula is presented as a maligned character who generally adjures the idea of drinking human blood and, in fact, represents a species of good vampires whose origins are

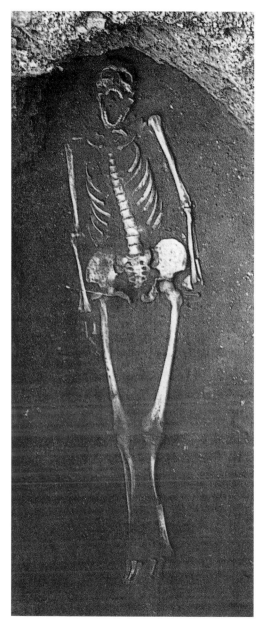

The 'Vampire Skeleton' uncovered at St Osyth in Essex

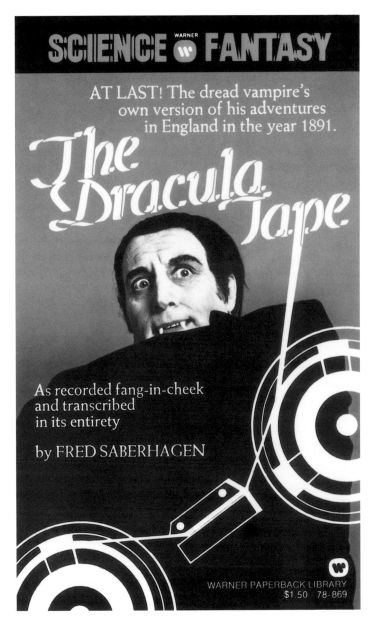

The first title in Frederick Saberhagen's revisionist series of
Dracula novels

rationalized in science fiction terms. Saberhagen was born in Chicago, served for a number of years in the US Air Force and from 1967–73 worked as an editor of the *Encyclopaedia Britannica*, for which he wrote the original entry on science fiction. He became popular with readers of science fiction for his long-running series of 'Berserker' novels, about alien robot fighting machines programmed to seek out and destroy life where it is found – including *Berserker* (1967), *Berserker's Planet* (1975), *Berserker Lies* (1991) – and he began the Dracula vampire series in 1975 with *The Dracula Tape*. In this he argued that it was the stupidity and incompetence of Prof. Van Helsing that was responsible for the death of Lucy Westenra and Dracula is quoted as saying: 'It was not I who hammered the great stake through her heart. My hands did not cut off her lovely head or stuff her mouth with garlic as if she were a dead pig. . . . Only reluctantly had I made her a vampire, nor would she ever have become a vampire if it were not for the imbecile Van Helsing and his work!' In the Count's eyes, the vampire hunter is nothing more than a racist, a sadist and a blasphemer. Subsequent novels in the series are *The Holmes–Dracula File* (1978) in which the Count helps Sherlock Holmes to save London from a plague carried by the Giant Rat of Sumatra; *An Old Friend of the Family* (1979) set in Chicago where he helps the police against some less benign vampires; *Thorn* (1980) which alternates between Renaissance Italy and contemporary Arizona; and *Dominion* (1982) featuring Merlin in modern-day New York. In the most recent books in the series, *A Matter of Taste* (1990), *A Question of Time* (1992) and *Seance For A Vampire* (1994), Dracula has become something of a superhero with special powers. In 1992, Saverhagen jointly wrote a novelization of the movie, *Bram Stoker's Dracula*, with James V. Hart.

'Salem's Lot

'Salem's Lot, an accursed small town in New England, is probably the most famous vampire-colony in twentieth-century fiction: a creation which author Stephen King (1947–   ) considers amongst his finest – while the novel that bears its name is widely regarded among fans and critics alike as the writer's best book. King's success as a novelist and short story writer is nothing short of a phenomenon and he is undoubtedly the top-selling horror writer of all time. His interest in the genre was already evident when he was a student at the University of Maine, and his first published short story, 'I Was a Teenage Graverobber' appeared in 1965. King has admitted that *Dracula* was a seminal influence on his work and *'Salem's Lot*, the book which established his reputation – his second, published in 1975 – has undeniable similarities with the Stoker classic. Indeed, King has readily admitted, 'It's my *Dracula* look-alike.' The story concerns an outbreak of vampirism in the small New England town of 'Salem's Lot' where the disease spreads from family to family as a result of the children infecting one another and their parents. Marsten House at the centre of the events could almost be Castle Dracula, while Barlow, the king vampire, is the Count, and his acolyte Straker resembles Renfield. Writer Ben Mears leads the battle to save the town helped by young Mark Petrie who knows all about the undead from reading horror magazines. The book is a landmark work in that it places the vampire legend in a contemporary setting, reveals the events through the eyes of a child and – in King's own words – 'When I wrote *'Salem's Lot* I decided to largely jettison the sexual angle.' He has revealed that there was also a second influence in the book's creation: 'In the early 1800's a whole sect of Shakers, a rather stranger, religious persuasion at best, disappeared from their village (Jeremiah's Lot) in Vermont and the town remains uninhabited to this day.' *'Salem's Lot* was adapted by CBS for a TV mini-series in 1979 directed by Tobe Hooper and starring David Soul and James Mason. The success of this prompted a sequel, *Return to 'Salem's Lot*, made in 1987, directed by Larry Cohen and starring James Discon. It was based on a short story, 'One for the Road' written in 1977. A third work, *Jerusalem's Lot* (1976), which also features the town, has yet to be filmed. King has also used variations of the vampire theme in his novels, *Christine* (1983) with a car acting as a vampire; the animated undead in *Pet Semetary* (1983) and *The Tommyknockers* (1987) with its energy-draining predator; plus short stories including, 'The Oracle and the Mountains' (1981), 'Popsy' (1987) and 'The Night Flier' (1988).

Sampiro (Albania)

The *Sampiro* is the Albanian species of vampire and sometimes referred to as a *Liugat*. It is a very distinctive-looking creature, wrapped in the shroud in which it was laid to rest, but now wearing shoes with enlarged heels to enable it to tower over victims. This vampire is said to have resulted from the mixing of the blood of different races – especially those of Albanians and Turks – and it is feared for the destruction it can cause as well as spreading pestilence. According to local tradition, the grave occupied by a *Sampiro* can be found thanks to some mysterious little night lights known as 'Will o' the Wisps', as they are avowed enemies of the vampire and will illuminate its hiding place so the undead can be dispatched by a stake through the heart.

Sarkomenos (Cyprus)

The *Sarkomenos* is the vampire species found on Cyprus, a creature said to bear certain similarities with the Greek *Vourkolakas* (*q.v.*). These members of the undead are said to be the souls of people who have led wicked lives and that they have returned after a hundred days in the grave to feed primarily on the blood of relatives. Referring to them in his study, *The Customs and Lore of Modern Greece* (1892), Sir Rennell Rodd explains, 'The name of the *Sarkomenos* of Cyprus implies either that the dead body from which the vampire issues has retained its flesh, or that it must be gorged with blood.' Burning the body in the grave is the only antidote for this vampire.

Schenectady Vampire

The city of Schenectady on the Mohawk River not far from Albany was first reported to be the haunt of a female vampire in the closing years of the nineteenth century. The undead was said to be young, blonde, with milk-white fanged teeth and a corpse-like pallor. Her slender hands had long fingernails like the talons of a hawk and she frequented the area of Green Street. According to Charles M. Skinner in his account of the 'Schenectady Vampire' in *Myths and Legends of Our Own Times* (1926),

> She used to sally forth at night in search of prey. Mostly she attacked children, digging her pointed fingernails into their flesh and sucking the wounds. Usually the children who suffered in this fashion pined away and died. Sceptical doctors who attended them attributed their deaths to consumption and other wasting diseases, but those who knew of the existence of vampires and the horror of Green Street knew different.

In fact, investigations brought to light that the street had been built on the site of an old Dutch cemetery, 'where some Hungarians and people from the Balkans had been buried and would, perhaps, account for the rumour of vampirism'. The attacks continued, Skinner says, until a figure that matched the description of the woman was seen entering and leaving a deserted house on Green Street. A service of exorcism was carried out at the propery and the attacks ceased – although that was not quite the end of the story as Charles Skinner explains: 'The day after the ceremony, the outline of a female vampire was found on the floor of the house. Every effort was made to remove it, but no matter how carefully this was done, the picture always returned.' The house was demolished in 1932, and with all traces of the event, although the legend of the female vampire of Green Street lives on in local folklore.

'Sending Vampires to Santorini'

The expression 'Sending Vampires to Santorini' is as commonplace throughout the Greek islands as 'Taking coals to Newcastle' in Great Britain. The reason behind the phrase about the little island some 60 miles north of Crete and named after Saint Irene who was martyred there in 304, has been explained by Professor N.P. Polites of Athens University in a recent study of vampirism.

The inhabitants of Santorini enjoy so vast a reputation as experts on dealing with vampires and putting an end to them, that people from far-off places troubled by these horrors will consult with them when all else has failed. Two instances of quite recent date – one of which occurred on the island of Mycomos and the other at Sphakia in Crete – both of which concluded with the dispatch of the body of the local vampire to Santorini to be cremated and finally disposed of there.

Shelley, Barbara (1936–)

Described by *Time Out* magazine as 'arguably the best actress Hammer [*q.v.*] used in its genre films', Barbara Shelley was probably the most classy female vampire seen on the screen in the 1960s. Born in London, she was educated at a convent school until she was 16, and then overcame what she described as 'psychopathic shyness' to become a fashion model and ultimately an actress. She worked initially in television before breaking into movies with *Camp on Blood Island* filmed in 1957. The following year she had her first taste of vampirism when she appeared with Sir Donald Wolfit in *Blood of the Vampire*, the story of one of the undead seeking a cure for his condition by developing a blood-group from the bodies of his victims. In 1966 Barbara Shelley made her big impact on fans co-starring with Christopher Lee (*q.v.*) and Peter Cushing (*q.v.*) in *Dracula – Prince of Darkness* as the prim and proper Helen who becomes the Count's first victim. She commented, 'I attacked the part of a vampire by looking for a peg to hang my hat on – or should I say fangs? I found in it a likeness to the Greek Furies and played it as the epitome of all evil. As to the eroticism of the legend, so much has already been said and written. But perhaps the eroticism is heightened by the night symbols and by the unbridled greed and determination of the vampire to achieve its ends. There is always something fascinating and repellent about a completely uncontrolled and rabid emotion.' Shelley has the distinction in this picture of being the first female vampire to be seen staked in full

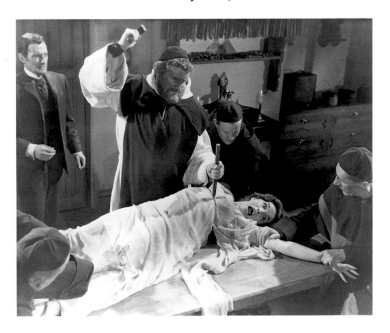

Barbara Shelley the first female vampire to be 'staked' on screen in
Dracula – Prince of Darkness (1965)

gruesome detail on camera. After excellent performances in
Rasputin – The Mad Monk (1966) and *Quatermass and the Pit*
(1967), Barbara Shelley gave up acting, although her reputation
among fans of vampire films has remained undiminished.

Slains Castle

The gaunt ruin of Slains Castle, which stands on the rocky headland
above Cruden Bay on the coast of Aberdeenshire in Scotland, is the
building that gave Bram Stoker the inspiration for Dracula's Castle.
Although for many years the Count's eerie and forbidding home in
Transylvania was thought to be pure imagination on the author's
part, the facts and the description in the novel itself clearly pin-
point Slains: details which are confirmed in *The Un-Dead: The
Legend of Bram Stoker and Dracula* by Peter Haining and Peter

Tremayne (*q.v.*) (1997). The authors say that Stoker visited Cruden Bay during a five-year period from 1892 to 1897 while he was writing the book and can hardly fail to have been inspired by the Gothic splendour of the castle. Indeed, the impact of Cruden Bay on his imagination can be judged from the fact that he featured it in two other novels, *The Watter's Mou* (1895) and *Mystery at Sea* (1902). At the period of his visits, the building with its battlements, tower and arched roof was still occupied by members of the Erroll family who had owned it for generations, and each night, lights from the windows shone down from its dark mass onto the beach below where Stoker often walked. Subsequently, the castle passed out of the hands of the Errolls and in 1926 was sold at auction: the roof being stripped of its lead and the building partly demolished. Today all that remains are the granite walls and an iron staircase, near which an unknown hand has scrawled in a case of mistaken identity the word, 'Frankenstein'.

The ruins of Slain Castle in Scotland which inspired Bram Stoker's
Dracula's Castle

Southey, Robert (1774–1843)

The name of the English writer Robert Southey, who was Poet Laureate from 1813, is generally better known than his works, though his Gothic epic, *Thalaba the Destroyer* (1797), is sometimes claimed to have introduced the vampire into English literature. From his youth, Southey was fascinated by politics and advocated the idea of 'pantisocracy' in various papers and as a contributor to the *Quarterly Review*. The sad death of his wife through insanity in 1837 deeply taumatized the author and led to his own death. The Thalaba of Southey's story is a man with considerable knowledge of magic and the supernatural who is forced into becoming a 'vampire hunter' with the terrible task of destroying his own dead wife, Oneiza, who has returned from the grave as one of the undead. In a footnote to *Thalaba*, Southey explained that vampire practises were common in Hungary, Greece and Turkey 'and the reader may be assured of the reliability of my description.' In August 1823, the work was adapted for the stage at the Royal Coburg Theatre in London with 'Mr Stanley' in the leading role and 'Miss Edmiston' as the vampire Oneiza.

Stagg, John (1770–1823)

The poet and essayist John Stagg, known alternately as 'The Blind Bard' or 'The Minstrel of the North', created one of the earliest ballads in English about the undead, *The Vampyre*, written in 1810, as well as producing an article about the phenomenon explaining its basis in reality which he entitled 'Argument'. Born the son of a tailor in Cumberland, Stagg was educated for the church, but was tragically blinded by an accident and instead chose to make his living by keeping a library in Wigton and augmenting his income by playing the fiddle at local gatherings. Despite his handicap, Stagg began to write poetry and prose in his 20s, and often travelled about the north of England collecting local folklore for use in his work. His first collection, *Miscellaneous Poems*, appeared in 1804, to be followed by *Minstrel of the North* (1810) and the three-volume *The Cumberland Minstrel* (1821), 'Being a Poetical Miscellany of Legendary, Gothic and Romantic Tales'. This included *The Vampyre* and Stagg's 'Argument' which is actually more notable for its use of exotic terminology than its scholarship: the author explaining at one point that a vampire 'phelbotomises' its victim by 'suckosity'. In the ballad, the heroine, Gertrude, is struck by the 'deadly pallor' of her husband, Lord Herman, and 'the fading crimson from his cheek'. When she tackles him about this, Herman confesses that a friend who died recently, Sigismund, has been visiting him every night to 'suck from my veins the streaming life/And drain the fountain of my heart'. Gertrude vows to guard him against the undead, but when the vampire appears once more she can do nothing to prevent her husband's untimely death. In the morning, she vows to open Sigismund's tomb and, discovering a body 'still warm as life, and undecay'd', drives a stake through its heart. To ensure the same fate does not befall her beloved, Lord Herman, Gertrude resolutely repeats the staking on him.

Stake

The use of a wooden stake driven through the heart of a vampire to kill it has been noted in accounts of vampirism for many centuries. The custom of 'Staking' (actually called 'Transfixation' by the Catholic Church) was regarded as something of an art and the stake had to be inserted in the prescribed manner. Tradition maintains that not just any piece of wood will do: throughout much of Europe the ash tree was believed to have the strongest magical properties, with maple also recommended. In Russia, the hawthorn (*q.v.*) was a favourite because of its thorns, to which vampires are apparently very allergic. The aspen was widely used, too, because of its association with the cross, as Felicia Hermans remarks in her *Woodwalk* (1928), 'The aspen-tree shivers mystically in sympathy with the horror of that mother-tree in Palestine which was compelled to furnish materials for the Cross.' According to folklore, the thrust of the stake into the body is not only intended to release the blood the creature has imbibed, but to free its soul from the eternity of a half-life. In a number of cultures, it is said the vampire's body must be turned face down before staking, so that should the creature get loose it will dig deeper into the earth rather than regain the surface. In England, until the time of George IV, it was also a regular practice for those who had committed suicide to be buried at crossroads between the hours of nine and midnight with a stake driven through the body, in order to prevent them returning as a vampire.

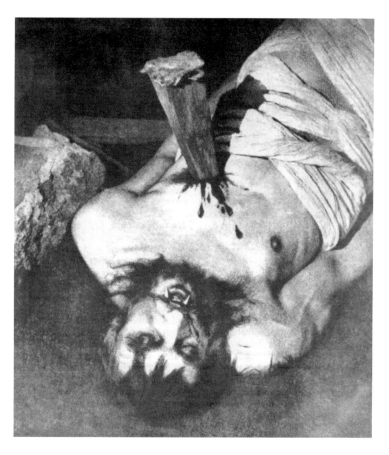

A graphic nineteenth-century picture of a staked vampire

Steele, Barbara (1938–   )

The British actress Barbara Steele has a cult status among fans of vampire films. Erotic-looking and aristocratically beautiful, she is known to English audiences as 'Alias: Miss Dracula' and in France, *le Marilyn des describes du Comte Dracula*. The American Count Dracula society has also awarded her a special commendation for her contributions to the genre. Never a prolific actress, her reputation has been built primarily on three outstanding vampire movies, *Revenge of the Vampire* (1960), *Castle of Blood* (1964) and *Revenge of the Blood Beast* (1965). Barbara Steele was born in Ireland where she got her first taste of acting as a child in a converted barn. Initially she tried to be a painter before deciding to become an actress and training at the Chelsea School of Art. Work followed in rep, and she joined the famous Rank 'charm school' but was only used in bit parts. Finally, her long raven hair and large green eyes caught the eye of the Italian director Mario Bava who was about to shoot *Revenge of the Vampire (aka Black Sunday* and *Le Masque du Demon)*. She was an immediate hit as Princess Asa, a 200-year-old

The cult actress Barbara Steel, 'Alias: Miss Dracula', in
Revenge of the Vampire (1960)

vampiress who wreaks a terrible vengeance on the descendants of those who originally buried her alive in a tomb. Her chilling portrayal of the undead got her labelled 'a female Christopher Lee', although what were described as its 'sadistic and nasty' elements prevented it from getting a certificate for showing in the UK until 1967! This success won her parts in several horror films before she was again cast as a vampire in *Castle of Blood* – also known as *Danse Macabre* and directed by Antonio Margherit – in which she played one of a family of vampires plaguing a haunted house. The last of her trio of movies, *Revenge of the Blood Beast*, saw her as another centuries-old vampiress who returns to Transylvania and is ultimately put to death by a Dr 'Von' Helsing, still boasting about how he killed Dracula. Since she stopped acting in 1979, Barbara Steele has worked as an associate producer on several movies as well as becoming a cult figure. She recalls her vampire films with affection: 'We had a marvellous time making them. But I did get a bit superstitious. I may not believe in fate, but those pictures were a bit chancy, a little spooky. I swear I'm never going to climb out of another coffin as long as I live!'

Stoker, Abraham (1847–1912)

In Count Dracula (*q.v.*), Bram Stoker created one of the great icons of popular culture and certainly the most famous vampire in literature. Despite the global fame of the novel which was first published in 1897, recognition for Stoker did not come until after his death and the endless series of films, plays, parodies and imitations of his book. Yet for much of his working life, he was content to work as the manager of the actor and impresario, Sir Henry Irving (*q.v.*) whose mesmerizing and dominant personality was undoubtedly influential in the development of Count Dracula (*q.v.*). Stoker was born on 8 November 1847 at 15, The Crescent, Clontarf, the son of Abraham Stoker, a clerk in the Chief Secretary's Department at Dublin Castle, and Charlotte Thornley, of Donegal, whose love of folklore and storytelling was to infuse her young son with a taste for the weird and the macabre and inspire him to become a writer.

Bram Stoker – business manager and author of the world's most famous vampire novel

Bram studied at Trinity College, overcame his rather sickly childhood to excel at sports, and then became a Civil Servant and spare-time theatre critic leading to his fateful meeting with Henry Irving

Number 15, The Crescent, Clontarf, the house in which
Bram Stoker was born

that changed the course of his life. During the 1870s Stoker
contributed a number of short stories and serials to Dublin period-

icals including 'The Primrose Path' a tale of horror which appeared in weekly instalments in The Shamrock magazine (February–March, 1875) and in which some authorities have seen the first stirrings of the ideas that would come to fruition in Dracula. Such were the demands of working for Irving, however, that Bram was only able to continue his writing during holiday periods, although this did result in several other works that may lack the power and originality of his vampire classic, but have been reprinted since his posthumous rise to fame, including The Mystery of the Sea (1902), The Jewel of the Seven Stars (1907), The Lady of the Shroud (1909) and The Lair of the White Worm (1911). A selection of his short stories, including an episode omitted from Dracula, were collected by his widow and published as Dracula's Guest in 1914, and further selections have been edited by Peter Haining as Shades of Dracula (1982) and Midnight Tales (1990). For all his subsequent fame, when Stoker died in Belgravia on 22 April 1912, just one obituary appeared in The Times two days later in which the anonymous writer observed, 'He was the master of a particularly lurid and creepy kind of fiction represented by Dracula and other novels. . . . But his chief literary memorial will be his Reminiscences of Henry Irving (1906), a book which with all its extravagances and shortcomings cannot but remain a valuable record of the workings of genius as they appeared to his devoted associate and admirer.' Among the several biographies which have been written about Stoker are A Biography of Dracula (1962) by Harry Ludlam (q.v.), The Man Who Wrote Dracula (1975) by Daniel Farson (q.v.) and The Un-Dead: The Legend of Bram Stoker and Dracula (1997) by Peter Haining and Peter Tremayne (q.v.).

Strigoiul (Romania)

The Wallachian area of Romania, for generations an independent agricultural region, has for centuries been the favourite hunting ground of the Strigoiul, a vampire that can be distinguished by its red hair, extremely pale features and large white teeth. According to folklore, it does not normally live in a grave or tomb, but prefers abandoned or ruined buildings which it leaves after nightfall to seek victims in neighbouring villages. A Wallachian tradition says the *Strigoiul* must be nailed into a coffin to prevent further attacks – or else it can be blown up with explosives carefully placed amongst the ruins where it lives! A third suggestion is to remove the vampire's heart and cut it in two. Wooden stakes are apparently no use against the *Strigoiul* – as W.R.S. Ralston reported in 1872: 'One who was transfixed with a sharp thorn cudgel in 1672, pulled it out of his body and flung it back contemptuously.'

Summers, Montague (1880–1948)

Although describing himself as 'The Reverend' Montague Summers, there is still doubt as to the origin of the holy orders that this enigmatic writer professed, though he was undeniably one of the most mysterious, colourful, even 'sinister' figures in the English literary world during the first half of the twentieth century. His friends and admirers described him as a genial and hospitable man, others saw him as a kind of clerical Dr Faustus, referring to him as 'The Witchfinder', and hinting that he was actually an unfrocked priest. Summers was, though, an undisputed authority on the Restoration theatre, Gothic literature and various elements of the supernatural, including witchcraft, black magic and especially vampires. His books, *The Vampire: His Kith and Kin* (1928) which examines the reasons for the ancient, worldwide belief in vampirism, and *The Vampire in Europe* (1929) dealing with the subject from a historical point of view, are considered among the most essential works on the subject and have been consulted by every successive generation of researchers, albeit that the author's strictly Catholic viewpoint is at times open to question. Little is known of his early life, though rumours have it that in his youth he may well have experimented with some of the elements of necromancy that he later wrote about with such insight and authority. Certainly he graduated from Trinity College, Oxford, tried unsuccessfully to become a Roman Catholic priest, and turned his intention instead to writing about the various historical subjects that interested him. Although it has been suggested

Montague Summers – one of the twentieth-century's leading vampirologists

that all Montague Summers' books were based on library research, there is evidence that he was in Greece in 1906 and 1907 collecting material on vampirism for his two books. It is said that as early as 1895 he had heard oral traditions about vampires and these may well have inspired his painstaking research. Though so much of his life is still clouded in conjecture, one of his admirers, Father Brocard Sewell, has offered this pen portrait in a Foreword to a new edition of Summers' *The History of Witchcraft and Demonology* (1926): 'During the year 1927, the striking and sombre figure of the Reverend Montague Summers in black soutane and cloak, with buckled shoes and shovel hat, could often be seen entering or leaving the reading room of the British Museum, carrying a large black portfolio bearing on its side a white label showing, in blood-red capitals, the legend VAMPIRES. This was just part of Summers' habitual *panache* and sense of fun, those qualities which made him such an admirable entertainer and *raconteur*.' More recently, R.W. Johnson wrote of him in *New Society* (9 December 1982): 'His books make it clear that he more than half believed in the vampires he studied – "the vampire tradition", he wrote (he always spoke of the tradition, never the myth), "contains far more truth than the ordinary individual cares to appreciate or acknowledge." I have, indeed, met those who were convinced that Summers believed himself to be a vampire.' Whatever the truth about this very strange man, his two works on vampires are essential reading for anyone interested in the subject.

Sussex Vampire

'The Adventure of the Sussex Vampire' (1924) is one of the most popular stories in the canon of Sherlock Holmes cases written by Sir Arthur Conan Doyle (*q.v.*). Set in the year 1896, it brings the Great Detective to rural Sussex where there is talk of a bloodsucking creature on the loose. From the very outset, Holmes is sceptical of this suggestion, though he does take the trouble to consult the section in his voluminous scrap-books on 'Vampires in London' – which, it has been argued, must surely contain the cuttings from the *Daily [Tele]graph* of 5 August 1890, and two others of the same year, the *Pall Mall Gazette* of 18 September and *Westminster Gazette* of 25 September, which describes the outrages perpetrated by Count Dracula and are referred to in *Dracula*. Nonetheless, the 'Great Detective' dismisses the idea to Watson: 'What have we to do with walking corpses who can only be held in their grave by stakes driven through their hearts? It's pure lunacy.' Despite the doctor's insistence that he has read of 'the old sucking the blood of the young in order to retain their youth,' Holmes travels to Sussex where, once again, he is proved right. The story has been adapted for films and television several times, most notably in 1993 as part of the Granada TV series, *The Casebook of Sherlock Holmes*, in which it became a two-hour special under the title 'The Last Vampyre'. Jeremy Brett and Edward Hardwick starred as Holmes and Watson with Roy Marsden as John Stockton, a mysterious figure who returns to the village where his ancestors were burned to death by the local people believing them to be vampires, and now, it is feared, has come back for revenge.

T

Talamaur (Polynesia)

The vampire of the Polynesian islands is known as a *Talamaur* and is part blood-and-energy-drinker and part cannibal. According to local tradition, after the creature has sapped the blood or energy of its victim, it has been known to tear out the heart and eat it while it is still beating. Folklore maintains that in the past some islanders have tried to become *Talamaurs* and benefit from their great strength and longevity by eating a piece of flesh from a victim. According to R.H. Codrington in *The Melanesians: Studies in their Anthropology and Folk Lore* (1891), 'The name *Talamaur* is also given to one whose soul was supposed to leave the grave and absorb the lingering vitality of a freshly dead person. There was a woman, some year ago, of whom the story is told that she made no secret of doing this, and that once on the death of a neighbour she gave notice that she would go in the night and eat the vitality. The friends of the deceased therefore kept watch in the house where the corpse lay and, at dead of night, heard a scratching at the door, followed by a rustling noise close to the body. One of them threw a stone and seemed to hit the unknown thing; and in the morning the *Talamaur* was found with a bruise on her arm, which she confessed was caused by a stone thrown at her whilst she was eating the vitality.'

Terry, Edward O'Connor (1844–1912)

The English comedian, Edward Terry, was the first actor to play a comic vampire on the stage: appearing in a burlesque, *The Vampire* written by R. Reece which opened at the Royal Strand Theatre in London on 18 August 1872. Born in London, Terry made his debut at the Christchurch Theatre in Dorset in 1863 where his slapstick style went down well with the seaside resort's patrons. He spent four years touring the provinces before playing London in 1867. His career proved to be one long round of comic successes which enabled him to open his own establishment, Terry's Theatre, in 1887. *The Vampire* – advertised as a 'Production of a Bit of Moonshine in Three Rays' – was claimed to be 'based on a German legend' and a story attributed to Lord Byron (*q.v.*), which was actually the work of the poet's doctor/companion John William Polidori (*q.v.*). In Reece's storyline, the vampire is aptly named Alan Raby, a grotesque figure in a long, black cloak, with an extremely pale face and bushy eyebrows and moustache. He lurks beneath Raby Castle and makes his presence felt to two female novelists who are staying there. But his intention is not to vampirize them, rather to listen to their conversations and steal their notes in order to write his own three-volume novel about the undead! Reviewing the play, which ultimately ran for almost a year, the *Illustrated London News* described Terry as 'the Hibernian plagiarist with the broadest of brogues and the most ghostly of faces' while another critic said, 'Mr Terry's make-up as the vampire was something extraordinary, and he worked with unflagging energy to add "go" to the novelty.'

Theodore of Gaza (1400–1478)

Theodore was a celebrated Greek Humanist and translator of Aristotle who laid a vampire to rest in an unusual incident related by Pierre Le Loyer in his *Quatre Discours et Histoires des Spectres* (1586). Born at Thessalonica, Theodore migrated to Italy in 1429 and taught Greek at several universities while translating Aristotle into the native language. Granted some land on which to live and continue his work, the Greek teacher was horrified to learn one day that a number of local people were complaining of being visited at night by 'a very thin man of harsh and forbidding aspect' and the next day finding themselves overcome by lethargy. When a young boy was discovered dead 'lying thin and waxy pale as though every drop of blood had been drained out of his body', Theodore suspected it might be the handiwork of a vampire and, on investigating, learned that the events had all occurred since a local man had dug up an ancient urn containing some curious ashes. The next night, the man of 'forbidding aspect', now plump and rosy-cheeked, was seen in the vicinity of the mysterious urn – and the facts seemed inescapable. Pierre Le Loyer writes, 'Whereupon Theodore hastened to the spot, buried the ill-omened vessel exactly where it had first been found, and the vampire was seen no more.'

Transylvania

Transylvania with its long history of vampires and famed as the 'home' of Dracula, is actually one of the three provinces of

Transylvanian coffin-makers ensuring that a corpse
does not rise again as a vampire

249

Romania (*q.v.*) – the others being Wallachia and Moldavia. The area is, though, separated from the other two geographically, historically and culturally. It is effectively cut off by the Carpathian Mountains, and although all three provinces were part of the kingdom of Dacia before Roman times, their later histories, which included numerous wars and migrations of people, finally drew them together. In the closing years of the nineteenth century when Bram Stoker (*q.v.*) was writing his novel, Transylvania was part of the Austro–Hungarian Empire and under the control of Hungary. The population was in excess of two million, consisting of 1.2 million Romanians, 530,000 Hungarians, 200,000 Saxons as well as several hundred thousand Armenians, Slavs and Jews. At the end of the First World War, Transylvania was finally combined with Wallachia and Moldavia to form the modern state of Romania. Among the locations, which now draw tourists on the trail of the vampire legend, is the town of Brasov where Vlad Tepes Dracula (*q.v.*) impaled hundreds of victims on Timpa Hill; Sighisoara where his birthplace is marked by a plaque; Castle Konigstein, where he was ambushed and arrested by the Hungarian King Matthias Corvinus; and Hundedoara where the young Vlad trained to be a soldier in the picturesque castle of John Hunyadi.

Travels of Three English Gentlemen (1734)

'The Travels of Three English Gentlemen, From Venice to Hamburg, Being the Grand Tour of Germany, in the Year 1734', was a curious article published two years after the events it describes in *The Harleian Miscellany*, 'A Collection of Scarce, Curious and Entertaining Pamphlets and Tracts'. The account is said to have prompted other European travellers to recount their experiences in vampire-infested countries as well as inspiring numerous tales of fiction. Very little though, is known of the three gentlemen, beyond the fact that the writer of the article was, by his own admission, 'a member of the Royal Society and of the University of Oxford' and had lived abroad in several countries. Of his observations on the journey, he said 'many are entirely new and all related with the utmost fidelity.' The relevant section of the essay deals with what the three men were told about the vampire tradition in Hungary while staying in the city of Laubach and what they learned from reading a dissertation on the subject written by an academic, Dr John Heinrich Zopfius (*q.v.*). After recounting with evident relish how vampires preyed at night on sleeping people and sucked out their blood, the anonymous gentleman added, 'Such a notion will, probably, be looked upon as fabulous and exploded by many people in England. However, it is not only countenanced by Baron Valasor and many Carnioleze noblemen, gentlemen & etc, as we were informed, but likewise actually embraced by some writers of good authority.' The extract appears in full in *The Vampire in Europe* by Montague Summers (*q.v.*) (1929).

Tremayne, Peter (1943–   )

Peter Tremayne is the pseudonym of the leading Celtic scholar, Peter Berresford Ellis, who has written books on a variety of popular subjects from the supernatural to biographies of H. Rider Haggard, Talbot Mundy and Bram Stoker (*q.v.*). Born in Coventry, he is the son of a journalist from Cork City, and was himself a newspaper-man for some years before becoming a full-time author. His pioneering research into Irish mythology revealed a strong vampire tradition in the nation and how this had influenced Dublin-born Bram Stoker in his creation of *Dracula*. Tremayne's admiration for the book also inspired him to write a series of novels covering the event that occurred before Stoker's tale begins. These, all told in the form of first-person narratives, are *Dracula Unborn* (1977) – published in the USA as *Bloodright: Memoirs of Mircea, Son of Dracula* in 1979 – *The Revenge of Dracula* (1978) and *Dracula, My Love* (1980), all three of which were assembled as an omnibus, *Dracula Lives!* in 1993. Peter Tremayne is also co-author with Peter Haining of *The Un-Dead: The Legend of Bram Stoker and Dracula* (1997) which has unearthed many new facts about the influences and creation of the most famous of all vampire novels.

ꕰ

The Un-Dead

The Un-Dead was the original title that Bram Stoker (*q.v.*) gave to his famous vampire novel when he delivered the manuscript to his London publishers, Archibald Constable & Company at 2, Whitehall Gardens, London in March 1897. Although the novel itself was typed – still something of a novelty for a manuscript at this time because the typewriter had only been in existence for a decade – the title page was handwritten by Stoker before it was handed to his editor, Otto Kyllmann, a 27-year-old from Manchester who can be credited with signing-up what is almost certainly the most famous horror novel of all time. Kyllmann was not entirely happy with the title *The Un-Dead* – perhaps because it was a little similar to Stoker's earlier collection of short stories for children, *Under The Sunset*, published by the rival firm of Sampson Low, Marston, Searle and Rivington in 1882 – and at his prompting, Stoker changed it to *Dracula, or The Un-Dead*, finally shortening it to the one evocative word now familiar all over the world. The editor also had strong reservations about the opening chapter of the book which seemed similar to the short story 'Carmilla' by Stoker's fellow Irishman, Joseph Sheridan Le Fanu (*q.v.*), and suggested it was omitted. Once again Stoker agreed – although many years later, after his death, his widow, Florence, included it as the title story in a collection of his short tales, *Dracula's Guest*, which appeared in 1914. Her explanation in an introduction to the collection that it was 'originally excised owing to the length of the book' is demonstrably not true as a few thousand words would have made little difference to the 390-page first edition which was, in actual

THE.UN-DEAD

By

Bram Stoker

author of "Under the
Sunset," "The Snake's Pass,"
"The Watter's Mou'", "The
Shoulder of Shasta."

Copyright 1897 By
Bram Stoker: All Rights Reserved.

Handwritten title page of *The Un-Dead* which would become a
classic as *Dracula*

fact, padded with eighteen pages of advertisements for other
Constable titles! For many years, no copy of the original manuscript
was believed to have survived, until a 529-page typewritten MS,
heavily revised and annotated, with various pages cut up and re-
pasted together, suddenly came to light in America in an old barn
on a Pennsylvanian homestead not far from Philadelphia. Though
doubts were initially raised about whether it was, in fact, the manuscript of *Dracula* – not the least of these being cast by the original
finders, put off by its title *The Un-Dead* – it had subsequently been
authenticated and now resides in a private collection in California.
The facts of this extraordinary discovery in an old trunk – in which

were also found the corpses of several withered and dried-out dead rats! – are given in *The Un-Dead: The Legend of Bram Stoker and Dracula* by Peter Haining and Peter Tremayne (*q.v.*) (1997).

Upierczi (Poland)

The Polish vampire or *Upierczi* (sometimes shortened to just *Upier*) is particularly feared in the more remote areas of the country, especially in the huge, low-lying, marshy land formerly known as White Russia. This ghastly bloodsucker may be either male (*Upier*) or female (*Upiercsa*) and is said to be the undead corpse of a person who committed suicide, died a violent death or practised witchcraft during their lifetime. Both sexes have the same characteristics: a hare-lip and a tongue which at its tip is pointed like an insect's sting. According to an old trdition, the *Upierczi* will sometimes gnaw their own hands and feet when they awaken from a long sleep in the grave to give themselves the strength to pursue living victims. The creature occasionally attacks cattle, but normally sucks the blood of sleeping men and women who are found the following morning with a very small wound on the left side of their chests, exactly over the heart. There are also stories in Polish folklore that the *Upierczi* have been known to ring bells at night and call out the names of people who then die shortly afterwards. An authority on vampires, Alexander Afanasief, has written in his authoritative work, *Poeticheskiya Vozzryeniya Slavyan na Pirodu* (1869) that the accepted ways of destroying an *Upierczi* are either to drown it in a lake or river, burying it face downwards well covered by earth, or else by staking it with a long, steel nail while it rests in the tomb. However this transfixion must be achieved with one blow or else the vampire will revive.

Utah Bloodsucker

A case of vampirism, which became known as 'The Utah Bloodsucker' occurred in a small town near Salt Lake City in Utah. The events, as subsequently reported in the *Weekly Budget* of 3 July

1867, began with a young man who came to stay in a local boarding-house. Each morning he awoke to find himself growing very pale and thin and also noticed some curious puncture marks on his arms from which blood had obviously been drawn. The same thing happened several times, although only once was he disturbed during the night and felt 'something cold pressing against him and bite'. The young man immediately left the boarding house, the *Weekly Budget* reported, but in the weeks that followed several other people who occupied the same room had similar experiences, until finally no-one would enter the building. The newspaper account concluded: 'People who live in the town believe it is haunted by a vampire, that is to say the accursed body of some former dweller in the house, who could find no rest in the neighbouring cemetery, and nightly left the grave to suck the blood of anyone who slept in the room which it had occupied when alive.' It is believed that the house was later torn down and the site redeveloped with no further visitations occurring.

Utukku (Egypt)

The *Utukku* of Egypt is one of the oldest vampires of all and records of it preying on human victims have been found in some of the earliest papyrus scrolls. According to Dr Campbell Thompson in *The Devils and Evil Spirits of Babylonia* (1903), 'The *Utukku*, or Departed Spirit, was the soul of a dead person who, for some reason, could find no rest and wandered over the earth lying in wait to seize upon men.' Local tradition maintained that these creatures 'moved like the wind' and were sometimes said to look more like ghosts than beings of flesh and blood. There are also stories of necromancers in ancient Egypt who attempted to raise *Utukku* to do their bidding – but because of the unpredictable nature of these undead, such activities were fraught with danger and there was a very real danger that those who summoned the beings would become their victims. According to tradition, the way to ensure such vampires remained in their tombs was to place regular offer-ings of food and drink where the undead could find them and thereby put them off the idea of searching for human blood.

Valek

Valek is a 600-year-old member of the undead who was originally buried in Europe in the Middle Ages and reappears in the late twentieth century in New Mexico. He is a master vampire, of incredible power and able to split people in half with a single blow of his razor-sharp hand. Valek has no fear of garlic or crosses, and in the film, *Vampires* (1999) is seen searching for a special crucifix which will give him and his increasing band of undead followers the power to walk in sunlight. Valek's nemesis is Jack Crow, a vampire hunter employed by the Catholic Church, who has to impress on the local population that real vampires are quite unlike those seen in films or read about in books. They are, he says, 'a new breed of evil'. Made by John Carpenter, the American director of several notable horror movies including, *Hallowe'en, The Fog* and *The Thing*, the screening of *Vampires* was awaited with great enthusiasm but proved to be a disappointment, despite the bloody duel between Thomas Ian Griffith as Valek and James Wood playing Jack Crow. An unusual element of the story was the suggestion that the Catholic clergy had been responsible for the creation of the first vampires. Critical opinions varied from *The Sunday Times*' description of *Vampires* as 'a workaday genre movie' to the *Daily Mirror*'s view that 'die-hard horror fans will revel in its monstrously violent special-effects mayhem.' Interestingly, the rock-style musical score was provided by the Texas Toadlickers, a group which included the director himself on synthesizer and rhythm guitar.

Vambery, Arminius (1832–1913)

Hungarian-born Professor Arminius Vambery was an expert on the folklore of Eastern Europe and is credited with having supplied information to Bram Stoker (*q.v.*) at the time he was planning *Dracula* – indeed one of Stoker's biographer, Daniel Farson (*q.v.*) has suggested in *The Man Who Wrote Dracula* (1975) that 'there is a touch of Vambery in the character of Van Helsing.' Born in Budapest, Vambery from an early age displayed a gift for languages and learned to speak sixteen, and then spent a number of years travelling, often disguising himself when in out of the way parts of Asia to avoid his real identity from being discovered. As a result of this travel, he wrote several highly regarded books including *Travels in Central Asia* (1864) and *The Story of My Struggles* (1886). Later Vambery accepted the less demanding post of Professor of Oriental Languages at the University of Budapest where his scholarship earned him a number of international honours including the Grand Cordon of Medjide, the Japanese Order of the Holy Treasure and, in 1889, a Commander of the Royal Victorian Order. In fact, Vambery was a great Anglophile and his influence in fostering British interests in Asia gained him access to the highest political circles, while his books – especially *Arminius Vambery: His Life and Adventures* published in 1883 – caused him to be lionized by English society. He was also a vain and rather pompous man, flattered to be part of this high society, and met Bram Stoker when he was invited by Sir Henry Irving (*q.v.*) to have dinner in the Lyceum's private dining hall, The Beefsteak Room, after a performance of *The Dead Heart* on 30 April 1890. Legend has it that Vambery regaled his fellow diners for hours with tales of his adventures in mysterious places such as Transylvania and, again according to Daniel Farson, 'There is good reason to assume that it was the Hungarian professor who told Bram, for the first time, of the name of Dracula.' Other biographers have suggested that Stoker actually corresponded with Vambrey for further information on vampire lore in Romania, but despite the fact his working papers have survived, there is no trace of any such correspondence. Nevertheless, Vambery does deserve a credit in the creation of *Dracula*, all the more so because in chapter 18 of the book, Van Helsing refers to 'my friend Arminius of Buda-Pesth University' and a request he had sent to him for all the information that 'he can tell me of what he [Dracula] has been'.

The part of Arminius Vambery in the creation of *Dracula* has been much debated

Vamp

A vamp is a woman who intentionally attracts and exploits men. She was first personified in 1915 by the Hollywood actress, Theda Bara (*q.v.*) in the film *A Fool There Was*, and the concept quickly became a stock character in plays and films, while many young women on both sides of the Atlantic deliberately copied these unashamed adventuresses. *The Vamp* became a famous stage play on Broadway in 1918 starring Enid Bennett and of it, the *New York Times* critic wrote,

> In this new 'Vamp' story, Enid Bennett appears as Nancy an ingenious wardrobe girl at a musical-comedy threatre where she hears sophisticated chorus girls tell how the female of the species may make the male buy her dinner and diamond bracelets by 'vamping' him – so Nancy takes a hint from the chorus girls and 'vamps' a man herself.

In an article on vamps in its issue of 24 January 1963, the *Listener* commented, 'Marilyn Monroe had all the physical equipment of the vamp, but the spirit of the girl next door – Marilyn was never truly vampiric on the screen and she was never a "taker" in life.'

Vampir (Hungary)

Vampir is the Hungarian word for vampire, although on occasions the term *Liderc Nadaly* has also been used in the country to describe the undead. The creature has glaring red eyes, sharp teeth and rises from its tomb during the night hour to suck the blood of living victims. There have been innumerable accounts of vampires in Hungarian history, although the persistence of the people working in collaboration with the clergy to put an end to the activities of these *vampirs* has been notably successful. Although staking a vampire through the heart is a method of disposing of them that has been recorded in a number of these instances, a local variation on the tradition is to drive a nail through the creature's temples while it sleeps in the tomb.

Vampire

The term *Vampire* (sometimes spelt *vampyre*) is from the Magyar, *vampir*, a word of Slavonic origin, which indicates a being who emerges from the grave at night to drink the blood of sleeping people. There are variants in many other languages to describe this supernatural resuscitated corpse, which has been recorded in all ages and all over the world as Montague Summers (*q.v.*) has written in his essential work, *The Vampire: His Kith and Kin* (1928),

> In all the darkest pages of the malign supernatural there is no more terrible tradition than of the Vampire, a pariah even among demons. Foul are his ravages; gruesome and seemingly barbaric are the ancient and approved methods by which folk must rid themselves of this hideous pest. Even today in certain quarters of the world, in remoter districts of Europe itself, Transylvania, the isles and mountains of Greece, the peasant will take the law into his own hands and utterly destroy the carrion who – as it is yet firmly believed – at night will issue from his unhallowed grave to spread the infection of vampirism throughout the countryside. Assyria knew the vampire long ago, and he lurched amid the primaeval forests of Mexico before Cortes came. He is feared by the Chinese, by the Indians, and the Malay alike; whilst Arabian story tells us again and again of the ghouls who haunt ill-omened sepulchres and lonely crossroads to attack and devour the unhappy traveller.

According to tradition, the vampire is said to be recognizable by its glaring eyes, long, pointed canine teeth and foul breath. The creature is gaunt in appearance but has almost hypnotic powers over victims which enables it to drink blood and sustain its undead existence. The vampire is said to rest in its coffin by daylight

Engraving of a Chinese vampire dating from the
seventeenth century

and can only be killed by a stake through the heart or by the head being cut off and burnt.

Vampire-Bat
See Bat, Vampire-

Vampire Cat
See Cat, Vampire

Vampire Lovers, The

The Hammer/American International film, *The Vampire Lovers* (1970) has been described by Jeffrey Frentzen in *The Penguin*

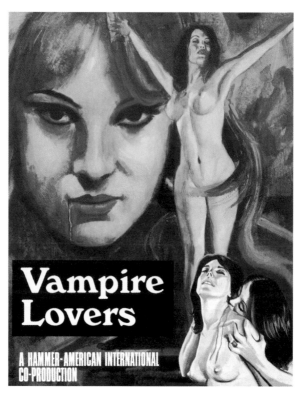

The Vampire Lovers (1970) which 'revolutionized the genre' according to critics

Encyclopedia of Horror and the Supernatural (1986) as the film that 'revolutionized the genre in many ways, setting a precedent for excessively perverse and bloody vampire films'. Although tame by today's standards, the picture did spawn a host of imitations. Ostensibly based on the classic short story 'Carmilla' (*q.v.*) by Joseph Sheridan Le Fanu (*q.v.*), the film was directed by Roy Ward Baker who explored the lesbian possibilities in the relationship between the vampiress and her female victims. Ingrid Pitt (*q.v.*) starred in her first vampire role with Pippa Steele and Madeleine Smith. The film was attacked by several English film critics – though it did excellent box-office business – and in America received an 'R' (for Restricted) rating. The movie inspired two sequels: *Lust For A Vampire* (1971) directed by Jeremy Sangster, starring the beautiful Danish actress, Yutte Stensgaard, and *Twins of Evil* (aka *Virgin Vampires*) made in 1972 by director John Hough with two exotic twins, Madelaine and Mary Collinson.

Vampirella [1]

Vampirella is a lovely, solitary female vampire, a descendant of Dracula, who has learned his dark secret and whose advice she must follow. She is the creation of the English writer, Angela Carter (1940–1992) and was first featured on BBC Radio in 1976. Carter, who was born in Eastbourne, Sussex, dazzled readers and critics alike with her imaginative, daring and explorative novels such as *The Infernal Desire Machine of Doctor Hoffman* (1972), *The Passion of New Eve* (1977) and *Nights at the Circus* (1984). Her writing has been termed 'Gothic Science Fiction' and she once declared of the genre, 'Only horror fiction is a true reflection of the times we live in; only fantasy is true to life.' Supernatural characters, including vampires, feature in several of her short stories in collections like *The Bloody Chamber* (1979) which includes *The Company of Wolves* filmed by Neil Jordan in 1985. Since her premature death, Angela Carter has become something of a cult figure, and 'Vampirella' was broadcast again as part of an evening devoted to classic horror in November 1992 with Anna Massey in the title role.

Angela Carter's *Vampirella* as visualized by Kasia Charko
for *Radio Times* in 1976

Vampirella [2]

'Vampirella' is also the name of a voluptuous American horror
comic-strip character who appeared in 1969 and became a virtual
icon of fantasy art with readers in the US and Europe during the
1970s. Created by the American writer, Forrest J. Ackerman
(1916–) as an unashamed imitation of the French comic-strip
heroine, Barbarella, and initially drawn by Tom Sutton (1937–),
she wore a red, one-piece costume cut to the verge of nudity and
calf-length, high-heeled boots. Just how she remained inside the
scanty costume with two tiny strips across her huge bosom so
narrow as to reveal a bat-shaped birthmark on her right breast –
considering the hectic nature of her adventures – was nothing
short of a miracle of design: though fans loved it! Vampirella is
said to come from the planet Draculon, have the power to trans-

form herself into bat-form at will, but requires a special serum every 24 hours or else she is forced to feed on human blood. During the series, a vampire hunter named Adam Van Helsing – a descendant of Stoker's Professor Van Helsing – became part of the stories and eventually became Vampirella's lover. Such was the popularity of her adventures published by the Warren Publishing Company, that they sparkled a whole range of merchandizing from T-shirts to posters as well as a series of novelizations written by Ron Goulart (1933–): *Bloodstalk* (1975), *On Alien Wings* (1975), *Deadwalk* (1976), *Blood Wedding* (1976), *Deathgame* (1976) and *Snakegod* (1976). The original magazine ceased publication in 1983, but the enduring popularity of the character resulted in her being revived in 1992 in a continuing series, *Vampirella: Morning in America*.

The voluptuous American *Vampirella* by Tom Sutton first appeared in 1969

Vampiro (Spain)

The Spanish member of the undead species, *Vampiro*, shares its name with those in Italy, and both are violent, bloodthirsty creatures who prey on isolated communities and solitary travellers. These vampires apparently rest for years on end before they require blood, and if unable to find a living victim quickly enough will reanimate the first corpse they can find. Tradition says there is no ideal remedy for disposing of the *Vampiro* in either Spain or Italy, although burning the corpse has reportedly been used on a number of occasions with apparent success.

Van Sloan, Edward (1882–1964)

The American actor Edward Van Sloan was the first man to portray Bran Stoker's (*q.v.*) vampire hunter, Professor Van Helsing, on the screen in 1931, having already played the character in the theatre in 1927 opposite Bela Lugosi (*q.v.*). Born in San Francisco of Dutch extraction – his real name was Van Sloun – he was educated at the University of California at Berkeley and was briefly a commercial artist before the lure of the stage made him join a local repertory company. He specialized in romantic and comedy roles and was surprised when offered the role of Van Helsing in the Broadway production of *Dracula*. It came as no surprise, though, when he was offered the screen role in 1931 because he was now very familiar with the character. Van Sloan said, 'I found him to be a fascinating and complex man – a man with as open a mind to superstition as he had to science. Nothing seemed too outlandish for him and he never treated even the wildest of his patients' stories with anything other than courtesy and the closest attention. I don't think I ever had such a demanding role!' Van Sloan was made to look much older by make-up, but with his Dutch ancestry found duplicating his character's manner of speech quite easy. He particularly enjoyed the epilogue to the film where he emerged from behind the curtain to warn the audience that 'vampires *do* exist'. Sadly this was cut from many prints of the film. Van Sloan appeared in only one other film in his favourite role, *Dracula's Daughter* made in 1936 and reputedly based on Stoker's story, 'Dracula's Guest'. Nonetheless, he continued to receive many fan letters from all over the world – some addressed simply 'Dr Van Helsing' – many asking for information about vampires and a few even appealing for his help in getting rid of members of the undead the writers believed were pursuing them! Even after his retirement, his house in San Francisco was often pointed out as the place where, 'the man who killed Dracula lived!'

The American actor Edward Van Sloan was the screen's first Van Helsing

Varney the Vampyre

Varney the Vampyre; or, The Feast of Blood, a serial story issued in penny-weekly parts that began appearing in the winter of 1847, represents a landmark in fantasy fiction: the first full-length fiction-alization of a vampire. A rambling, chaotic and often badly written saga, set mainly during the time of Oliver Cromwell, it features Sir Francis Varney of Ratford Abbey, a vampire who emerges by night from his tomb to prey on terrified villagers and nubile young

'The vampire arises!' – a typical 'penny dreadful' illustration from the long-running serial, *Varney the Vampire* (1847–9)

women. It was launched as just another 'penny dreadful' serial by the London publisher, Edward Lloyd, but it became so popular that the usual extent of these publications – on average 12 weeks – was extended until it had run for 109 issues, each with a dramatic engraving on the front. At this point, the vampire, who had escaped countless cliff-hanger situations, finally committed suicide by leaping into the lava pit of Mount Vesuvius. However, despite this success, the weekly parts – by their nature very ephemeral – rapidly became scarce and today few complete copies of individual issues, let alone the whole set, still survive: although the reputation of *Varney the Vampyre* has become legendary. For years the authorship of the work has been in dispute – no credit was ever given on 'penny dreadfuls' – and initially one of Edward Lloyd's most prolific writers, Thomas Peckett Prest, was credited with the work. However, subsequent research into Prest's stories and those of another of his contemporaries, James Malcolm Ryner (1814–1881), has established that stylistically, grammatically and in aspects of characterization, it is more probably the work of Rymer, who was already known for serial stories of blood and gore such as *Ada The Betrayed* (1842) and *The Black Monk* (1844). A two-volume facsimile edition of *Varney the Vampyre* was published in 1972 with an informative introduction by E.F. Bleiler.

Velden Haunt

The story of the 'Velden Haunt' and one man's encounter with a vampire in the Carinthia district of Austria during the winter of 1945–6 was told by S.J. Saunders in *Prediction* magazine, June 1969. Saunders was a warrant officer in the 78 Divisional Signals when a creature of 'evil intent' began prowling about the senior officers' mess at Velden, a handsome building overlooking Lake Worthersee. According to the report of one officer, Major P., a terrifying apparition like an old woman dressed in black had grappled with him one night, attacking his throat. After hearing several other similar stories, Saunders decided to investigate by sleeping in Major P.'s room. During the night he was suddenly aware of a drop in the temperature and the emergence of a fetid odour. He also got the distinct feeling of 'someone constantly peering down on me . . . and an increasing asphyxiation and a pain in my right forearm'. Although Saunders experienced nothing else, he was startled to be informed the next day that some 'infant human remains' had been found in the grounds at Velden. The author concluded his article, 'A Vampire ghost? Carinthia shares, with parts of present day Hungary and Yugoslavia, the reputation of being traditional vampire country, and in 1732 the outbreak of vampirism was so widespread in Central Europe that investigations were instituted by the government. . . . The bruise on my arm suggests a potentiality of deliberate evil, and the feeling of being watched by something unclean haunts me yet.'

Vetala (India)

The Indian species of vampire known as the *Vetala* differs from its compatriot, the cannibalistic *Rakshasa* (*q.v.*), in that it resembles an old woman and very often only attacks other females. Folklore maintains that this species of the undead is associated with the goddess Kali, infamous for generating destruction, plague and violent death, and believed to drink the blood of some of her victims. According to tradition, the *Vetala* possess supernatural powers and will use a special ritual involving a magic thread to immobilize victims before drinking their blood. Because of the creature's habit of appearing as an elderly woman, over the centuries many unfortunate old ladies have been burnt alive in the mistaken impression they were a *Vetala*.

Vlad Tepes, 'The Impaler' (1431–1476)

Vlad Tepes was the Romanian prince of Wallachia whose remarkable exploits as patriot, tactician and bloodthirsty sadist provided Bram Stoker (*q.v.*) with material for the creature of *Dracula* – as well as the all-important name of his central character. Born Vlad Tepes

Dracula, he was the second son of Vlad II, better known as 'Dracul'. The boy's character was undoubtedly shaped during his childhood when the constant wars Vlad II was forced to fight against the Turks caused him to offer the young Dracula some simple advice, 'It is better for you to be feared than loved.' After one battle, Vlad had to send his two sons, Dracula and Radu, as captives of the Turkish Sultan, Murad II, and during his imprisonment the boy developed an overwhelming hatred of the enemy which would shape his later life. After the death of his father, Prince Dracula ruled Wallachia three times: briefly in 1448, then from 1456–1462, and again during the last two months of 1476 just before his assassination. It has been alleged that during this time, he killed in excess of 40,000 people, the majority of them Turks. He was also utterly ruthless to his own countrymen. When some local landowners seemed about to threaten his power, he had them brutally executed, *en masse*, by being impaled on stakes, hence the nickname, 'The Impaler'. Subsequently, he appointed a number of peasants to positions of authority and determined to make Wallachia free of poverty. With this in mind he invited all the beggars in the country to a huge feast in his castle and, once they had been wined and dined, asked if they wanted a future 'without care, lacking nothing in this world?' On receiving a mighty cheer of affirmation, Dracula ordered his palace to be boarded up and set on fire. 'I did this so that no one will be poor in my realm,' he explained. In the end, however, the prince's sexual abnormality and cruelty – he would watch the sexual organs of women being mutilated and often ate his dinners surrounded by impaled bodies – caused the country to turn against him. But his reputation as a tyrant and monster was already assured, as Radu Florescu and Raymond T. McNally have written in their painstaking biography which links the man to his part in the Bram Stoker classic, *Dracula: A Biography of Vlad the Impaler* (1973); 'He may well vie with Ivan the Terrible for the title of the most gruesome psychopath of history – in fact, it is believed that Ivan the Terrible modelled some of his own tortures on those of Dracula.' The story of Vlad has been filmed as *Drakula Istanbulda* (1953) based on *The Impaling Voivode* by Riza Seyfi, directed by Mehmet Muktar and starring Atif Kaptan; and produced on the stage in 1978 as *Vlad the*

Impaler in which the Romanian playwright Marin Sorescu satirized Romania's most recent sadistic megalomaniac, Ceausescu. In November 1992, the British actor John Hurt gave a bloodcurdling performance in the title role in an adaptation for BBC Radio 3.

Vlad Tepes, 'The Impaler', liked to dine among his victims

Vourdalak (Serbia)

The Serbian vampire known as a *Vourdalak* has been described as having 'the congested face of an impenitent drunkard and blood-coloured skin,' according to Ornella Volta's study, *The Vampire* (1965). The species is always a middle-aged man and tradition says they remain active for seven years and then become human again and repeat the process somewhere else in the country. The committing of incest is said to be one of the causes of this type of vampire, or else by the practise of witchcraft or being attacked by a werewolf. The *Vourdalak* can only be stopped by driving a nail into its neck and cutting off its thumbs and toes.

Vrykolakas (Greece)

The Greek work *Vrykolakas* originally meant a revenant (*q.v.*), but in recent times has come to indicate a vampire. In some parts of the nation the word is spelt *Vroukolakas* or even *Vompiras* – the later form also being used as a term of abuse. According to tradition, the creatures lived either evil or immoral lives and have been reanimated by the Devil who causes them to rise from their graves and plague their next of kin. These hapless victims invariably fall ill and usually die. *Vrykolakas* are said to be able to appear in the daytime and have the power to transfix a victim with just a glance. The way of ridding the countryside of them is described by William Martin Leake in his *Travels in Northern Greece* (1835): 'The remedy is to dig up the body, and if after it has been exorcized by the priest, the demon still persists in annoying the living, to cut the body into small pieces, or if that be not sufficient, to burn it.'

W

Waterford Vampire

The picturesque Irish town of Waterford in Munster is claimed to be the haunt of the country's most famous vampire. The overgrown graveyard beside the ruined church is where the undead creature is said to lie, although some local people believe it may actually be underneath the edifice known as Strongbow's Tower. What makes this particular vampire unique is that, centuries ago, it was supposed to have been put to death in the traditional manner with a stake, yet still returns to attack anyone foolish enough to stray into the churchyard at night. Indeed, there have been several instances over the years of young men and women experiencing terrifying phenomena in the area. These accounts vary as to whether the undead is male or female, which helps to explain the different suggestions as to the vampire's identity. Some people believe it to be Richard de Clare, the Second Earl of Pembroke, who occupied Waterford in 1171 and was known as 'Strongbow'; while those who are convinced the figure to be female, think she could be Aoife, the daughter of the King of Leinster whom de Clare succeeded. Both were certainly notorious for their cruelty – Aoife having cut her own son in half for cowardice.

Weir, John (c.1512–1568)

John Weir was a celebrated German demonologist who conducted a special enquiry into the ways of vampires as part of his life-long study of the occult. Born in Cologne, Weir became interested in the undead while a pupil of Cornelius Agrippa (1486–1535), the cabalistic philosopher notorious for his defence of witchcraft and labelled a magician by the people of Germany following the publication of his famous book, *De Occulta Philosophia* (1531–33). John Weir wrote several pamphlets on occultism, in one of which, *Der Vampyre* (1548), he outlined a 'method for the repelling of vampires'. Weir instructed that samples of earth should be taken from the first three spadefuls of consecrated soil used at a Christian burial. If this earth was then trodden into the entranceway of a church, he said, the holy soil would prevent any vampire from entering. He also suggested that if the same kind of earth was spread around the grave of a suspected vampire it would be unable to leave the tomb.

Whitby, Yorkshire

The seaside resort of Whitby, huddling in a cleft of the River Esk, is famous as the place where Captain James Cook (1728–1779)

Whitby in Yorkshire has created a tourist attraction from its association with the Dracula legend

served his apprenticeship before setting sail to become one of the world's great navigators (in two vessels, *Resolution* and *Endeavour* both built in the local shipyards) and – in fiction – the place where Dracula makes his landfall in Britain on board the Russian schooner, *Demeter*, complete with 50 boxes of native soil. Generations of curiosity seekers have visited the little port to trace the footsteps of the undead Count and those of his first victim, Lucy Westenra. Scarborough Borough Council now publishes an informative leaflet, *The Whitby Dracula Trail*, complete with map, which takes walkers to all the major spots: starting at the Bram Stoker Memorial Seat on West Cliff, via 6 Royal Crescent where he stayed while researching the book, through the town and finally up the 199 stone steps to St Mary's Churchyard with the towering ruins of Whitby Abbey behind. On Marine Parade is a waxwork museum, 'The Dracula Experience'.

Wilkinson, William (1758–1830)

William Wilkinson was the English author of *An Account of the Principalities of Wallachia and Moldavia* published in 1820, a copy of which Bram Stoker (*q.v.*) found in Whitby Library and used as a source for background material in the writing of *Dracula*. The author, a Cambridge University educated career Civil Servant, had been the British Consul in Bucharest for ten years until his retirement in 1819. He wrote his 320-page book mixing travelogue with historical detail all based upon years of personal experience. In it, Stoker found much valuable information including the reference which gave him the name for his central character. For on page 19 of the *Account* he copies down this paragraph: 'Dracula in Wallachia language means Devil. Wallachians were accustomed to give it as a surname to any person who rendered himself conspicuous by courage, cruel actions or cunning.'

William of Newburgh (1136–1201)

The historian and canon, William of Newburgh, was the first writer to attempt to chronicle in detail some of the vampire legends of his

AN

ACCOUNT

OF

THE PRINCIPALITIES

OF

WALLACHIA AND MOLDAVIA:

WITH

VARIOUS POLITICAL OBSERVATIONS

RELATING TO THEM.

By WILLIAM WILKINSON, Esǫ.

LATE BRITISH CONSUL RESIDENT AT BUKOREST.

Dobbiamo considerare queste due provincie, Wallachia e Moldavia a guisa di due nave in un mar' tempestoso, dove rare volte si gode la tranquilita e la calma.   DELCHIARO—*Revoluxione di Wallachia.*

LONDON:

PRINTED FOR LONGMAN, HURST, REES, ORME, AND BROWN,
PATERNOSTER-ROW.
1820.

Title page of William Wilkinson's seminal book which provided a valuable source for Bram Stoker

native England. Born in Bridlington, he was educated at the Augustinian Priory of Newburgh in the North Riding of Yorkshire. At the age of 25, he married the wealthy Emma de Peri which gave him financial independence and allowed him to pursue his interests in history. However, in 1182, William left his wife and returned to the priory where he eventually became the canon. Here he continued his historical researches and wrote prodigiously. William's major work, the two-volume *Historia Rerum Angelicarum (History of English Affairs)*, which recounts the history of England from 1066 to 1135, is today acknowledged as one of the most forceful and polished works to be written in the twelfth century. Several sections of the book are specifically devoted to vampires and all are presented with William's scrupulous attention to the facts. These include 'The Vampire of Alnwick Castle' in Berwick-on-Tweed which features a 'deadly monster' who nightly hunts for victims with a pack of dogs at his heels; 'The Hundeprest', a former chaplain of Melrose Abbey in Scotland who seeks the life-blood of his congregation until finally staked in his tomb; and 'The Buckinghamshire Vampire' who returns from the dead to plague his wife until sealed forever in his tomb by 'an episcopal absolution placed under his breast'. These accounts are reprinted in *The Natural History of the Vampire* by Anthony Masters (1972).

Wright, Dudley D'Auvergne (1867–1948)

Dudley Wright was a house surgeon at the London Homoeopathic Hospital who lectured, wrote and expounded on the value of healthy eating. He was also the author of the first twentieth-century history of the undead, *Vampires and Vampirism*, published in 1914, and which subsequently ran into several editions. Although the Eton-educated surgeon was more familiar with the use of fruit, vegetables, cereals, dairy products, even nuts and seaweed in dieting, he was prompted to write the book, he said in his Preface, 'because of the awakened interest in supernormal phenomena which has taken place in recent years and has included in its wake the absorbing subject of vampirism'. He believed vampires were 'regarded more seriously today than they ever were even a decade since', and warned readers that 'a certain amount of scientific truth may underlie even what may be regarded as the most extravagant stories.' *Vampires and Vampirism* covered the history of the undead from Ancient Babylon through Europe and the Far East to the start of the twentieth century, including a special section devoted to 'The Vampire in Literature', all in a similar style – though far less scholarly in tone – than Montague Summers (*q.v.*) adopted fifteen years later in his two classic volumes.

Wume (America)

The *Wume* is a variety of vampire associated with the negro slaves who were uprooted from Africa and brought to the United States. The creature is said to have a proboscis which it plunges into the ear or mouth of its victim to suck out the person's life-blood. Southern folklore claims that the *Wume* is a person who was cursed during their lifetime and is doomed to plague relatives and friends. Unlike most other vampires, it does not have to be staked or burned to put an end to its undead life, but merely 'buried on its face in a secret place', according to tradition.

XYZ

XXX

In a number of European countries the bite of a vampire is reported to look like XXX – which, it is said, suggests the thirty pieces of silver that Judas was paid to betray Christ. Several traditions also refer to vampires as the 'Children of Judas' because like him they are supposed to have red hair. This whole concept fascinated an English writer, Julian Osgood Field, who in 1894 wrote a remarkable vampire novelette, *The Kiss of Judas*, under the pen name 'X.L.' – pronounced like 'excel' – which was first published in the July 1893 issue of *Pall Mall Magazine*. Little is known of Field beyond the fact he was a Londoner and a friend of Oscar Wilde and Aubrey Beardsley (who illustrated the story) and also the writer of a number of exotic and decadent stories in the style of the 1890s, the best of which were published as *Aut Diabolus Aut Nihil* (1894). His vampire story is set in Moldavia where it is said some descendants of Judas still live and have a habit of making pacts with the Devil, after which they commit suicide, and then return as the undead to kill their enemies with a kiss. On each of their victims they leave the tell-tale mark XXX.

Yarbro, Chelsea Quinn (1942–   )

The American authoress, Chelsea Quinn Yarbro, is a professional tarot reader and committed believer in occultism, who has created

Aubrey Beardsley's illustration for 'The Kiss of Judas' (1893)

a very popular vampire fiction series, 'The Saint-Germain Chronicles'. The hero of these stories is a 4,000-year-old nobleman believed to be loosely based on the mysterious eighteenth-century figure, the Count de Saint-Germain. A dark, saturnine, yet sympathetic figure, he is irresistible to women, but because he is technically impotent he passes on immortal life with a vampire kiss. During the series of novels in which he has featured – begun in 1978 with *Hotel Transylvania* – Saint-Germain has moved across the ages from Ancient Egypt through the Roman Empire, Renaissance Italy, eighteenth-century France and into twentieth century England. His great knowledge, paranormal strength and evident inclination towards human beings are what sustain him rather than a lust for blood, and admirers of the Yarbro novels see him as a figure of allure rather than horror. Other novels in the series are: *The Palace* (1978), *Blood Game* (1980), *Path of the Eclipse* (1981), *Tempting Fate* (1982), the collection of linking stories, *The Saint-Germain Chronicles* (1983), *Out of the House of Life* (1990), *The Spider Glass* (1991), *Darker Jewels* (1993), *Better in the Dark* (1993) and *Mansions of Darkness* (1996). *The Vampire Stories of Chelsea Quinn Yarbro* published in 1994 is also relevant to the series as are the spin-off trio of novels about the Count's lover, Atta Olivia Clemens: *A Flame in Byzantium* (1987), *Crusader's Torch* (1988) and *A Candle for D'Artagnan* (1989).

Ye Vampyres!

Ye Vampyres! was the first of a series of books published in the 1870s by the London publisher, Samuel Tinsley, of Southampton Street, which utilized the fear of vampirism in a crusade against gambling, drunkenness and immorality. All the books were written anonymously and bore a decorated series stamp which carried the words, 'Mind is Stronger than Matter'. *Ye Vampres* was published in 1875 and attacked bookmakers and the profits they were 'sucking' from hapless betting men; the title page is self-explanatory: 'A Legend of the National Betting-Ring, Showing what became of it. By "The Spectre" '. The following year, Tinsley published the most successful book in the series, *The Vampyre*, 'By The Wife of a Medical Man', a diatribe against the demon drink set in 'The Vampyre Inn'. Just one paragraph of dialogue by the drunken hero illustrates why the book proved so popular with the teetotal fraternity: 'They fly – they bite – they suck my blood – I die. That hideous "Vampyre"! Its eyes pierce me through – they are red – they are bloodshot. I dare not lie down. It bites – I die! Give me brandy – brandy – more brandy!'

The tradition of *Ye Vampyres!* being continued half a century later in moral little booklets like *Trail of the Vampire* (1949)

Yorga, Count

Count Yorga was another of the screen vampires created in the 1960s and intended to be a series character. Although only two movies were shot, both are now cult favourites among younger audiences and are regularly re-shown on television. Created by the American producer, Michael MacReady, the Count, a sauve, hypnotic vampire from Eastern Europe, who is introduced arriving in his coffin in contemporary Los Angeles, was actually conceived as a character for a soft-core pornographic movie! But when MacReady showed the script to an actor-friend, Robert Quarry, he was persuaded by the star to make the film into a straightforward horror picture. Joining forces with the ingenious scriptwriter and director, Robert Kelljan, the entire production was made for just

$20,000 – a record for a genre movie. The success of the film in bringing vampires – especially a bevy of sexy young members of the undead all vampirized by the Count – into an urban setting fascinated audiences and prompted a big-budget sequel, *The Return of Count Yorga*, in 1971. The second picture is more violent than its predecessor, with the Count's tribe of vampires massacring an entire family before being cornered in Yorga's castle. Although the master vampire is apparently destroyed at the end of the picture, one of his pursuers has already been turned into one of the undead and the signs are the cult will live on. Yet despite the superiority of the second picture with its sly observations in Kelljan's script (he was also the director again) on Middle America's preoccupation with fantasy and violence, plans for a third outing for Count Yorga have not so far materialized.

Zacharias, Lamia

Lamia Zacharius is the beautiful, evil vampire heroine of a series of novels by the American author and editor, Gerald Neal Williamson (1932–) who signs himself J.N. Williamson. Coming to the notice of readers in the 1980s, Williamson has written on all aspects of the supernatural from banshees to haunted houses, though his stories of Lamia and her quest for blood in contemporary USA have been the most successful. The series began with *Death-Coach* in 1981 and has been followed by *Death-Angel* (1981), *Death-School* (1982) and *Death-Doctor* (1982). Vampires also feature in Williamson's chilling tale, *Bloodlines* (1994).

Zaleska, Countess Marya

Countess Marya Zaleska is the daughter of Count Dracula who comes to Carfax Abbey in England to claim his body after his death and then burns it in an attempt to escape her fate. She was the creation of scriptwriter, Garrett Ford, writer of the original 1931 Universal movie, *Dracula*, who had been commissioned by the studio to prepare a sequel *without* the Count, and turned to Bram Stoker's short story, 'Dracula's Guest' for his inspiration. The beautiful English-born actress, Gloria Holden, a former model who had moved to Hollywood and appeared in a number of *femme fatale* (*q.v.*) roles, starred as *Dracula's Daughter* (1936), and utilized her marble-like features and restrained style of acting to convey the torment she suffered in her undead existence, suggesting that she was not the wantonly evil creature her father had become. As the screen's earliest female vampire of note she had, initially, been startled by the role as she told a reporter from *Variety* in an interview: 'The author has made me a ruthless vampire, a beast in human form. I don't believe any woman has ever been asked to play such a poisonous role before. I would just like to meet the man who wrote such an inhuman role for me. He must be a monstrous, horrible person.' In fact, Holden got on well with Garrett Ford, as she did with Edward Van Sloan (*q.v.*) repeating his role as Professor Van Helsing, and director Lambert Hillyer who used her sensitivity to suggest a mixture of bloodlust and lesbian tendencies in a crucial scene where she was seen posing a young girl for a painting. But

Countess Marya Zaleska played by Gloria Holden
in *Dracula's Daughter* (1936)

unable to find a cure for her vampirism, the Countess can only return to Transylvania where Van Helsing is again present as she meets the same end as her father. On its release, *Dracula's Daughter* was enthusiastically reviewed and in the eyes of many critics it is a superior picture to *Dracula*. It remains Gloria Holden's best screen performance and the sole appearance of the magnetic Countess Marya Zaleska.

Zopfius, John Heinrich (c.1675–1749)

The German scholar, Dr John Heinrich Zopfius, is regarded as one of the foremost eighteenth-century authorities on vampirism, and his book, *Dissertatio de Vampiris Seruiensibus* was published at Duisburg in 1733 has been one of the most influential and widely consulted works by later writers on the subject. Born in Halle, he attended the university in nearby Leipzig and developed a passion for history and all its curiosities. Later Zopfius became the director of the gymnasium for education in the imperial city of Essen where he proved himself 'a person of great erudition' according to one contemporary account, and a man whose work was not to be taken lightly even when he published his 'extremely learned and curious volume on vampires'. In the *Dissertatio*, he quoted numerous instances of vampirism from across Europe and provided a definition of the undead which has been endlessly repeated:

> The vampyres, which come out of the graves in the nighttime, rush upon people sleeping in their beds, suck out all their blood and destroy them. They attack men, women and children; sparing neither age nor sex. The people, attacked by them, complain of suffocation and a great interception of spirits; after which they soon expire. Some of them, being asked at the point of death, what is the matter with them?, reply that such and such persons, lately dead, have arisen from the tomb to torment and torture them. Their countenances are fresh and ruddy; and their nails as well as hair, are very much grown. And, though they have been much longer dead than

An early eighteenth-century case of suspected vampirism as recorded
by Dr John Heinrich Zopfius in his dissertation

many other bodies, which are perfectly putrified, not the least
mark of corruption is upon them. Those who were destroyed by
them, after their deaths, become vampyres; so that to prevent so
spreading an evil, it is found requisite to drive a stake through
the dead body, from whence, on this occasion, the blood flows,
as if the person was alive. Sometimes the body is dug out of the
grave, and burnt to ashes; upon which all disturbances cease.

Zugun, Eleonore (1913–   )

Eleonore Zugun was a 13-year-old Romanian peasant girl who
became a cause célèbre in 1926 as a result of claims that she was the
victim of a 'vampire spirit' who was constantly leaving bite and scratch
marks on her face, neck and arms. The attacks began on the little girl
in her native village of Talpa where she became known as 'The Devil
Girl' because she claimed the assaults were being made by a creature
she called 'Dracu'. Stories of these vampirish attacks reached the
world's Press and in October 1926, Zugun was brought to London for

investigations to be conducted at the National Laboratory of Psychical Research run by the occult investigator, Harry Price. For several days, she was observed by Price and his assistant, Neil Gow, and what occurred only added to the mystery. An account written by Gow at the time states:

> Monday, October 4. 3.20. Eleonore cried out. Showed marks on back of left hand like teeth-marks which afterwards developed into deep weals . . . 4.12. Eleonore was just raising a cup of tea to her lips, but suddenly gave a cry and put the cup down hastily: there was a mark on her right hand similar to that caused by the bite. Both rows of teeth were indicated.

Harry Price was convinced there was no fraud involved and tells the unsolved story of 'The Vampire Ghost's Victim' in his book, *Poltergeist Over England* (1945).

The hand of Eleonore Zugun the Romanian girl who was scratched and bitten by a 'vampire spirit' in 1926